AF324067

BISHOPS, WIVES AND CHILDREN

Bishops, Wives and Children
Spiritual Capital Across the Generations

DOUGLAS J. DAVIES
Durham University, UK

and

MATHEW GUEST
Durham University, UK

ASHGATE

© Douglas J. Davies and Mathew Guest 2007

All rights reserved. No part of this publication may be reproduced, stored in a retrieval system or transmitted in any form or by any means, electronic, mechanical, photocopying, recording or otherwise without the prior permission of the publisher.

Douglas J. Davies and Mathew Guest have asserted their moral right under the Copyright, Designs and Patents Act, 1988, to be identified as the authors of this work.

Published by
Ashgate Publishing Limited
Gower House
Croft Road
Aldershot
Hampshire GU11 3HR
England

Ashgate Publishing Company
Suite 420
101 Cherry Street
Burlington, VT 05401-4405
USA

Ashgate website: http://www.ashgate.com

British Library Cataloguing in Publication Data
Davies, Douglas J.
   Bishops, wives and children: spiritual capital across the
   generations
   1. Church of England – Bishops 2. Church of England –
   Bishops – Family relationships 3. Children of clergy –
   England 4. Children of clergy – England – Family
   relationships 5. Bishops' spouses – England
   I. Title II. Guest, Mathew
   283.4'2'0922

Library of Congress Cataloging-in-Publication Data
Davies, Douglas James.
   Bishops, wives and children: spiritual capital across the generations / Douglas J. Davies and
Mathew Guest.
         p. cm.
Includes bibliographical references and index.
ISBN-13: 978-0-7546-5485-8 (hardcover : alk. paper)
1.   Church of England–Bishops–Family relationships. 2.   Children of clergy–Great Britain
–Social conditions. 3.   Bishops' spouses–Great Britain–Social conditions.
4.   Christian sociology–Church of England. 5. Christian sociology–Great Britain.   I. Guest,
Mathew. II. Title.
   BX5176.D38 2007
   262'.12342--dc22
                                                                                      2006021157

ISBN 978-0-7546-5485-8

Printed and bound in Great Britain by MPG Books Ltd, Bodmin, Cornwall.

Contents

List of Plates

1   The Rt Revd Edward Henry Bickersteth, Bishop of Exeter (1885–1900).
    Reproduced by kind permission of the Rt Revd John Bickersteth.

2   His son, the Rt Revd Samuel Bickersteth, Residentiary Canon of Canterbury
    Cathedral (1916–36) and Chaplain to King George V (1916–37).
    Reproduced by kind permission of the Rt Revd John Bickersteth.

3   His grandson, the Revd Canon Edward Monier Bickersteth, Secretary of the
    Jerusalem and the East Mission (1915–35).
    Reproduced by kind permission of the Rt Revd John Bickersteth.

4   His great-grandson, the Rt Revd John Bickersteth, Bishop of Bath & Wells
    (1975–87), his wife, Rosemary, and their youngest son, Sam, outside the Bishop's
    Palace in Wells.
    Reproduced by kind permission of the Rt Revd John Bickersteth.

5   The Rt Revd Robert Bickersteth, Bishop of Ripon (1857–84).
    Reproduced by kind permission of the Rt Revd John Bickersteth.

6   'The tasks of a bishop', as noted by one of our respondents while he was
    in office during the 1990s. This is a copy of the note, written for his own reference,
    which he kept on his study desk during this time. In the absence of an official 'job
    description' as such, it is interesting when bishops forge their own understanding
    of their Episcopal ministry. Here, vision coupled with ministerial engagement
    take precedence, with 'public affairs' notably at the end of the list.
    Reproduced by kind permission of a bishop who took part in the study.

7   Bishops' timeline. This timeline details the lives and careers of the 107 retired
    bishops who formed the basis of our study. The light shaded blocks indicate their
    pre-episcopal ministerial careers, while the darker shaded blocks indicate their
    time as active bishops. The list was compiled from public records published in
    Crockford's Clerical Directory, and includes all those ordained clergymen who
    – at the outset of our study in 2001 – were both retired and had served as bishops
    in the Church of England.

8   Auckland Castle, residence of the Bishop of Durham.
    Photograph by Douglas J. Davies.

Note: Plates 2–6

The Bickersteths are a dynasty of clergy, representing five generations (Robert Bickersteth was a first cousin of Edward Henry Bickersteth). Examination of these photographs reveals changing fashions of clerical dress from the late nineteenth to the late twentieth century. The succeeding generations also represent changing patterns in clerical recruitment, from a strong tradition of clerical families in the Victorian period to greater secularization and fragmentation in the present day, when such clerical continuity is rare indeed.

List of Tables

Acknowledgments

This book is the direct outcome of The Clergy and British Society Project, 1940–2000, funded by the then Arts and Humanities Research Board with Prof. Douglas. J. Davies as Project Director and Dr Mathew Guest as Senior Research Associate. I take this opportunity to thank Dr. Guest for his enormous effort on the project and in the preparation of this present book.

Together we wish to thank the following individuals for preliminary discussions, suggestions and various contributions: Neil Burgess, Robin Gill, Tim Jenkins, Ken Medhurst, John Nelson and Stephen Sykes. The following attended an early research seminar at Durham in the Spring of 2002 as part of the funded project: Anders Backstrom, Else-Maj Falk, Mike Hornsby-Smith, Martha Middlemiss, David Martin, Per Pettersson and John Wolffe. At the close of the project, within the context of a further seminar, Callum Brown, Robin Gill, Hijme Stoffels, Bob Towler and Helen Waterhouse also generously offered their time and academic comment. To all these we extend our gratitude for critical conversation and participation. We are also grateful for the support of Durham University, to colleagues in the Department of Theology and Religion for many passing comments, and to Sarah Lloyd at Ashgate Publishing for her sound advice and continued support throughout the production process.

Earlier versions of Chapter 5 were presented by Mathew Guest as 'The Role of the Clergy Wife as the Guardian of Christian Tradition?' at *Religion and Gender*, the British Sociological Association's Religion Study Group Annual Conference, University of Lancaster, April 2005. He, similarly, presented earlier versions of Chapter 6 as 'Raised by the Spiritual Elite: The Religious Identities of Clergy Children' at the Staff Seminar of the Department of Religious and Theological Studies, University of Cardiff, April 2004, and as 'Clergy Children and the Transmission of Spiritual Capital' at *The Sociology of Spirituality*, the British Sociology Association's Religion Study Group Annual Conference, University of Bristol, April 2004. Thanks are due to those who offered constructive comment and criticism at those events.

Finally, we owe a great debt to the bishops, wives and children who took part in this study for sharing their life experiences with us. For ethical reasons, they cannot be named individually, but we hope this acknowledgment will go some small way towards conveying our sincere gratitude to them and to their families.

Douglas Davies
Mathew Guest
Durham, 2006

Chapter 1

Religious Leadership in a Changing Society

Introduction

Episcopacy, family, and religious values – at first glance these all seem well known to us, with bishops, their image, as well as that of their wives and children, all holding a place in English cultural life. On further consideration, however, these caricatures transform into a trio of complexity, challenging analysis yet promising distinctive insight into the Church of England and its social world.

Churches exist at different levels and need to be studied as such. Take a senior diocesan bishop of the Church of England in full regalia at great national events compared with the same man, leisure-shirted in retirement, telling the story of his life with all its successes, failures and doubts. On the public stage he stands hierarchically surrounded by clergy: domestically recalling the event, he is accompanied by his wife, surrounded by photographs of their children, now making their own way in the world. As he tells of his life, his wife adds her account of his, of hers, and of their family, and the complexity of religious influence grows. When their children contribute their own memories of the family's past and their self-reflection on their engagement with contemporary life we begin to see the social, institutional and personal intricacies that this book seeks to explore. It is in its own detailed way a contribution to that 'general sociology of the problems of transmission in modern societies' that Danièle Hervièu-Léger sought in her influential reflections on *Religion as a Chain of Memory* (2000: 176). It is a contribution made possible by the accounts of their lives granted us by a large number of bishops active in the Church of England between 1940 and 2000, and by their wives and children.

We begin by addressing the theoretical context of our study, devoting our first chapter to a discussion of spiritual capital and gift theory before offering a sketch of the cultural and historical contexts in which the bishops, wives and children of our study have functioned as individuals. Chapter 2 focusses specifically on the biographical and ecclesiastical background of our bishops, thus furnishing a picture of the resources from which these men have drawn in constructing their identities as senior churchmen. Chapter 3 addresses the particular challenges these bishops have faced in the latter half of the twentieth century, focussing on issues arising from managerial approaches to leadership and the prominence of the mass media, while Chapter 4 turns to the internal politics of the Church of England itself, in a discussion of the difference between diocesan and suffragan bishops, both in status and experience. In Chapter 5 we turn our attention to the experience of clergy wives through an examination of the lives and roles adopted by the bishops' wives who took part in our study. Chapter 6 broadens this focus to the domestic context of the clergy family itself, reflecting on the nature of the clergy home as portrayed in accounts offered by our respondents, and drawing inferences about its role as a context for the negotiation of personal values. Chapters 7 and 8 address the concerns of bishops' sons and daughters within the context of their adult lives, beginning with their religious identities, then turning to their professional and vocational experience. Our focus throughout is on patterns of influence between the generations, and our central aim is to comment on the very process of transmission and value-formation as exemplified in the lives of our respondents, concerns revisited in relation to our theoretical framework in the concluding chapter.

Method and Perspective

In sharp focus, then, the three interrelated aims of this study were to: (a) chart the ministerial development of senior Anglican clergymen; (b) assess how the responsibilities of leadership shape the home life of clergy families, and (c) trace how each of these factors contributed to the developing identities of the sons and daughters of these clergy. Each required the collection and analysis of empirical data and, as our intention was primarily to furnish a sociological study of living individuals, this material was gathered through a social survey and in-depth interviews as described in the Appendix.

Through this material we sought to explore the vocation of these men to the priesthood and their mode of engagement in ministry as well as various issues attending their episcopal elevation. Paralleling this ecclesiastical and social domain lay our interest in their family life. How did a 'father in God' treat his own wife and children, and how did a public guardian of the faith hand it on within his own home? And what of the complex roles and career development of their wives and the emergent identities and life-styles of their children? Because these complex questions require appropriate appreciation and analysis we complemented our sociological outlook with selected perspectives from other disciplines including anthropology, psychology and theology. All of this material was pondered with an eye to historical issues surrounding British society in general and the Church of England in particular. Constraints of space demand that while many of these theoretical influences underlie the ongoing argument they are sometimes restricted to footnotes. We have often found our material influencing ongoing modes of analysis as much as our awareness of discrete academic disciplines fostered our initial venture. We approach the church as an institution embedded in English social processes through the individuals whose personal and interpersonal endeavors have given it life. In a complementary fashion we align husbands, wives and children to demonstrate the importance of the family as a base from which most bishops gain additional legitimacy to act in society, to explore the wife's role in the maintenance of Christian leadership, and to consider how values are transmitted across generations.

Society depends for its flourishing upon the mutual action of individuals as individuals and as members of institutions who embody and enact prime cultural values. Here we are reminded of Georg Simmel's distinctive sociology, part

German idealism, part Protestant self-affirmation before God, in which, as one of his advocates described it, 'society is the product of human movement towards its Being, towards being who one really is, toward salvation' (Erickson, 2001: 112). In this process various degrees of individual self-interest need to be negotiated, controlled or curbed, indeed, the history of political thought and social theory is replete with analyses of just how these mixed motives may be best categorized, debated and implemented. Bishops of a state church are one means of bringing such issues to a sharp focus.

Theoretical Approaches

As James Beckford comments, not all ventures in the sociology of religion are concerned with simply identifying causes and effects; sometimes 'the aim is, rather, to identify a syndrome or a constellation of interrelated elements without any clear assignment of causal priority' (2005: 126). This reflects our aim in this book – to examine the constellation of factors surrounding Anglican bishops and their families in advancing an exploration of the social expression of Christian identity. Our project concerns the construction of identity among the hierarchy of the church, and the question of how the values and experiences of these men contribute to an embodiment of Christian identity among their wives and children. In this sense it is concerned with a complexity of leadership, with how the influence of church hierarchy is generated and with how it functions. This takes us from the formation of bishops to the dissemination, evolution and embodiment of their values within the lives of their families, as we explore the influence of a clerical household upon professed convictions and lived practices.

The two major theoretical perspectives underlying our analysis are those of spiritual capital and symbolic exchange, notions that require some elaboration since those familiar with one may well be unfamiliar with the other since it is unusual for them to be employed together. Their alignment, however, allows a more penetrating analysis of our material and highlights the complexity of influence as conceived and explored within this book. The first conceives of a resource created, accumulated and deployed in and through social networks whose relationships enable certain people to accumulate various forms of 'capital' that can then be deployed for varied purposes. The second approach deals with ideas of symbolic exchange, often described as gift-theory – where 'gift' can assume a great variety of forms. Here, too, we are engaged with networks of people, but with a greater emphasis upon the *use* of resources, whether in the establishment of families or of churches. Given that both 'capital' and 'gift' theories share an interest in society and the processes by which human relationships are mediated, we are interested in how they complement each other in furthering our knowledge of the complexity of both religious leadership and family life.

Spiritual Capital and the Influence of Religion

Throughout the twentieth century sociological studies of religion have emphasized issues concerning the influence of religious phenomena. The dominant secularization thesis resulted in numerous attempts to measure the extent to which religion remains a socially significant force in contemporary life, asking whether religion still influences how people conduct their lives as professionals, educators, citizens, parents, and individuals seeking meaning in the world. Various conclusions have been drawn, from the negative arguments of the hard-line secularization theorists, who see religion rapidly disappearing from the public, followed by the private, sphere (Bruce, 2002), to those who see religion evolving in dialogue with cultural change, becoming less institutional, less fixed, more deregulated, but not necessarily less important as a consequence (Davie, 1994; Lyon, 2000). Historians have adopted a more mixed approach, acutely aware of detailed cultural differences (McLeod, 2003: 1–26). While all are concerned at some significant level with the capacity of religion, in whatever form, to shape people's lives, the actual influence of religion within social life remains woefully under-theorized, not least in the sociology of religion. Few venture any detailed account of how religion might shape identity over time, and, by logical extension, of how it might function as an intergenerational phenomenon. Many have attempted to measure religious commitment over time, and some have attempted to use survey data to gauge the effectiveness of religious socialization, as with Robin Gill's excellent work on Sunday School attendance and its potential effect on the future low profile of the religious belief of the nation (Gill, 1999: 290). Still, little has been written on exactly how religious values function: how they emerge, evolve, achieve meaning, develop, thrive and decay.

James Beckford's work on the changing status of religion in advanced industrial societies offers one means of rectifying this tendency, notably his claim that one major change in recent decades charts how 'religious symbols and meanings have floated free from their origins in religious traditions and organizations' so as to become available for 'appropriation by non-religious agencies'. This prompted him to suggest that it is useful to 'think of religion less as a social institution and more of a *cultural resource* susceptible to many different uses' (2001: 233; our emphasis). His innovative analysis has been used to explain and develop understandings of contemporary religious change, from the exploratory impermanence of what some call the 'New Age', and what Colin Campbell (1972) has called the 'cultic milieu', to the Anglican context in which churchgoers adopt changing habits of congregational involvement according to how experiences offered by specific churches resource their Christian identities. Here religion functions as a resource, to be mobilized and deployed by individuals in accordance with their needs. For our purposes, Beckford's analysis offers a way into the problem of religious influence because it provides a means of talking about what is inherited, nurtured, transmitted, accepted or rejected. By re-conceiving of religion as a cultural resource, we become more sensitive to its potential as a fluid and shared phenomenon rather than as an established institution or creedal scheme. And yet Beckford only takes us so far, leaving us with the desire to develop the 'resource' theme further, specifically in terms of 'spiritual capital'.

The notion of 'spiritual capital' is complex and builds on a tradition that can be traced back at least as far as Karl Marx's argument that economic capital be seen not just as a commodity but also as a social relation. This conceives of capital in terms of a process of exchange between social agents, an exchange that extends well beyond the economic. Capital may, for example, appear as a mobile human resource embracing social relationships, education, political acumen or symbolic prestige. All refer to resources that may be acquired and then deployed in order to achieve some individual or group advantage.

More recently James Coleman has discussed the achievement of goals by virtue of the possession of various social resources – 'social capital' – taking the form of social relations between persons and including the notion of trust and reciprocal obligations (1990: 302). One feature of this perspective lies in consequences that are often byproducts rather than intended goals, and offers one way of viewing social class, as ongoing social relations and engagement in institutions produce an accumulated social capital. An Oxbridge education or theological college training may, for example, yield many subsequent consequences for ecclesiastical preferment. One valuable feature of Coleman's account lies in his claim that social capital is inalienable, being something that is not easily exchanged, a feature developed below (Coleman, 1990: 315).

The most well-known and topical example of capital theory is found in Robert Putnam's ground-breaking volume *Bowling Alone* (2000) which refers to North America's declining levels of 'social capital' within the context of a debate about the breakdown in community. For Putnam, 'social capital refers to connections among individuals – social networks and the norms of reciprocity and trustworthiness that arise from them' (Putnam, 2000: 19). Social capital is the 'connective tissue' that holds society together, so that when individualism becomes a dominant influence, and people act alone rather than as part of an integrated collective, there is a serious breakdown in social cohesion.

For Putnam, if economic capital refers to money, and human capital to properties of individuals, social capital refers to the connections that exist between individuals, to significant social relationships that allow certain things to be achieved that would not otherwise be achievable. In this sense 'capital' is conceived as an empowering resource that may be harnessed in the service of individual advancement or for the collective good, issues that help furnish the moral frame within which Putnam's work is set. A further and cognate development is that of 'cultural capital', a notion that has been used to refer to skills and knowledge, acquired through education of some kind, which can be used to acquire jobs, money and status, as portrayed in the work of French sociologist Pierre Bourdieu (1977). He has done most to develop this term through his writings on how social inequalities of power are sustained through the education system. According to Bourdieu, particular social classes tend to acquire the cultural dispositions required to excel in the academic world because they possess the appropriate cultural capital, that is, forms of speech and modes of behavior instilled through what he calls 'familiarization'. In simple terms, members of the privileged classes learn how to behave in ways that are associated with intellectual prowess, status and respectability from their parents and through their upbringing, what sociologists call 'socialization'. Academic merit is accorded in a way that favors these forms of behavior and thereby sustains an unfair advantage of the privileged over the less wealthy or working class (Bourdieu, 1977: 495). With Monique de Saint Martin he has also developed this theme in relation to Catholic Bishops in France. In an important and subtle study they show how an appearance of unity of purpose and mode of life develops amongst such senior clergy for whom the unity of the Church is of paramount concern, irrespective of their social or educational background (Bourdieu and de Saint Martin, 1982). Their suggestive treatment of celibacy notes its potential consequences for the organization of the Catholic Church as well as for the clerical presentation of self and invites a useful comparison with the married clergy of the Church of England.[1] Influenced by Bourdieu, but deployed within British social class contexts, Basil Bernstein's seminal studies also demonstrated the close connection between the cultural resources of the family transmitted as styles or 'codes' of communication and wider educational opportunities or limitations.[2]

If economic capital refers to money, social capital to human relationships, and cultural capital to skills and knowledge, what of 'spiritual capital'? Does it refer to a special kind of knowledge, relationship or individual resource? Here Bourdieu is instructive for within his diverse range of publications lies a handful of articles on religion developing what he calls 'religious capital'. This he associates with various other forms of power, and demonstrates a sensitivity to the ways in which religious groups borrow from other sources of capital – economic, social or symbolic, for example – in order to advance their goals, not to mention the ways in which secular institutions adopt religious symbols and connections in order to nurture a more morally respectable image. In this sense, religious capital is embedded in a complex matrix of power that effectively blurs the boundaries between religious and non-religious forms of legitimation; some might argue that the established status of the Church of England provides us with a striking contemporary example, with its presence in the House of Lords, liturgical deference to the monarchy and historical privileges related to its status as the 'state church'. But Bourdieu takes his argument further, describing what he sees as distinctive about 'religious capital', that is, the 'goods of salvation', which are most obviously the sacraments, but they may also refer to a form of recognized membership of a church. In the widest sense, the goods of salvation – that which is constitutive of religious capital - are *the resources deemed by a religious tradition to be requisite to salvation*. These might be ritualized practices, bodies of doctrine or access to sacred spaces, but most importantly for Bourdieu, they are under the control of religious specialists, who only understand and thereby control religious capital because they have been privy to what he

---

1   Their discussion of the mother's role in influencing the vocation of sons is also valuable, especially when related to the loss, absence or inadequacy of a father figure. This relates to theories of early bereavement and adult charismatic personalities (Davies, 2000: 102–4) but concerns few of the bishops studied.

2   His work on the 'mode of establishing relationships' within different social class groups in relation to the long-term options they make available to children is an important background factor in this book (Bernstein, 1971: 50). For Bourdieu's influence see Bernstein (1975: 14–17).

calls 'knowledgeable mastery', that is, specialist training and initiation into the priesthood. Hence, for Bourdieu, religious capital signifies the power differential between official religious specialists and those they purport to serve; it expresses the spiritual dependency of the lay upon the priesthood.

Given our interest in senior clergymen, Bourdieu's discussion of religious capital is of obvious concern as he draws attention to the special resources possessed by the hierarchy of the church. From where do they get these resources, and what is most significant in shaping them: the personal histories of individual bishops, for example, or the institutional status accorded to them? Despite these inroads, Bourdieu's treatment of power in the church is limited and requires some modification if it is to be of value for our study. The main problems of his model relate to his conception of the kind of resource to which the term 'religious capital' might refer, especially his emphasis upon knowledge as a cerebral, intellectual phenomenon; he does not consider that the capital associated with religious orders might be embodied in charisma, emotional literacy or refer to a more multi-faceted understanding of religious identity. This is especially important within this study because, as we shall discover, if we are to use capital to understand that which is transmitted between generations – as an inter-generational resource – then we must accept that it takes a wider range of forms: not just knowledge as such, but experience, making itself manifest in a range of skills, predilections, tendencies and frameworks of meaning (Guest, 2007). As Bernstein showed, children inherit from their parents not just ideas, but a complex set of resources, not all of which are met with a positive response in adulthood, and we shall explore the ways in which such resources affect professional and religious identity in our later chapters.[3] In addition to this problem, Bourdieu's model of religious capital is restricted because it is centered around the priest–laity distinction and therefore is unable to capture the complexities of religious influence within the contemporary world. As one commentator on Bourdieu's work puts it:

> this model treats religion as an institution but not as a disposition, as an intricate system of coercion but not as a liquid species of capital. In short, it employs categories that are too rigid to account for the fluidities of today's spiritual marketplace. (Verter, 2003: 151)

In recognition of the more deregulated state of religion within the contemporary west, both within religious institutions and among individuals outside of them, we prefer to speak of 'spiritual capital'. In so doing we retain Bourdieu's focus on the 'goods of salvation' but set it within the context of an understanding of contemporary Britain that takes religious meanings and influences as more free-floating than they once were. If the intergenerational resources circulating among bishops and their families are to be conceived in a fashion that recognizes their complexity and propensity to evolve into other forms of capital, then 'spiritual capital' is, we believe, the preferable expression. For here is a phenomenon not defined and strictly controlled by the hierarchy of the Church of England, but one that, while rooted in this tradition, lies open to development and transformation by those with opportunity to deploy it within the course of their lives. Given how profoundly the lives of sons

---

3   For a brief theological application of Bernstein see Davies (1981).

and daughters of Anglican bishops are shaped and infused by this capital, they provide an illuminating case study for exploring how spiritual capital functions within the broader context of the Church of England. That same 'cultural resource' is also a means of describing how the Church of England remains a pervasive influence within English society and, in this sense, we are interested in the contention that bishops provide a major matrix of spiritual capital for the Church of England and for English society at large.

The Limits of Capital Theory: Turning to the Gift

Capital theory, then, takes us some way towards formulating an approach to understanding religious leadership and influence in contemporary Britain. It highlights the social networks through which a person gains experience, capacity, and opportunity to act effectively in relation to desired goals. In this sense it also embraces the resources brought by different members of a group to the life and, thus, potential effectiveness of that group. In embracing Bourdieu's insight into the transformability of capital alongside Beckford's sense of religion as a cultural resource, we are enabled to explore how factors supposedly generated by religious institutions are in fact related to politics, education and symbolic prestige, and how power and authority acquired through ecclesiastical connections may be subsequently deployed in a way that generates cultural, social and symbolic capital. However, capital theory risks perpetuating assumptions about human action that leave little room for morality or community, overemphasizing the individual as an agent of power. Our presentation of the church and of British society would remain stark and impersonally individualistic if based solely on this approach. More importantly, such a fragmented and self-driven picture of British culture would not reflect the evidence obtained from those we have studied.[4]

A similar sentiment is expressed by Jacques Godbout who, in his strongly philosophical and ethical anthropology, argues forcefully that an appropriate understanding of human life in its depth of relationships requires that:

> we must break with the explanations of human behaviour proposed by both utilitarianism – methodological individualism or rational choice theory – and by the various versions of Nietzscheism – those that see humans as natural egoists as well as those that see them, at least in their modern, Western guise, as interested only in power. (Godbout with Caillé, 1998: 16)

Godbout's relevance for our study lies in the fact that he exemplifies scholars who have developed an approach to society – that of symbolic exchange – that gives serious weight to the personal and human qualities of social relationships. This relevance is exemplified in the reasons he adduces for why so many think symbolic exchange or gift-theory absurd or irrelevant in today's world. One is deeply rooted in a historical and theological view that since the Reformation the very notion of grace has been 'banished, relegated to the outer limits of transcendence' (Godbout with

---

4   Bloch argued that people ought to be able to recognize their lives within social scientific accounts (1992: 127–45).

Caillé, 1998: 16) where it became too 'religious' a notion. He would prefer to see thinkers 'evolve a more realistic' notion of grace, one that is neither exiled to 'some other world' nor reduced to 'profane, self-interest'. Moreover, he sees modernity's rejection of tradition and the language of tradition, all within its excessive focus upon the present and the isolated self, as conducing to a 'caustic sarcasm' and a discrediting of 'noble acts, such as Christian love' (1998: 17). In other words, many aspects of life that people know to be important to their very existence are easily ignored and should not be so ignored.

Godbout's importance here, then, lies in his call for an understanding of human action that makes room for both ethical self-giving and for the role of reciprocity in the building of institutions. While Bourdieu talks of various forms of capital as residing in collective bodies, he does not speak of how capital may be deployed positively in the construction of them, in the forging of moral identities and in the ongoing development of moral communities. It is possible to develop an analysis of spiritual capital in this direction, however, by appealing to the well-established insights of symbolic exchange theory, a body of ideas ultimately derived from Marcel Mauss's seminal work *The Gift* (1954). Mauss was concerned with how the personalized reciprocity of traditional societies gave way to an increasingly impersonal market-led economy in developed industrial societies.

For our analysis it is important to draw a distinction between what Mauss saw as the *threefold obligation* to give, to receive, and to give again in return, a scheme he reckoned to underlie a great many aspects of social life involving human beings, and the *fourth obligation* of giving to or being involved with the gods. The 'gifts' involved in the threefold scheme can bear a market value and be estimated as part of the overall scheme of giving, receiving and given back again in due course. The 'gifts' or phenomena involved in the fourth obligation carry a different kind of value, one that is culturally regarded as inestimable or inalienable. In popular terms we might speak of the 'sentimental value' of something irrespective of its monetary worth. Godelier explored how such inalienable gifts might help link the present with the past or furnish an 'anchorage in time': they, 'concentrate the greatest imaginary power and, as a consequence, the greatest symbolic value' (1999: 32–3).[5] In more specifically sociological terms, inalienable factors would be identified as the prime values of a society, those that normally pass as unquestioned and unassailable.

Others have developed Mauss's work and applied it to modern cultures as a means of interpreting the nature of persons in their self-understanding and in their mutual relationships. Drawing theoretical distinctions between bureaucratic and legally grounded institutions such as the state on the one hand and groups existing

---

5   One of the authors has, for example, employed this approach for analyzing different theological ideas, including the idea of grace (Davies, 2002: 53–80, 195–209) and also of the 'gift of the Spirit' in the Acts of the Apostles' (Davies, 2004a: 259–80), both as inestimable and inalienable gifts that could not, for example, be bought with money. This is why, in theological terms, the betrayal of Jesus, himself interpreted as constituting an inestimable gift, through the medium of mere money was particularly heinous: the more so when money paralleled the use of a kiss, itself more a symbol of the inalienable domain of human value (Luke 22:48).

through personal relationships and governed by moral concerns on the other, they describe how many people thrive 'on such things (as) affinities and privileged and personalized ties that are not only proper to personal relationships but also underlie the functioning of organizations grounded in the principle of the gift' (Godbout with Caillé, 1998: 62).

Here, the 'principle of the gift' describes 'the embodiment of the system of interpersonal social relationships' and serves to summarize the idea 'that the drive to give is as important to an understanding of humanity as the desire to receive ... compassion and generosity' (1998: 18–19). The gift principle also assumes that human beings do not seek freedom from others but, rather, a sense of security that accompanies social engagement enabling Godbout, for example, to argue trenchantly that 'friendship cannot replace family' (1998: 34). This perspective allows us to see the social and spiritual resources surrounding the Anglican hierarchy in terms of a complementary relationship between the centrality of moral commitment and the necessity of formal authority. We do this within a broader account of church and social life that takes seriously not just issues of power, but also the moral and theological traditions that invest the church and its leaders with meaning and significance.[6] Bishops and their families are not merely passive receptacles of kinds of capital but play an active part in shaping them for deployment in developing social life. It is precisely our intention to explore both as significant dimensions of spiritual capital and, in so doing, reflect on potentially fruitful theological topics to which our more social scientific perspectives draw attention.

In the present discussion, for example, we should take these very lives as potential embodiments of Christian belief and of the history within which that belief has been shaped. Tradition is embodied and, in this sense we can speak of bishops as part of the symbolic resource of a tradition now available for contemporary engagement. However, many of them are also husbands and, as such, are symbolic resources – or gifts – for wife and children, as their wives and children are for them. Here a potential conflict emerges between episcopal consecration that extends the social demands implied in priestly ordination and the marriage rite that marks a committed personal relationship of man and woman and creates new forms of community involvement for them as a couple. The married bishop is placed in a potentially problematic position with two demanding spheres of responsibility before him, diocese and family. Who, then, is the beneficiary of the spiritual capital that he represents and embodies? Must 'the gift' be divided, or can apparent tensions be reconciled? The answer to these questions has to be explored within a church that has long conceived of itself as a universal community and often also as a family of God with god-fathers and god-

---

6   One might view this approach as the 'thick description' associated with Geertz. Issues of competence in describing those studied is an ongoing anthropological debate and becomes complex in studies of one's own society where many possess informed opinion (Geertz, 1988: 129–49). Though much ignored, we note that in 1960 Isaiah Berlin used 'thick description' to account for a humanities approach allowing historians access to material with a 'texture constituted by the interwoven strands' of people and events (Berlin, [1960] 1997: 17–58). He contrasted this with the single-stranded 'thin' approaches of psychological, economic or even sociological work as he saw it.

mothers and members addressed as 'brothers and sisters': with God as its heavenly father, priests called 'father' and with the bishop as a father in God.

Generations and Value Transmission

Our interest in the emergence and transmission of spiritual capital as 'gift' also takes us into the domain of generational analysis and its concern with social change as played out from one generation to another. Here the pioneering work of Karl Mannheim (1952) remains influential, informing recent studies of the wartime generation, baby-boomers and Generation X. Still, the identification of the factors that distinguish any one generation of individuals from another remains a complicated task. Alessandro Cavalli is helpful in identifying three dimensions to the process:

> ... (1) the 'age effect' (depending on the developmental process – values, opinions, attitudes change because individuals grow up through various life stages); (2) the 'generational effect' (depending, as we have seen, on the selective exposure to historical situations and events during the formative phase of the life cycle); and (3) the 'time period effect' (depending upon the historically contingent situation at the moment the data were collected). (Cavalli, 2004: 159)

While Cavalli acknowledges that all three elements are often difficult to differentiate as significant variables it is important to be aware of them as they alert us to the complexities of the task and the limitations of certain research methods. For example, consideration of the 'time period effect' highlights the filters that inevitably shape interview responses. While enquiring about specific experiences we have, obviously, often asked individuals to recount details many years after the event. The elderly bishop telling the story of his appointment to an inner city parish forty years earlier is not simply furnishing us with historical fact; his account is colored by subsequent life experience, both personal and professional. He may choose to focus on his personal anxiety at being offered such a post, triggered by contemplation of its many unfamiliar demands or the knowledge that this parish embraced a style of church liturgy rather different from his own background. He may emphasize family upheaval, how upset the children were when moving from their rural village school, where they were settled and content. Both memories may be eclipsed by the nostalgia of a man pondering his career from the standpoint of retirement and it is left to us to contend with such historical filters, not to mention the insurmountable problem of memory, how it errs, selects, erases and forgets, in reflection of the subjective predilections of the individual, and the sometimes destabilizing effects of old age.

Such complexities, inevitably associated with in-depth interviews, properly demand critical reflection on the status of the information gained and take us beyond the assumption that oral history is simply another source from which a factual account may be constructed. Here recent studies of narrative are helpful in developing a critical perspective towards interview data and the way it reflects the subjective negotiation of identity. Narrative approaches also offer ways of dealing with the problem of the truth status of claims made in interviews. Charlotte Linde's innovative volume *Life Stories* (1993), for example, argues against approaches that focus on narrative only in so far as it may be correlated with external 'facts' or with the psycho-social identity of the speaker. The additional issue of how the interviewer and interviewee relate to each other, and develop a mutual understanding of what they are about also makes such correlations impossible to demonstrate with any degree of certainty. Linde prefers to work from the position that all we have to work with are 'texts', which she approaches not as indicators of truth but as sites for the achievement of coherence (Linde, 1993: 12–19). While not uncritical of Linde's approach to discourse, we do acknowledge the importance of coherence when trying to make sense of the narratives expressed during interviews. Asking individuals to reflect on their lives and identities provokes a variety of stories and accounts, but most are united in seeking to offer a coherent narrative. Moreover, such coherence is achieved not only through conformity with established rules and conventions of storytelling but also through an appeal to norms and reference points embodied in what Linde calls 'coherence systems' (Linde, 1993: 18). These are often shared by those of the same profession, and have certainly emerged among the bishops, wives and children of our study: coherence systems that are grounded in a position of institutional leadership in the Church of England and in family experiences consequent upon it. Indeed, we might argue that in appealing to such coherence systems, they are contributing to the emerging oral history of the church itself.

Echoing what we said earlier about exchange theory, this consideration of narrative also highlights the way our study places the individual rather than any group at the heart of our analysis. Informing our surveys and interviews, our presentation and interpretation of verbatim material, lies not just an acknowledgement of the importance of narrative theory in relation to religious experience (Yamane, 2000: 171–89), but also a real desire to pay 'serious attention to the individual as a category of analysis', especially to 'those individuals who are engaged in explicit or implicit religious life as an idiom of lived experience' (Hutch, 1997: 2). It is precisely this emphasis that shades our use of capital and symbolic exchange theories, where the individual accumulates and embodies networked experience and prime values. These individuals are set within broader networks of experience, as members of the episcopate, of the upper middle classes or products of a clergy family. Survey data help us determine the extent to which these clerically grounded groups are more or less representative of broader patterns among the British population during the late twentieth century, and allow us to see whether a spiritual elite expresses a distinctive identity in terms of its social attitudes, civic practices or religious convictions.

Studies of generational change have tended to group individuals together on the basis of shared and similar *formative experiences* (Cavalli, 2004: 156). Numerous books on the baby boomer generation, for example, focus on the significance of growing up after the Second World War through the period of post-war depression and on the experience of coming into adulthood during the vibrant 1960s. Our work does not allow such a neat analysis, as the individuals we are interested in are not united as generational cohorts in this sense; it is paternal occupation rather than strictly a period of biographical development that defines our population. It is therefore impossible to treat these bishops and their children as representatives of two identifiable generational groupings. However, two factors that are key to our concerns may be identified: the clerical family, and ecclesiastical changes from 1940 to 2000.

The first formative experience – the clerical family – is shared by all our clergy children, a good number of the bishops and some of their wives. It may not be surprising that many of those who go on to be or to marry clergymen originate from clerical families themselves. There is a clear tendency for some to gravitate towards the familiar, especially when social networks and personal faith present the right opportunities. These gladly embraced the life embodied by their father, and the model of faith and service that he represented for them. For some others, however, their clerical choice was in spite of efforts to act to the contrary and against more negative memories of a clerical home life. These patterns of response appear in chapter six, where the experience of being raised in a clerical family reveals a foundation upon which many clergy children later formulate a stance towards religion and the church, as well as towards work and the family.

The second formative experience is less clearly defined because it concerns the cultural and ecclesiastical changes encompassed by the period 1940–2000. While the varying ages of the bishops and their family members mean that different aspects of this sixty-year period will be of varying significance for different individuals, it is worth sketching the main elements that furnish an important cultural backdrop for the biographical experiences of both generations. As Cavalli comments: 'individual biographies are localized historically, influenced and conditioned by the historical context' (2004: 157). Given the very particular professional identities of these senior clergy, and the fact that their families experienced a life shaped by identifiable peculiarities, it is possible to isolate a series of key cultural factors which affected this group more than most others in British society, factors which, in some cases, reveal a kind of shared memory, forged out of common experiences and encounters. Table 1.1 shows the decade of birth of bishops covered in this study.[7]

Table 1.1   Bishops by decade of birth

Born	Number	% (Adjusted)
1900–1910	2	2
1911–1920	23	21
1921–1930	57	53
1931–1940	25	23
Total	107	100

All but eight were born between 1915 and 1935, with the eldest bishop born in 1907 and the youngest in 1936. The eldest bishops' child was born in 1944, the youngest in 1981. For both sub-groups there is a lengthy period between eldest and youngest, which accounts for well over a generation, and encompasses significant cultural change. Accordingly, we cannot assume that members within each group have been subject to the same cultural pressures, and therefore cannot reasonably

---

7   A full account of the criteria used in selecting the bishops, wives and children within this study is provided in the Appendix.

be categorized within the same generational cohort, however defined. However, it is worth noting the period 1935–55 because of its distinctive first-hand or family-related experience of the Second World War and its aftermath, and because this was when most of the bishops were between the ages of 15 to 25, a formative period for many as far as their vocation was concerned.

Cultural Context

Our concern lies, primarily, with the narrative accounts of these bishops, their wives and children, and with how their formative experience may have lead them to embody particular orientations to their social context in terms of moral and religious outlook and professional identity. As a cultural background for this we sketch some salient social features of British life over our period 1940–2000 (see Plate 1), from a period beset by war through a brief post-war increase of religious activity into a more secular ethos that increasingly seemed to typify wider British society from the 1960s.

Social Welfare and Religious Ecumenism

The Second World War between major Christian countries, thoughts on its aftermath and planning for a new social and religious order frame the beginning of our period. Archbishop Lang resigned, aged 77, in 1942, aware that 'great problems of reconstruction' would lie ahead for both church and state and would require a younger man (Lockhart, 1949: 439). Edward Norman is one who has furnished a clear account of the intertwined theological and political concerns debated during and after that war, including the considered opinions and visions of church leaders such as William Temple, Archbishop of Canterbury from only 1942–44, who 'could not envisage the notion of a secular State' and whose *Christianity and Social Order* of 1942 was influential and widely read (Norman, 1976: 368). Christian commitments to social welfare, justice and reform were expressed in such events as the Malvern Conference of 1941 or groups such as Christian Action in 1945 with its concern for post-war Germany and later with Apartheid in South Africa. The emergent Ecumenical Movement, a conjoint venture of many churches to seek increased unity and collaboration, was expressed concretely, for example, both in the inauguration of the British Council of Churches in 1942, with its own influence upon the later Christian Aid charitable venture,[8] and The World Council of Churches in Amsterdam in 1948. Significant for many of our bishops was the Parish and People movement created at Queen's College, Birmingham in 1949 which sought to place the Eucharist and a sense of communal life at the heart of British parishes.[9] The Liturgical Commission would follow in 1955. In 1960 the Christian Socialist

---

8   Suggate (1994): 467–87, explores ecumenism and social concern from 1945.

9   Not all gave wholehearted support. In the early 1960s Edwin Morris, Archbishop of Wales, was critically aware that Morning Prayer and, especially, Evensong would suffer because of the morning Eucharist's centrality (Peart-Binns, 1990: 180).

Movement was founded.[10] That year, too, Archbishop Fisher visited Pope John XXIII at Rome and, shortly after, non-Catholics were invited to be observers at the Second Vatican Council (1962–65) whose 1964 Decree on Ecumenism helped redefine non-Catholics more as 'separated brethren' than as dissidents beyond the pale. While in 1969 (and again in 1972) the Church of England rejected a scheme of union with Methodists, much to the dismay of some committed Anglicans, it entered into a new Anglican-Roman Catholic International Commission (ARCIC) that would go on to address a series of theological-ecclesiastical issues.

Bryan Wilson's influential *Religion in Secular Society* (1966) devoted three of its 12 chapters to 'Ecumenicalism', interpreting it as 'a growing recognition of the essential weakness of religious life in the increasingly secular society' (Wilson, 1966: 154). By contrast, while some of our bishops recognized changes in social attitude in which 'the climate has driven us back to the wall a bit', leaving them with a position that 'doesn't count for much these days', many remained positive about ecumenical experiences. One potentially creative aspect of ecumenical work was that it pre-adapted the churches for their subsequent response to non-Christian religions in Britain, initially with Sikhs and Hindus but, especially in the 1990s, also with Islam as it rapidly assumed social significance. Here, an increased secularization was paralleled by the emergence of a religious identity of a shared kind and bishops tended to operate at precisely the level of public action that encountered these issues. As we will see below, they generally met it in a more positive than negative spirit.

Liberal, Evangelical and Charismatic Shifts

Following the social theology of the 1930s–1940s there emerged a shift to more individual concerns manifest, for example, from the later 1950s in psychotherapeutically marked perspectives including Clinical Theology, headed by Frank Lake,[11] and in the 1960s to individual possibilities of belief with suffragan bishop of Woolwich John Robinson's 1963 *Honest to God* prompting extensive popular discussion.[12] Such critical and relatively popular theological writing would be followed with David Jenkins, as Bishop of Durham, posing all sorts of questions to jangle any self-satisfied Anglican contentment while, from Cambridge, Don Cupitt's work, as in *The Debate about Christ* (1979), fostered The Sea of Faith movement with its conferences and network through its radical form of human-centered religiosity. Feminist, Black and Gay Theologies would all develop the theme of oppressive power in relation to the widely espoused notions of the freedom and maturity of the self-in-community. Looking back over his period of service, one who had been both a suffragan and a quite well-known diocesan bishop said he 'was

---

10   Preston (1988): 24–31, furnishes some insightful comment on its subsequent 'becalming'.

11   Lake acknowledged the help of 41 bishops in facilitating training in this approach in their dioceses (1966: xii). His early work included 'a heavy reliance on the use of lysergic acid (LSD) long before it became the suspect drug it now is' (Hare Duke, 1982).

12   Even prompting a rapid response from Archbishop Ramsey (Carey, 1995: 159–75).

always very conscious of how much we were just getting by, theologically at least, we couldn't have done with much less'.

Through the 1970s and 1980s the Church of England also witnessed an evangelical resurgence, especially amongst clergy and bishops, as well as the rise of the Charismatic Movement. Yet again the individual assumed the social focus of discourse as a growth in religious interest, zeal and commitment amongst significant minorities of middle-class, churchgoing and a few peripheral individuals offered a new sense of community for many whose social worlds were increasingly fragmented. This force affected evangelicals in a distinctive fashion but also embraced some catholic constituencies in the church. Bishops now had to cope with this new dimension amongst their clergy and parishes. New pressures also came from issues over the ordination of women and of homosexual clergy, moves that sometimes brought the otherwise antipathetic evangelical and Anglo-catholic factions into alliance against what some supposed to be a liberal conspiracy (cf. Burgess, 2005). Surrounding all these issues lay theological matters and the necessity to engage with them. From the later 1970s, too, the Oxford-based Alastair McGrath wrote prodigious amounts of theology of a more evangelical kind while the pastorally and politically focussed work of Bishop David Sheppard in Liverpool, often in partnership with Derek Warlock, Liverpool's Catholic Archbishop, fostered a kind of Liberation Theology hallmarked by its bias to the poor and applied to a British context. Some of these trends took firm root within the church at large, and Sheppard's perspectives influenced the Church of England's *Faith in the City* report (1985), and in turn its ensuing Urban Fund that sought to channel money from richer to poorer areas.[13] The momentum behind Sheppard's initiative also illustrates how, at certain times, the established church has come into conflict with the state and certain of its 'policies of confrontation', exemplified in comments critical of the government made by the bishops of Birmingham, Durham and Canterbury in the 1980s (Heelas and Morris, 1992: 260). Evangelical theology coupled with Charismatic revitalization shaped the Alpha Course (cf. Hunt, 2001), subsequently more influential than the Decade of Evangelism proposed by Archbishop George Carey in the 1990s. Alongside this we have the rising significance of the laity, often increasingly well educated yet decreasing in number, for the financial welfare and broad social capital of the church. To note these many social, ideological and organizational changes is to gain some sense of the pressures faced by bishops as leaders amidst a changing world.

There was over this period, too, an increasing groundswell of wider ethical discourse fired by notions of human rights and increasingly explicit concerns over ethics drawing from broad principles rather than simply from religious roots. This echoes, in some respects, Callum Brown's historical analysis of secularization in Britain. He aligned this change with a shift in modes of perceiving and publicly addressing religious themes allied with the place of women within British society and the life of churches. He sees the 1960s as marked by a 'sudden and culturally violent event', which is none other than a dramatic shift in the decreased role taken

---

13   *Faith in the City* (1985); see also the progress report *Living Faith in the City* (1990). The subsequent *Faith in the Countryside* (1990) also involved social welfare issues (Davies, Watkins and Winter, 1991).

by women in maintaining and transmitting religious practice (Brown, 2001: 175). Perhaps the ordination of women was both a reflection and a denial of this thesis in that, at one level, it marked a degree of increased feminization of the church[14] at a time when clerical status was declining in society at large. Certainly, theological shifts were accompanied by appropriate liturgical reform with the *Alternative Service Book* introduced in 1980 and *Common Worship* in 2000 while, in the intervening period, women were admitted to the Diaconate from 1987 and to the Priesthood from 1992. Politicians, too, came to be interested in engaging with and in supporting 'faith communities', not only because of matters of conflict but also because of their potential as voluntary agencies of social welfare provision provided. The Church of England often played important roles in these changing interests, not least because of the recognized place of bishops as social networkers with a recognized political voice.

Family

Our period also involved changes in the nature of family life (Davies, 1993), from the Christian definition of marriage (Segalen, 1986) through changes in sex and marriage patterns (Gorer, 1973) and working-class generations and the way they depict their family history (Cornwell, 1984) to post-modern notions of discrete selves maintaining increasingly voluntary relational networks (Giddens, 1991: 176–7). Of most relevance here are those social shifts of emphasis and practice that impact upon many ordinary families and call into question or highlight features in those of bishops. Callum Brown, for example, refers to the 1930s and 1940s as a period when, 'contented marriage and home, though decreasingly discussed in 1930s girls' magazines, was still an embedded meaning, especially evident in what Tinkler classifies as mother-daughter magazines'. He argued that what,

> changed in the 1930s and 1940s was that contentment displaced anxiety in moral discourse. The artefacts of male temptation – drink, betting and pre-marital sex – were no longer the problem; it was discontented rather than immoral manhood which the woman had to combat in the home, and to do this she had to make the home an unremittingly happy place. (Brown, 2001: 87)

Another, though quite different, family-related issue, running throughout our period concerns the difference between celibacy and marriage among the clergy in relation to their mode of ministry and social acceptance. The fact that church leaders may possess an immediate family of their own may well affect the way a church is perceived by its laity as by wider society. Major religions all hold a relatively clear attitude to how ultimate goals may be negotiated through the practicalities of family life,[15] and within Christian history itself, the shift from the medieval Catholic

---

14 Nesbitt (1997) offers a major study of *Feminization of the Clergy in America*.

15 Sikhism sets the householder as the ideal-type religious person, Hinduism holds a fourfold scheme including but not prizing the householder, while Buddhism's ideal is celibacy.

ideal of the celibate priest to the Protestant permission of leaders to marry was a significant innovation.[16] The fact that Orthodoxy allows marriage for priests but not for bishops further illustrates the practical importance accorded to marriage and the family within both the life of the church and the economy of society at large.

Visions of Episcopacy

As with models of marriage so, too, with models of episcopacy, for the Church of England possesses no single and fixed theology of bishops, a fact that has borne upon discussions with other churches, especially with Methodists, the Nordic Lutherans and, at present, in considerations of the possibility of women as bishops (Podmore, 2006). Here we outline a series of germane but not exhaustive theological and ecclesiastical accounts of bishops, indicating some of the changing historical emphases, but paying particular attention to those that bear most upon our period.

Late in the sixteenth century, Richard Hooker transacted important theological business over bishops as the Church of England began to establish its new identity within English society. In countering extreme Protestant views opposing episcopal governance, he employs an extensive analysis of Patristic material to affirm the office of bishop as essentially consonant with the emergence and growth of Christian churches. 'Prelates are the Apostles' successors' (*Laws*: VII.xvii.4.), their principal role lies in ordaining priests, in being pastor to these pastors, and in the governance of clergy and laity (*Laws*: VII.ii.3). Indeed, this pastoral care of the clergy is something that is 'the first thing looked for', as is the 'severity' they should show to both high and low when occasion demands critical judgment. Without that, bishops will appear to many 'as bees that have lost their sting' (Laws: VII.xxiv.11). He also considers how honor is due to bishops because, theologically if not historically, 'bishops are now as high priests were then' in biblical Israel. Hooker holds the opinion that 'a bishop's estimation doth grow from the excellency of virtues suitable unto his place' (*Laws*: VII.xxiv.15). Since 'devotion and the feeling sense of religion' are often absent in secular rulers it is, for him, all the more important that bishops should embody just these elements because such a religiously formed character will evoke a respect, 'a stooping kind of disposition, clean opposite to contempt' amongst rulers (*Laws*: VII.xxiv.15). Hooker's view of bishops is one of Christian continuity, an embodiment of faithful, devotional and learned spirituality made present in society at large and capable of judicious criticism, and of pastoral care for the clergy. His relative uncertainty over whether 'prelates are the apostles' successors' because of simple continuity of Christian practice or of apostolic fiat was not matched by a growing view in the seventeenth and eighteenth centuries that emphasized the latter (cf. Norris, 1988: 303). Transformations in the relationship between the 'godly prince' and the church probably necessitated an increasing emphasis upon the bishop as the effective power of princes declined and that of parliament increased. Such changes would need to be interpreted by recourse to increasingly theological ideas,

---

16   Taken to the Protestant extreme in Mormonism's necessity of marriage for ultimate salvation.

whether in some model of Apostolic Succession, of universal unity or of servanthood. Certainly, the relative weight of religious and political factors framing episcopacy would change from the days of Elizabeth I to those of Elizabeth II. As Richard Norris describes these changes, Anglican episcopacy 'has come to count as a factor that grounds the identity of the Church', indeed it comes to be 'an institution which counts as part of the definition of "church"'. Despite that emergence, he stressed how 'little energy has been devoted to examination of the actual workings of episcopacy' (1988: 306–7). This point needs emphasis, especially when we realize that, within Anglicanism, the very notion of episcopacy is still in the process of formulation and development. It is, in fact, one key arena within which images and ideals of the notion of 'church' and 'orthodoxy' are worked out. This becomes especially clear when Anglicans engage with other denominations, as Joseph Britton (2003), for example, has shown for Anglicans and Lutherans.

From the nineteenth century one telling account of bishops, diocesan and suffragan, was furnished by John Henry Newman just before his attitude to Anglicanism changed.[17] Responding to a contemporary Ecclesiastical Commission concerning the 'more equal distribution of Episcopal duties', he advocates an increase in the number of bishops in a 'resident Episcopy', through a restoration of the 'primitive institution of Suffragans', and in response to the 'local wants of an overgrown and disaffected population'.[18] Newman argues not for innovation but for developments grounded in a sense of history, citing Constantinople as a large and needy city in the fourth and fifth centuries. He reminds us that Cranmer had advised Henry VIII to endow some fifteen to twenty new sees with the proceeds from the disestablished monasteries, and that five were thus established. He also notes that an existing Act of Parliament (26 Henry VIII c. 14) would allow for an immediate appointment of some 26 suffragan bishops if the church agreed to it. More critically, he cites Bishop Ussher's failed plan of 1641 to furnish suffragans 'equal to the number of rural deans'. Newman interestingly sees the episcopal role as closely related to that of an evangelist and would have been happy for each city to possess one. What is historically important about Newman's account is his observation that bishops were, in some sense, marginal in the actual life of the church. He asks rhetorically: 'are we not, if the truth be spoken, tending to this – to learn to dispense with the episcopal system altogether?' Many of the laity and clergy could not give an answer to the 'use of having bishops', and there is a 'painful growing separation of feeling, on the whole, between the Episcopal Bench and the Clergy' (Newman, 1835: 25–7).

The transformation from that nineteenth-century image to the twentieth shows just how dynamic a focus the episcopacy has been and is within the Church of England. Kenneth Medhurst and George Moyser's careful social-political study of the Church of England in the early and mid-twentieth century, for example, traces the

---

17 Newman says he viewed the Church of England as 'a mere national institution' from 1836 (1946: 219).

18 He bases his paper statistically, comparing the population of 1378 (2,300,000) and 1588 (4,400,000) with 1831 (13,897,187), and even provides a statistical appendix with dioceses in rank order of population in which Chester's population (1,883,958) exceeds that of London (1,722,605).

transformations in the episcopate from the 'prince' bishops of the English Reformation period into the 'prelate' form of the eighteenth and nineteenth centuries. Whereas each of these types could express a 'monarchical' perspective on life, the prince-bishop was more directly involved in the political life of the nation as one party to its central elite, while the prelate-bishop was less so. Medhurst and Moyser argue that this shift in degree of involvement is one example of increasing secularization, drawing particular attention to the pastoral aspect of the prelate-bishop's work. Even if driven monarchically to control his diocese to the full extent of his authority, he was increasingly concerned with the clergy under his charge. Accordingly, Medhurst and Moyser describe the *pastoral model* as typifying 'the more recent, redefined, and now common model of episcopacy', locating the main transition into this form of 'modern bishop' within the 1960s (Medhurst and Moyser, 1988: 98). Factors influencing this change are many but include the clergy's experience of military service, including active war experience and the post-war transformation in British life. One bishop in our study could even speak of his Cambridge theological college in the post-war period as preferring not to take young men lacking wider experience of 'the world'. Others note the distinctive influence of individuals like William Temple who refocussed pastoral concern in the nation at large. Complementing these changes was a new commitment to ecumenism and to the wider world of Anglicanism, of which some influential bishops of the mid-twentieth century had personal experience. These important elements furnish a backcloth of institutional values against which our generation of bishops emerged as the next wave of church leaders.

Paul Avis provides a complementary though brief account of transformations in the English church and its bishops in a threefold scheme of development. This begins with the 'nation-as-church' model, typifying the church between the Reformation and the Oxford Movement of the earlier nineteenth century, though with some elements still reflected today with, for example, some bishops in the House of Lords and the sovereign as supreme governor of the church (Avis, 2000: 15). His second model – 'the Episcopal succession model' – he identifies as emerging in the late seventeenth century and gaining impetus from the Oxford Movement. It draws on the notion of apostolic succession, claiming that 'bishops are essential' for the very nature as well as the organization of the church (Avis, 2000: 20). Though seeing many historical and contemporary weaknesses in this outlook, he retains the value of the bishop as 'the effective symbol of unity', a retention that enhances his preferred scheme of the contemporary English church – 'the communion-through-baptism' model. He identifies an increasing egalitarianism in the shift from the focus on one monarch in his first model through to several bishops in his second, to the many baptized members in the third. Whatever the model, however, bishops are there playing a significant if changing role as reflected in the widely influential Chicago-Lambeth Quadrilateral of 1886–88, in which the historic episcopate is listed alongside (i) the Holy Scriptures, (ii) Apostles' and Nicene Creeds and (iii) the two sacraments of Baptism and Lord's Supper (Hankey, 1988: 209).

These historical and theological sketches of Anglican ecclesiology afford a firm background against which to ponder both the contemporary theological and practical significance of bishops in the church. As Chapter 2 intimates, while bishops are rarely present in today's parishes this is not an unprecedented trend as Anthony Russell argues, 'the role of the eighteenth century bishop stressed his political function as a member of the House of Lords, which required him to reside in London for the greater part of the year' (Russell, 1980: 133). He notes that this, along with poor roads and the 'extreme age and infirmity' of many bishops, meant that they appeared in parishes very infrequently for confirmations, perhaps every three years. Russell's astute historical and sociological study, *The Clerical Profession*, is of particular interest because of the absence of bishops in its account of the emergence of a clerical profession and in the operation of the church in the nineteenth and twentieth centuries. Almost echoing Newman, they play a very small part indeed in the operation of the clerical profession as he analyses it. Still, amongst his suggested models of the future church, the bishop emerges in 'The Church of the Reformist Future' in which 'the stipendiary ministry forms a closely knit team, centered on the leadership and authority of the bishop' (Russell, 1980: 304). Because Russell's focus was on the *clerical* profession it might be expected to exclude any particular concern with bishops, but that is not the point we make here. Rather, it is in reflecting upon, for example, Hooker's affirmation of the bishop as a pastor of the pastors that we might have expected the relationship between bishop and parish clergyman to have a significant profile. The fact that it is given hardly any serious description or analysis suggests that it was, in fact, of relatively minor importance during the period Russell addressed, not least the mid-twentieth century, the time when our population of bishops was in training and, later, in ministry and episcopal office.

If, during our period, the role of the bishop has remained implicit rather than explicit, then we might ask what the role is. Trevor Beeson's *The Bishops* (2002), based on biographical accounts of 48 bishops over the period 1832–2000, offers one possibility, that 'all of today's bishops fall into the single category of pastoral-manager' (2002: 1). One of his goals is to analyze this category and, critically, suggest creative ways of exploiting it as the church moves into an increasingly problematic future where mission is more important than maintenance, larger units of church organization are necessary, and in which the bishop has time and opportunity to ponder development, direct specialist clerical staff, and engage with 'society's influencers and decision-makers' as part of a strategy in which society at large may be 'infiltrated and improved' by Christian values (2002: 233, 231), desires that resemble those of Newman some 170 years earlier. To achieve this Beeson would have an increase in area bishops with delegated responsibility for the 'twin Episcopal roles' of pastoral and administrative work. He sees a corresponding need for a higher caliber of diocesan bishop than currently exists, one whose strategic thinking and networking capacity is framed by spiritual and theological intensity.

We, too, will explore this category of 'pastoral-manager' in a variety of ways in Chapters 2, 3 and 4. Historically speaking, Beeson sees English bishops as being largely unpopular, more often bastions of a political establishment than saints devoted to the needs of church and people. Though Gladstone was the first Prime Minister to have an ecclesiastical advisor, Beeson still judges the nineteenth century a largely negative period of episcopal leadership, including the loss of the working classes to the church throughout the Industrial Revolution, despite programs of church building and an attempt at replicating the parish system in large urban contexts. He claims that the inability of bishops to cope, for example, with the scientific advances of the nineteenth century left them discredited, resulting in a 'serious reduction in the number of able men seeking Holy Orders and providing a strong cadre from which bishops could be chosen'. He cites the influential priest Dick Sheppard, writing in 1927: 'Frankly, I doubt if any bishop on the present Bench is capable of really leading the Church on the road to sacrifice. The Church needs a bigger man than any of its present Bishops' (Beeson, 2002: 4–5). Despite changes in the twentieth century, including recruitment of bishops with university backgrounds beyond Oxford and Cambridge, Beeson judges that 'the Church of England entered the twenty-first century with an alarming lack of bishops of widely acknowledged ability' (2002: 6). It is this sense of 'ability' that poses a challenging question for our study. What does it mean? It is easy to talk of ability in terms of scholarly, managerial or interpersonal competences. It is also easy to speak of a person's prior experience as furnishing an optimum background for a leadership post. But it is also possible to see in this notion of 'ability' a different kind of concern, one partially revealed in Beeson's desire to see bishops 'liberated from a role which has become a denial of the true purpose of their sacred office and a serious hindrance to the church's mission in the twenty-first century'. Beeson's theological statements about Christianity are few, yet references to Christ as 'the founder of their faith' and to 'the poor man of Nazareth' who was 'for the most part despised and rejected' are illuminating and point to a Jesus-focussed, open-ended, theology (2002: 2, 3). Perhaps Beeson does not say or know what today's form of message should be, but he wants men who can find and implement it. Here we are faced with bishops possessing a sacred office, related to a despised founder, who are a sign of contradiction and whose mission is to infiltrate a networked world with a faith that they must interpret in ways that may 'influence those elements in modern culture that militate against any form of religious belief' (2002: 207).

We do not present Beeson's desire for a distinctive category of 'visionary leader' as simplistic idealism, but as reflective of the complexity involved in a religious institution cognizant of the equally complex cultural change in which it is set and aware that its major resource of response lies in individuals. In fact, it is a description that easily resonates with the concepts of spiritual capital and embodied 'gift' that underlie much of this book.

These varied models and interpretations of episcopacy offer a valuable background for contemporary research, being rooted in the ecclesiastical and social experience of the authors concerned: experience that also influences their reading of history and application of theology. We, too, have been similarly influenced, not least by the impact of the individuals who generously allowed us to survey and interview them and their families. It is with the central importance of these individuals in mind that we introduce the first of a series of case studies that will bring theoretical issues to life at the same time as they challenge any simplicity of explanation.

Case Study: School and College Influence

One former suffragan and diocesan bishop saw amongst the major influences on his life that of his father – 'a quiet and shy man who loved his work' as a 'doctor to … a whole community … an example of unfussy dedication'. His mother was the daughter 'of a Christian Socialist parson' and, although the household was churchgoing, he did not particularly 'love church services as a boy'. It was his boarding school – 'not particularly prestigious' – that made a considerable impression upon him. The 'staff were the best English stock, yeoman stock, and somehow they were all a community'. Then, his housemaster's view of life, 'very much sparked by the sense of the good, and the moral imperative', added its influence to one who was 'a born prefect' who then received a commission during his national service which included service abroad when he would 'go to some length to get to church services', something that had 'quite surprised' him and caused him to laugh in the interview.

Going up to Cambridge, he encountered in his college 'amazing figures of influence', a feature to which we return in Chapter 2, and it is in this atmosphere that he was 'able to tie the whole thing up with the Christian gospel … that was it … yes.' Here a long pause in the interview seemed to mark the importance of that reflection in which home, school, the military and Cambridge had united in some way in his making sense of Christianity.

It was the combined influence of the dean and chaplain of his college that turned his mind to ordination. He admired these men – 'Clever, oh how they worked together' – one a most distinguished scholar and the other a dedicated pastor, 'a remarkable person who would sit up till two o'clock to speak to students' and who went on to become a bishop himself. It was the chaplain who (in that form of typically Anglican spiritual direction of 'reserve' or of an 'aside' in life that we analyze later) 'casually said to me as we were going on a reading party in Derbyshire, "there is always a school chaplain as well as a schoolmaster you know"'. He added: 'coming from a world-class person like him [this] … was very fortunate'. The idea of vocation to the priesthood did not seem strange because a general sense of vocation within life 'was there anyway through the influence' of home, school and army. 'Ordination was one other way of pursuing the vocation to be a human being according to the Christian Gospel.' This took the form of 'a subtle combination between the leadership thing and the servant thing', and echoed his memory of a school report entry: 'he's learned that the master of all is the servant of all'. He added: 'now you don't always get that. There is a tradition that if you get to the top you make a big thing out of it for yourself. This was a different tradition.' He then explicitly talked of how this value 'combined with the moral imperative' from school and with the Cambridge influence to enable him to appreciate the Christian Gospel. While his theological college helped him frame his sense of identity within 'Anglican Catholicism' but clearly not that of the more 'Roman' variety, it did so through wider church groupings, especially Parish and People and journals such as *Prism* (later *New Christian*). The college was not the great influence it was to numerous other bishops in our study; for him it was the vicars with whom he served as a curate who were to be influential upon his own developing ministry. So, too, with figures such as Eric James, Nick Stacey and Trevor Beeson, whom he identified as 'tremendous influences on a number of parish clergy' because of the 'boldness of the stuff they were bringing to light' and who did not become bishops, 'whereas unknown people like me did'. As for his vicars, both of whom went on to become church dignitaries, one was 'a very vital person' who fostered artistic ventures and another 'a pure parish priest who knew his stuff and this was a real eye-opener ... who knew everything ... first in the way he approached things, the policy, and the way he moved his church forward, and had the ability to see inside me and pull my leg'.

This bishop is interesting for his sense of the cumulative development of his life. For example, his sense of ministry as both vicar and bishop did not come 'as a clap of thunder', but through 'hard work years after ... learning what it is like to be this embodied figure', one that 'must be more than a symbol ... [who] must produce good work'. This last comment was amplified when he said that a parish priest 'can always go back the next day', presumably to correct an error, whereas the next day finds the bishop 'in a different parish'. He had also been much influenced through the church's provision of training courses, as at St George's House, Windsor, and described his own development as coming more from 'the group route' than from, for example, any individual spiritual director. He was keen to use the 'secular skills' and input from specialists as part of diocesan programs through which people might 'see themselves as a family, a valued group that made sense of life'. What he sought in people was a 'change from going to church and taking away a message for oneself and a New Testament sense of being committed to each other and yet retaining that openness to those round and about and not being a tight group as is the tendency of some traditions'. He felt he had managed this both as a suffragan and diocesan bishop, and felt that both he and his wife had been genuinely missed when he left both posts. In this he contrasted the type of bishop valued 'for the high profile thing' with his own style of 'affecting people' through more direct contact. His view and experience of the Church of England in the 1960s was one in which 'teaching was part of group learning', in which, as far as a leader is concerned, 'the less he says the more effective he is'. At a more personal level this bishop noted his own sense of personal development and, 'a very significant part of the pilgrimage' coming from a growing engagement with a psychological understanding of himself. His wife had also been a major influence. From a medical family, she had 'thrown herself into having children' and later developed a career and clear identity of her own while also being extremely supportive of his ministry not because she was married to him but 'as a matter of her vocation to the church and Christian cause'. Her siblings included influential businessmen. The children were in either teaching or community-focussed jobs.

One feature of this case lies in the way in which direct references to God or Christ or, indeed, to any specific formulation or expression of Christian doctrine does not occur as a matter of course. It is not avoided, but when asked about religious and spiritual development he replied: 'As a question this is absolutely straight down the line isn't it? It's obvious you have this question and it's fine ... Here you go into personal history ... so you want a bit of that do you?'

We mention this because the way the bishop then discussed his life as we have outlined it above was in and through people and circumstance, in a networked complexity of influence, out of which a sense of 'the Christian Gospel' emerged.

This scheme of development, almost a *bricolage* of faith emerging from life, then becomes a kind of model for his own mode of operation in ministry when seeking to 'talk little' and encourage the development of others in a group focused fashion. So, too, with his children and religion, he and his wife had 'certainly not tried to pump it in. Its more a case of let them take it'.

This case study highlights the feature of a networked life that cumulatively developed a sense of what the Christian message is, of how it is related to groups (family, school, the military and college), influential individuals (parents, schoolmasters, chaplains, wife), within a growing experience of parish life in one curacy (with two different yet influential vicars), two incumbencies, and theological-practical church movements (Parish and People). This before the experience of suffragan and diocesan ministry fostered new experiences and introduced further church-focussed training and support groups. As such this case, with its sets of cohering experiences, exemplifies the process in which social and spiritual capital interfuse in life.

Conclusion

This kind of detailed complexity could be reproduced for many other bishops. Its importance lies in portraying the personal interfaces between individual and profession, and in the caution it brings to any consideration of the more fixed models and partial classifications of bishops outlined earlier and which tend to be employed when describing institutions and their personnel within a larger framework. The bifocal task of pondering such situations in terms of capital and symbolic exchange theories is also worth reiterating in relation to such models. Joseph Britton, for example, describes how the nineteenth-century Phillips Brooks, Bishop of Massachusetts, viewed American Episcopal 'attachment to the symbolic formalisms of polity and ritual … as running the danger of creating a stagnant reservoir of power and tradition, rather than emanating in a flowing river of love and obedience to Christ' (Britton, 2003: 611–12). Ignoring the dual valuations in this quotation, it illustrates well the pitfalls and potential of capital images of 'reservoirs of power' and symbolic exchange motifs of 'flowing rivers'. While there is no need to align 'tradition' with a static image, as Brooks obviously did, it is important to have a theoretical means of comparing and contrasting more institutional motifs such as tradition and the more personal images of, for example, 'love' and 'obedience'.

The relationship between bishop and church can, then, be interpreted from different perspectives. Social scientific, historical and theological approaches have all made contributions to understanding bishops not only as symbols of the universal church – power elites with authority over leadership, doctrine and practice within the changing philosophical, political and economic fortunes of churches over two millennia – but also as pastors with roles in evangelism. While our approach will, when appropriate, engage with both theological and some historical material, its main perspective remains sociological as we seek to describe more contemporary aspects of episcopal life in church, family and in English social worlds during the second half of the twentieth century. In all, this our goal is to provide at least some response to Richard Norris's call for 'exploration-theological and practical – of the relation between the bishop's role as one who speaks to the Church and his role as one who speaks for the Church and with it' (Norris, 1988: 308).

Chapter 2

Bishop and Church:
Changing Times and Institutions

Beginning with bishops as mediators between national and local church, this chapter then moves to examine their childhood, parents, schools, churches, university and theological college training. The spatial contexts of their diocese and palace-home are then pondered before concluding with a combination of case studies and further theoretical reflections on personal influences and the constraints inherent in formal sociological categories.

Bishops are central to contemporary Church of England organization despite their infrequent presence in any one parish.[1] When at Confirmation services or licensing new clergy their theological significance becomes liturgically explicit as a symbol of the universal faith and as the pastor responsible for its local administration. New incumbents share in this ministry as both ordination rites and parish licensing make clear. As substitute-representatives, the bishop charges vicars to teach, administer the sacraments and care for the people committed to their charge. The bishop's place within the grand narrative of Christian history and practice is also rehearsed in his absence when the people pray for their bishop in the regular liturgy. In both theological tradition and liturgical practice, then, bishops symbolize the universal nature of the faith and manifest it through their practical ministry. These two 'directions' of ministry, outward to the world at large and inward to the locality, combine to furnish the prime dynamics of episcopal life within the Church of England, their relative emphasis depending upon particular contexts.

This pivotal episcopal significance is not, however, without its difficulties, as evident in the crisp self-criticism of the official 2001 report, *Resourcing Bishops*. There bishops expressed three key anxieties: excessive administration, increasing 'introversion' in church work rather than engagement with the wider community, and the problematic balance between '*leading* the Church and *running* the Church' (2001: 86; original emphasis). All three relate to our concern with bishops as universal and local. In Chapter 4 we explore these tensions within diocesan–suffragan bishop relationships but here we remain with the ways in which territory-grounded identity affects their work and family life. For, though a bishop's geographical diocese might appear to be only an enlarged version of his former parish, with several bishops emphasizing this point, other factors mark a difference, especially issues of place of

---

1   Even a bishop writing a manual for clergy in the 1970s gives very scant attention to Episcopal profiles within parishes (Martineau, 1972: 19, 31, 55). Forder's influential manual is similarly stark (1949: 48, 257–8).

work in relation to identity and the location of the home in relation to the family's networks of work, school, leisure and friendship.

Residence, Work and Identity

By the twenty-first century the theme of work and place became increasingly complex. The taken-for-granted sense of 'place of work' that reflects traditional notions of work-location now readily contrasts with contemporary possibilities of working 'from home'. Telephones apart, developments in electronic communication that make distance-working perfectly feasible for many professionals were not generally available to bishops for much of the period 1940–2000. Moreover, much of a bishop's work depends upon his physical presence and immediate contact with people.

A prime theological frame for diocesan bishops returns us to that double-direction of their local and universal significance. Anglican thought has often stressed the catholicity from which bishops bring a valid Christian authority to a locality while also representing that local ministry at regional and world levels. Indeed, the Church of England increasingly interpreted and sought to practice its theology through episcopal frames in the centuries after the Reformation. This inevitably turned the geographical fact of space into a theological interpretation of place. Even though this perspective may be more representative of Catholic rather than Protestant thinking it is very evident in the formularies of the Church of England, fostered historically in mutually reinforcing ways through the English Reformation, the dynamics of statehood, monarchy and empire. Even though such a perspective may play a subsidiary role in the thought of many Evangelicals, if it plays any part at all, it is likely to grow in significance as Evangelicals increase amongst the bishops.

These theological interpretations of ministry bear, quite dramatically, upon the identity of the bishop when approached more anthropologically through the notion of embodiment. While each and every individual comes, in a sense, to embody the values of their social world, the bishop does so in a distinctive fashion because his embodiment is rooted in a spatial context. But to these theological views of the bishop as expressing the ministry of Christ and his church here and now needs to be added the status of a bishop in a state church. This adds a political dimension to his embodiment of religious and social values in what emerges as a heavy responsibility reflected in the rite of consecration as in subsequent experience.

Placing Identity

Human beings are place-related in complex ways. That growth of meaning that infuses a degree of well-being in life is, itself, intimately associated with adaptation to environment. New and strange places both tax and excite us, eliciting high levels of attention that enhance perception of our surroundings. The widespread denominational practice of training specialist leaders and sending them to new places is, theoretically speaking, very significant for, in heightening an individual's awareness, it may foster both wariness of established patterns of life and the desire to repeat familiar patterns.

The move from parish to parish, to some other duty or to a diocese is likely to involve a degree of stress, with the energy demanded by new circumstances needing to be met from personal resources. This is not to say that such stress may not be creative, on the contrary, the very attitudes that emerge to face new challenges are likely to be those that foster vision and the desire to enact it. What is more, in terms of church members new leaders often foster a sense of hope and possibility. And hope is central to a great deal of individual, community and institutional life, it is also a central dynamic within Christian spirituality. Sociologically speaking, this is one way of interpreting the negative stories sometimes told about priests that have just left a post: stories expressing anticipation of better things to come.

In terms of mobility, Ranson, Bryman and Hinings' 1970s study of Church of England clergy designated as 'hierarchs' a certain group of 'organizational men' who tended to be more highly educated than others and to have occupied more positions in several dioceses. These they contrasted, for example, with 'traditionalists' who had 'not been particularly mobile geographically or socially' and emphasized 'an ethic of service and feelings of vocation' (Ranson, Bryman and Hinings, 1977: 160–61). They also found a distinction in the hierarchy between archdeacons as 'products of parish and organisational work' and bishops as 'products of educational work in public schools, theological colleges and universities' (1977: 34). That distinction, subsequently, changed with the promotion of diocesan bishops from the ranks of suffragans who, in turn, are likely to have been from the archdiaconal class of clergy and certainly not from the public school headmaster or university don. Our bishops reflect a mixture of the mobile 'hierarchs' and more static 'traditionalists' but also include some who reflect Ranson, Bryman and Hinings' third classification of 'youth': these were 'hierarchs' with strong radical theological tendencies and favoring a 'reformed and ecumenical' church. These bishops match, perhaps, those who were young priests at the time of Ransom, Bryman and Hinings' study and who maintained their attitude into older age.

Irrespective of type, one of our interests concerns the move into the bishop's house or, as we shall speak of it, the palace, a description that more clearly invests the dwelling with a distinctive ethos. Palaces should not be passed over too quickly either as a familiar fact of cultural life or as a well-known economic conflict between local church leaders and central financiers. One significant frame for their significance lies in the growth of popular interest in home-making, interior design, furniture and gardening amongst expanding sectors of society in the closing decades of the twentieth century. While, initially, it may seem ironic that such domestic concerns expanded in parallel with a declining pattern of marriage and increasing incidence of co-residence of partners – indeed the very term 'partner' rapidly expanded in use over this period – more serious anthropological analysis might interpret homemaking as another form of meaning-making through the cementing of relationships. At this point social scientific and theological considerations bear strongly upon each other through such interrelated ideas as home, home-making, homecoming, hospitality and welcoming the stranger.[2] Remaining with sociological factors, however, we

---

2   Notions of home, homecoming and homelessness have been fruitfully explored in sociological analyses of the human condition from Schutz's phenomenology (Broderson,

might interpret mutual concern over and investment in domesticity as a symbolic alternative to formal wedding vows, especially given the background reality of divorce in British society. Somewhat analogously, more Britons than ever now live alone, their home and garden may easily become a symbolic screen, not for displaying 'conspicuous consumption' to friends or neighbours but as a means of asserting an identity.

What, then, of the palace and its occupants? It, too, will announce its occupants to those who visit or otherwise engage with it, and different issues arise depending upon whether the bishop is single or married and upon the age of any family members. Here we ignore the official church concern over financial aspects to focus more upon personal and social aspects of palace-homes. It is, however, worth recalling Hensley Henson's reflection on the financial state of bishops, the houses and families on the very eve of the Second World War, and the period at which our study begins. He records that, then, 'many of the bishops are unmarried or childless, and few are wholly without some small income of their own' (Henson, 1939: 144). These constraints he considered to be quite significant given the fact that many were, even so, 'financially embarrassed'. In characteristically trenchant fashion Henson even spoke of the 'sin of simony' as having 'crept back in disguise' since 'the possession of private means tends to become an important qualification for an appointment to an English bishopric' (1939: 144). But times have changed.

Most bishops move from their prior post, usually a parish rectory, vicarage, or now from a suffragan bishop's residence to the palace. Spatially it is likely to be separate from other residences, imposing, and in its own grounds, and it may carry a weight of history. Even if of a more modern construction it is likely to be of a considerable size and quality. Though many bishops have already occupied large vicarages, they differ from palaces in one major respect, especially for the generations in our study: the vicarage is geographically and socially central to parish life while the palace is often not so structurally related to a diocese. The parishes from which these priests were promoted to the episcopate were generally very active, with parishioners and others coming and going to the vicarage. As something of a hub of activity it made complementary sense in relation to the parish church and other activities the vicar 'went out' to complete. It is here that the vicar's family played an important role in a way that, for example, was not the case for a local medical practitioner, even if 'he' held his surgery at premises adjacent to his home. The vicarage was a complex institution in which father, mother, children, perhaps curates, and certainly parishioners interacted. Ease of access and possibility of access fostered this, not least because the vicar's study was at home and he might elect to see people there. Parish offices at the church or elsewhere are, relatively speaking, of very recent emergence. In the kind of thriving parishes from which many of these men came it was possible that the vicar said the offices of morning and evening prayer at church

---

1971), Peter Berger's early argument that 'the mythic motif in these quests is the hope for a redemptive community in which each individual will once more be 'at home' (1977: 390) and Bauman's portrayal of postmodernity (2000). Theological parallels exist, for example in Winquist (1978), and are echoed when Rowan Williams talks of 'enabling the stranger to be heard' (2000: 289).

and not in his study. For both theological and sociological reasons it is worth noting that private chapels do not exist in vicarages. But even if he said the offices in his study that would not have been the case with the Eucharist.

Palaces, by contrast, often contain a private chapel for the bishop's use. Although, for work purposes, we might link vicarage and parish church it would be difficult to extend that analogy to palace and cathedral. Indeed, the bishop's relationship with his cathedral is quite unlike that of the vicar and his parish church. The ritual symbolism of his knocking with his pastoral staff to gain admittance for the enthronement might even be, very occasionally, reflected in an ongoing attitude of the cathedral authorities of dean and chapter to their bishop. Certainly, a major aspect of a bishop's complex life concerns his new colleagues within the diocesan organization. Though only a few bishops commented upon elements of resistance to himself, as newcomer, it remained that a diocesan's capacity to appoint his own suffragan, when opportunity presents itself was, if not something of a relief, at least a valuable means for establishing his own perspectives.

Much of the bishop's work throughout his diocese touches local parishes without reference to the cathedral, unlike the vicar whose work throughout his parish is often related to the parish church, as with funerals, baptisms and marriages, or even with school events. Accordingly, the bishop stands apart from the cathedral to a far greater degree than many might assume. This, in a sense, brings his palace more to the fore as a potentially important operational site. If people, especially his clergy, are to 'meet the bishop' in anything other than a formal context it is likely to be at the palace. This may have consequences for his family, as Chapter 6 shows.

Cumulative Biographical Experience

But what of the man moving into this palace and new diocesan territory? What of his previous experience, not least his religious experience? From his previous life he not only brings different kinds of social, cultural and spiritual 'capital' but can also be thought of as part of the inalienable 'gift' of the Christian tradition. That is to say, he is an embodied representative and symbol of the ongoing Christian faith. And, in most cases, he does not come alone but with his family, each of whose members also contributes to the bishop's identity and his ability to relate to those with whom he works and those he seeks to serve. Bishop and family form an axis for the transmission of spiritual capital. So what of the backgrounds resourcing each?

Family Background

In terms of their fathers' occupation the great majority of bishops, some 90 per cent, came from a diversity of middle-class and professional families, and only 10 per cent owned working-class roots. For example, the following majority occupations (in percentage terms) marked out bishops: civil service (13), business (13), senior and junior management (11), accountancy (7) and teaching (5). Two individuals had doctors as fathers, and two farmers. Single individuals had stockbroker, bank manager, military, architect, engineer, and surveyor fathers. Beyond all these, however, the

single most represented occupation was that of clergyman for approximately a fifth
of our total responding sample (of 60 individuals) had such a clerical background. To
this we will return. The great majority of their mothers (73 per cent) did not follow a
separate career and were, in effect, housewives, but with all the qualification of that
term involved in the middle and clerical classes from which they came.

As for church attendance of their parents, both their fathers and mothers
demonstrated relatively high levels of active participation, as Table 2.1 shows (with
figures rounded up and non-responses ignored). But it must be recalled that 20 per
cent of the fathers were themselves priests.

Table 2.1   Church attendance by bishops' parents

Attendance	*Father (%)*	*Mother (%)*
Sundays and weekdays	47	52
Sundays only	20	20
Once a month	3	8
Major festivals	8	7
Rarely if ever	18	7

The composition of bishops' families of origin showed some 66 per cent as nuclear
families including siblings; 18 per cent were extended and included grandparents,
while 11 per cent focussed on parents and an only child. Interestingly, practically 45
per cent of these families employed some member of staff, reflecting the middle- and
upper-middle-class world of the earlier twentieth century.

Their childhood experience of formal religion revealed some 62 per cent
attending Sunday and some weekday church events, while 29 per cent only attended
Sunday services. As far as Sunday School as a distinct activity was concerned, some
43 per cent registered attendance while 57 per cent did not. This, however, needs
consideration in relation to the 59 per cent who attended public schools and for
whom Sunday School as such was, in a sense, built into school religion. Of these
bishops 93 per cent were childhood Anglicans, 5 per cent were Congregationalist,
and one individual Presbyterian.

Education: An Arts World

For their education 59 per cent of the bishops attended a public school (roughly 40
per cent Clarendon Schools,[3] and 20 per cent other public schools), with roughly
48 per cent being boarders. A further 37 per cent attended grammar and the small
remainder secondary modern schools. The great majority proceeded to university

---

3   The Clarendon Schools were first grouped together for the purposes of the Clarendon
Report, published in 1864, which investigated the finance, management and curriculum of nine
of the most prestigious public schools. These were Eton, Harrow, Winchester, Westminster,
Rugby, Charterhouse, Shrewsbury, St Paul's, and Merchant Taylors. All were boarding schools
except the last two. Since then it has become shorthand for the elite public schools in the
system, and is used here to highlight the especially privileged backgrounds of some bishops.

or to military training, either as professional soldiers or on National Service, and thence to further university and theological college contexts. Cambridge was the main focus with some 52 per cent, with Oxford at 20 per cent and Durham and London at 7 per cent each. Others went to Trinity College Dublin, Bristol, Leeds and Manchester. Just over half (54 per cent) read for a non-theological degree prior to theological training. Some 47 per cent studied only theology, whether prior to or as part of explicit theological training. Of those gaining a degree separate from their theological education only a small minority read subjects beyond the arts and humanities: only about 8 per cent in natural sciences, and 4 per cent in philosophy, politics and economics. The major non-theological subject pursued was history (at 14 per cent).

To give some historical context for their education and training it is worth recalling that between 1900 and 1919, 10 per cent of diocesans had received private tutorship as young children, itself a sign of some aristocratic status, but this dropped to a single bishop between 1920 and 1939. By then, it was common for bishops to have been educated at one of the top public schools and, during the inter-war years, some 48 per cent of bishops had passed through such institutions. The past headmasterships of archbishops Tait, Frederick Temple, William Temple and Geoffrey Fisher also mark the public schooling system as significant in forging the ecclesiastical elite (Medhurst and Moyser, 1988: 86). A decline follows this and, according to the public records analyzed by Rubinstein, of those diocesan bishops who held a see between 1920 and 1939, 72 per cent had attended public schools. By the 1940–1959 period this had dropped to 55 per cent, and by 1960–70 to 40 percent (Rubinstein, 1987: 195). As for our retired contingent, some 62 per cent had been to public school, but here it is important to recall that these include people with thirty years' age difference between them, and who therefore do not constitute a single 'generational' group as in Rubinstein's sample. A similar though more tempered decline can be detected in the proportion of diocesan bishops attending Oxbridge colleges. Of bishops in post between 1920 and 1939, 98 per cent had attended Oxford or Cambridge Universities, by the 1940–59 period this had dropped to 90 per cent, and by 1960–70 to 76 per cent (Rubinstein, 1987: 198). A very similar profile, 74 per cent, held for our group, with Oxford at 22 per cent and Cambridge 52 per cent.

As far as our bishops and their theological college training was concerned the following obtained, with approximate percentages attending each. Once more Cambridge and Oxford predominate: Cambridge – Ridley Hall (17), Westcott House (15); Oxford – Cuddesdon (10), Wycliffe Hall (8), Ripon Hall (2), St Stephen's House (2). Other colleges included: Lincoln (8); Wells (8); Durham – St John's College and Cranmer Hall (5); St Chad's College (2); Chichester (3); Mirfield (3); Oak Hill (5); Ely (3); Clifton (2); Sarum (2), and Kelham (2); these 2 per cents generally represent a single individual.

Science and Faith

Given the general absence of science in their education it is worth noting their general sympathy with science, something that was probably fostered both by the general liberal theological tradition of many and the impact of years of experience in a society upon which science has made a dramatic impact in terms of social welfare. This is evident in several science-related issues posed in our questionnaire, beginning with environmental problems. We found that 34 per cent strongly agreed and 64 per cent agreed that environmental matters are important social issues that should be addressed (even at the expense of economic growth), and this is a significant issue, not least because it involves links between scientific observation and strong ethical and political concerns. It also functions as a 'religion and science' bridge. But, to evoke their attitudes to modern science more directly, we asked if they thought it did more harm than good. With some 25 per cent strongly disagreeing and 62 per cent disagreeing with this, a large majority was in favor of science and its broad effect. Only two individuals 'didn't know', while three thought science did more harm than good.

Over and against this broad support for 'science' we found a degree of ambivalence or uncertainty when pressing the issue in a different direction and asking whether they thought people believed too often in science and not in faith (see Table 2.2).

Table 2.2   People believe too often in science and not in faith, according to bishops

Response	Number	% (Adjusted)
Strongly agree	3	5.0
Agree	24	40.0
Don't know	12	20.0
Disagree	14	23.3
Strongly disagree	4	6.7
No response	3	5.0
Total	60	100

Here a degree of difference of opinion emerged, with 30 per cent disagreeing or strongly disagreeing and a corresponding 26 per cent either strongly agreeing or agreeing that people do believe too often in science and not in faith. At least this suggests that just under a half of these bishops saw some problem over science and religion as alternative interpretative resources.

A further question asked if they thought religion causes more harm than good (see Table 2.3). As might be expected for religious leaders, we found 78 per cent disagreeing or strongly disagreeing with the question. But it is not without interest that nine individual bishops 'didn't know' and three more thought that religion did, indeed, cause more harm than good. Though we are dealing with very small numbers here we are still dealing with a significant group of men with very extensive practical life experience and influence as professional religious leaders.

Table 2.3 'Religion causes more harm than good' – bishops' responses

Response	Number	% (Adjusted)
Agree	3	5.0
Don't know	9	15.0
Disagree	35	58.3
Strongly disagree	12	20.0
No response	1	1.7
Total	60	100

Churchmanship

From educational background and attitudes to science and religion we now focus on the idea of 'churchmanship', the notion that expresses the combined diversity of religious perspective related to doctrine, ministerial priesthood, liturgical performance and pastoral approaches in the Church of England. Though other denominations also possess variations of attitude and practice, churchmanship remains something of a distinctive feature within Anglicanism, reflecting its dual Catholic-Protestant heritage distinctively shaped through nineteenth-century Anglo-Catholic, Evangelical and Liberal positions partially institutionalized through new party-linked theological colleges. Although a few twentieth-century churchmen, such as Winnington-Ingram (Carpenter, 1949: 16), Bishop of London from 1901 to 1939, attended no such college, they did become the normal path to ordination until the 1970s when various regional training courses were established.[4] Still, at the beginning of the twentieth century there had been many, 'including not a few Diocesan Bishops', who regarded theological colleges as 'at the best luxuries, and, at the worst, obnoxious redundancies, which had a positively harmful effect upon a man's character, tending to make him into a hothouse plant, and probably a partisan' (Headlam, 1944: 51).

Hothouse or no, not all our bishops had, however, felt entirely comfortable at their theological college so we should not assume perfect degrees of fit between personal outlook and college tradition nor be surprised at subsequent shifts of emphasis within their personal ministry. With these dynamics in mind we expressly explored the issue of churchmanship, recognizing that as far as bishops are concerned churchmanship raises distinctive problems of how party commitment might detract from being the focus of unity for all clergy and people. As a background complement for this issue, however, we should not ignore the broad British cultural fact that, in the political world, though members of parliament are elected as party-political persons, once elected they exist to serve members of all parties and none. Though the analogy of member of parliament and bishop is, certainly, partial it is not entirely inappropriate within the British scheme of representative leadership.

As far as bishops' views of church-party issues were concerned interviews proved important in assessing the subtler aspects of commitment and contrast, for example,

---

4   Initially these tended to train non-stipendiary ministers, but they also came to train stipendiary priests (Vaughan, 1990).

with earlier studies of clergy, churchmanship and their theological colleges, and the assumption that earlier attitudes continue throughout ministry (Ransom, Bryman and Hinings, 1977:44). Our material also allows a response to Sophie Gilliat-Ray's call for further research to track any change in theological understanding 'during the various stages of the ministerial career, from ordination to retirement' (Gilliat-Ray, 2001: 216). Certainly we can demonstrate that changes do occur over a lifetime, and not only in that short-term sense demonstrated by Towler and Coxon (1979) among ordinands of the 1960s during their time at theological college. Indeed, it is likely that some of the ordinands they studied then were amongst our group of bishops.

Several questions asked of the bishops sought to explore these issues. One considered the churchmanship of their childhood church. Table 2.4 shows this as a broad balance of Evangelical (23 per cent), and Catholic (25 per cent) around a solid Central core position (42 per cent).

Table 2.4   Churchmanship of childhood church

Churchmanship	*Number*	*% (Adjusted)*
Central	25	41.7
Open Evangelical	7	11.7
Conservative Evangelical	7	11.7
Traditional Catholic	9	15
Modern Catholic	4	6.7
Prayer Book Catholic	2	3.3
Mixture	2	3.3
Could not say	2	3.3
Total	60	100

Another question compared their churchmanship at time of ordination with their current position in retirement: the results present both numbers of individuals and their percentage amongst those studied (see Table 2.5). Here it is worth noting not only how their classification of positions is more complex than for their 'childhood church', but also how they have consciously distanced themselves from the 'central' category.

These responses indicate a shift from more to less conservative attitudes in general, but with an interesting divergence between the more evangelical and the more catholic. So, while 16 (26 per cent) noted an early evangelicalism of some sort, only 9 (15 per cent) saw themselves as such now: conservative evangelical and liberal evangelical descriptors now found no adherents. This is telling in relation to the fact that, in terms of spiritual self-identity, some 27 per cent spoke of having had a born-again style of conversion compared with 65 per cent who saw their history as perennially Christian: some 7 per cent spoke of a gradual identity change.

Though belonging to an earlier generation than our bishops one clear account of a shift away from a childhood and early adult evangelicalism is found in Joost de Blank's brief autobiographical account of his first being ordained as an Anglican 'for utilitarian reasons', viewing the Church of England as 'the best boat to fish from'

Table 2.5 Churchmanship at ordination and in retirement

Churchmanship	At Ordination	In Retirement
Central	3 (5%)	3 (5%)
Evangelical	6 (10%)	3 (5%)
Open Evangelical	6 (10%)	5 (8%)
Liberal Evangelical	2 (3%)	0
Conservative Evangelical	2 (3%)	1 (2%)
Anglo-Catholic	5 (8%)	1 (2%)
Modern Catholic	6 (10%)	11 (18%)
Catholic	2 (3%)	0
Liberal Catholic	5 (8%)	7 (12%)
Moderate Catholic	3 (5%)	2 (3%)
Open Catholic	0	1 (2%)
Affirming Catholicism	0	1 (2%)
Radical Catholic	0	1 (2%)
Prayer Book Catholic	7 (12%)	2 (3%)
Liberal Evangelical-Catholic	1 (2%)	2 (3%)
Too vague to define	9 (15%)	17 (28%)
Comprehensive	0	1 (2%)
Other	0	2 (3%)
Too long ago to remember	2 (3%)	0
No answer	1 (2%)	0
Total	60 (100%)	60 (100%)

and then gaining a sense of 'liberation' through the church's 'sacramental emphasis (Morgan, 1959: 31–2). He had been born in 1908 and subsequently became the influential Archbishop of Cape Town. Quite different was retired Archbishop Cosmo Lang's retrospective desire to pinpoint a boyhood moment of belief even that there was a God, and a later sense that he had really received 'an inward sense of vocation' (Lockhart, 1949: 13, 443).

It was, however, amongst Catholic descriptors that the greatest degree of change had taken place. This reinforces Gilliat-Ray's findings for ordinands of the late 1990s (2001: 212) and suggests a contemporary cultural change shared both by ordinands and retired bishops. While the direct 'Anglo-Catholic' became less popular the opposite was the case for 'Modern Catholic'. 'Open Catholic', 'Affirming Catholicism' and 'Radical Catholic' all marked innovative descriptions. It seems as though the diversity of catholic descriptors provided appropriate identification for catholically minded priests when they became bishops.

The 'Vagueness' Factor

The most direct expression of change, however, concerns the nine who, at ordination, reckoned they were 'too vague to define', a number that had now grown to 17.

Interestingly only three defined themselves as 'Central' both at ordination and at present. We think this notion of 'vagueness' rather important, and will return to it in our concluding chapter; here we note it as a description of how some people reflect upon their own, complex, lives, upon what they want to do in life and, indeed, upon the very fact of complexity of the activities into which they entered as bishops. 'Vagueness' may also help describe some people for whom the church, its parties or some specific special interest group were not driving forces, individuals who possessed a broad sense of vocation, of being called to serve people and society at large. Some of our bishops saw that attitude as perhaps more typical of their generation than it is today. One expressed it in terms of: 'wishing to be of service to people and to be doing some good ... to spend my life in a career which had that as an element in it ... for myself and others at the time public service was quite a factor'.

That bishop also spoke of the way in which he had to force himself into some parts of his clerical life, especially hospital visiting, and wondered if today some young curate might 'get behind their computers ... produce something (and hide) from the costly business of personal contact'. The necessity of engaging in many activities and, sometimes, of coming from one set of backgrounds into another so that many factors played upon one's sense of identity can all relate to a degree of 'vagueness'. It is important not to cast 'vagueness' into an inevitably negative category, as might be easy for those with a very firm doctrinal or party stance. On the contrary, there is a valuable 'vagueness' possessing an adaptive potential to enliven a variety of different life-situations as they emerge. The late Hugh Montefiore, before becoming a bishop, saw in such a 'certain loss of definiteness ... a resulting comprehensiveness' that was, to him, 'a very wonderful and very Christian quality' (Morgan, 1959: 119). The open potential of 'vagueness' was reflected in a further question on churchmanship party alignment held when in episcopal office. Nearly half (48 per cent) reckoned they had no such alignment while a further 22 per cent said there had been such, but only occasionally or on certain issues. Some 17 per cent more acknowledged alignment but 'only to a limited extent'. This left only a small minority of approximately 13 per cent who saw themselves as belonging to a church faction for much of their time as a bishop.

Another aspect of 'vagueness' can be assessed in terms of multiple influences upon individuals. When asked which movements had so influenced their ministry in some way we found that many had done so, often overlapping or being significant at particular phases of life. The following percentages give some sense of this complex picture of positive influences: Modern Catholicism (59), Evangelicalism (48), Anglo-Catholicism (42), Radical Theology (37), Liberal Theology (27), Celtic Spirituality (25), Charismatic Renewal (20), Russian-Greek Orthodoxy (15) and Confessing Church (10). From a slightly different perspective the following percentages indicate another kind of influence attached to particular projects or movements and should be read in conjunction with Chapter 1's brief historical profile of theological and other trends affecting the period covered by our bishops' ministries: Faith in the City (53), Parish and People (48), Clinical Theology (32) and Liberation Theology (19).

Need for Change

Given these influences, often associated with changes within their own experience, and the centrality of these men in church organization, with several in particular in the decision-making agencies of the church, it is worth seeing how they responded to a question on whether the church needed to modernize itself. The majority felt that it did, as Table 2.6 indicates.

Table 2.6   'The church needs to modernize itself' – bishops' responses

Response	Number	% (Adjusted)
Strongly agree	9	15.0
Agree	33	55.0
Don't know	2	3.3
Disagree	9	15.0
Strongly disagree	3	5.0
No response	3	5.0
Mixed response	1	2.0
Total	60	100

Here some 70 per cent agreed that modernization was necessary, with 55 per cent broadly agreeing and 15 per cent strongly thinking that it was necessary. By contrast some 18 per cent, whether broadly (15) or strongly (5), did not think modernization necessary. One individual had a mixed response while five did not know or did not answer. This overall profile seems to indicate much more of a wish to see change occur than to leave the church as it is. It also reflects the actual experience of many whose ministry spanned, and some whose activity fostered profound changes within, church organization and liturgy.

Emphases in Episcopal Ministry

Given the changes these bishops had either desired or effected we now turn to what the bishops considered they were actually doing in their work. We asked how they would evaluate particular descriptions of episcopal ministry and, while, doubtless, all of these features would have been included in a compound list of duties, the following picture emerged when single features were preferred.

Pastoring Diocese and Clergy

Half placed 'providing for pastoral needs of the diocese' at the head of their list, followed by those (23 per cent) who opted for 'providing pastoral care for the clergy'. Together they combine a geographical commitment infused with pastoral concern and, it could be argued, they indicate how a local pastoral concern is brought into the episcopal role. The clerical formation of the parish priest expands into the episcopate. Like the bishop, the parish priest has pastoral care of a geographical territory and, even during the second half of the twentieth century, this 'cure of souls' remained a guiding principle for many clergy.[5] On becoming a bishop it is understandable that such values are retained; it is equally understandable that these principles should seek appropriate points of application so that as the diocese replaces the parish so its clergy replace 'parishioners'. Theologically speaking these two transformed applications make good sense in that the bishop, aware of his diocesan territory, should seek to enable the locally distributed priests to engage in the pastoral task that belongs, symbolically, to the bishop but which is shared with his priests. Here, certainly, we see evidence supporting Beeson's account of bishops as 'pastor-managers' discussed in the previous chapter.

Catholicity of Church

Of equal theological interest is that another aspect of episcopacy, that of 'maintaining the catholicity of the church', was adopted as first choice by a relatively small group (10 per cent). All choices presented by and taken in a questionnaire survey are, of course, open to a variety of explanation, and that is the case here. Our interpretation turns on the opinion that the prime values acquired and embodied as and by a parish priest are the ones most likely to be developed and applied when he becomes a bishop. While it can be argued, theologically, that the parish priest is, to a degree, a symbol of the universal church, not least as a dynamic representative of the bishop, in practice that feature is seldom dominant: it gives way to the local concerns and, indeed, preoccupations of parish life. This helps us understand why only such a minority of our bishops selected as first choice their representative role as leaders within the universal church. Still, it was often present as one element of self-reflection, sometimes appearing within a different framework as with those who had visited or been involved with ventures such as the Taizé and Iona Communities and who saw in them a vision of the openness and world-wideness of Christianity. In such a context the sense was more of being an immediate part of that catholicity than of symbolizing it at a distance. As is so often true, practice fosters attitude more profoundly than does abstracted theology.

Moral Leadership

Another minority of only two (3 per cent) took as their central role that of 'providing a voice of moral leadership for English people'. This, too, we might view as an obvious extrapolation from parish to diocese, arguing that few parish priests probably see their duty as consisting in being the moral leader of their parish or have opportunity or inclination to be such. While it is the case that there are priests, in many parts of the country, who employ the media to express their views on moral or social issues, they are relatively few in number and are seldom the type of person selected for episcopal status. Historically speaking, it may be that bishops whose previous

---

5   In Davies, Watkins and Winter's (1991: 111) Rural Church Project, some 70 per cent of interviewed clergy saw themselves as 'serving all parishioners' (43 per cent), or gathered congregations plus other parishioners (27 per cent).

priestly career was not substantially parochial and which might, for example, have been more academic or school-based were more naturally disposed to adopt this wider stance. The circles in which priests move influence their sense of identity to a marked extent, including their sense of natural competence for engaging in national debates. To a degree this is also the case as far as engagement within national church circles is concerned. Some bishops, for example, saw their own technical theological competence as relatively low and were relatively ill-inclined to participate in certain debates when in the presence of bishops with extensive and high-profile theological expertise. While this is perfectly understandable it must not be overlooked when also pondering issues of national involvement nor, perhaps, when considering career trajectories of potential bishops.

Complex Outlooks

A final minority of 12 per cent who did not answer this question (with a single individual who insisted on a multiple response) prompt a renewed emphasis on the complexity of ministry and individual identity or, perhaps, it might even be better to speak of 'character' as the ascribed evaluation of an individual. This is germane in a church and society where the sense of someone's 'character' was important over the period in which our bishops were formed and served their ministry.[6] Nor must we forget the sense of God implicated in their vocation and ministry and helping to frame their character as evaluated by community and church. We emphasize these issues through two case studies interpolated by a theoretical sociological discussion of this notion of 'character': a concept grounded in the development of personality through interpersonal relationships and within a sense of life framed for these bishops by the divine.[7] This progression from case study to theoretical reflection to case study will foster a cumulative sense of the kind of sociological description and analysis underlying a great deal of this book.

Case Study: Dream Change

One bishop talked of his family's ecclesiastical background with practically all males being clergy. When, amidst this conventionality, his college chaplain suggests ordination to him he moves in that direction as a matter of course but is devoid of any particular sense of vocation. Through this redirection of studies he encounters Michael Ramsey as a professor of divinity: 'the effect on me and on my closest friends ... was absolutely electric: I'd never heard a lecturer like that before in my life'. Despite this his sense of vocation remains bland, even through his diaconal year. Into this life comes what he variously described as a 'sort of dream/fantasy/ nightmare where a whole lot of people were lining up at the pearly gates and they were all looking at me, and they were saying, "It was because of him that I didn't

---

6   As in Cunningham's pastoral theology lectures at Cambridge (1908: 92–3).

7   It lies beyond our competence to consider 'character' in terms of its psychological motive and its affinity with doctrinal perspectives as was favored, for example, by psychologists such as Fromm ([1942] 1960: 54).

follow Christ." And that really shook me.' This trauma seems to reflect a powerful anxiety dream in which the tensions of a conventional life, already challenged by exciting theological thinking and the new experience of diaconal life, come to a crisis. He notes that being made deacon and the diaconate itself 'just sort of passed over me'; by sharp contrast, 'the experience of being ordained priest absolutely hit me and was an antidote to what had happened' during his diaconate, including that dream. It may well be that many find the act of ordination significantly different from that of being made deacon even though to the public at large 'ordination' is often seen as applying equally to both rites. The embodied experience of diaconal ministry seems to prepare a person for priestly ordination in a way that earlier training cannot. This itself is an area ripe for further research. In this case, personal experiences brought the individual to a pastoral outlook that was exercised through a liberal catholic perspective. With others it was through different forms of churchmanship that an increased personal alertness to pastoral needs emerged.

Theoretical Interpolation: Influences and Asides

This example provides opportunity for a brief description of a kind of personal encounter, often associated with influential figures, that not only relates to a sense of vocation but defines a style of engagement that frames important religious self-assessment, life-direction and reference to God within the Church of England. We categorize this as the 'divine aside' of the 'influential figure'. Approaching 'divine asides' through our earlier statistics we highlight the role of Oxford and, especially, of Cambridge on our generation of bishops, and doubtless on many other priests. At those universities, much theological education was provided by active church members, often in holy orders and often in the process of a developing clerical career of their own. They brought the influence of the Church of England to bear upon many who would, in due course, become bishops. These university and college contexts were of wider scope than the theological colleges to which graduates proceeded as ordinands. These personal experiences are easily overlooked when Oxbridge is cited as part of episcopal backgrounds only to stress social-class issues of privilege. The role of thinking clerics who embodied attractive features of their faith and religious tradition was of enduring importance to numerous 'ordinand-bishops', named examples included Michael Ramsey, Ian Ramsey, John Robinson, Owen Chadwick, Charles Moule, Geoffrey Lampe, as well as several well-known parish priests such Bryan Green of St Martin's, Birmingham and Eric Abbot of Westminster Abbey.

Influential figures exist in all religious traditions, their significance varying according to distinctive organizational features of groups. Within the Church of England it is the diversity associated with churchmanship and theological variation, as well as the complex interplay of theological teaching and pastoral presence at certain universities, that accentuates their significance. At more than one level these figures 'become' Anglicanism; they embody an ecclesiastical ethos and frame an attitude to doctrine and practice. As people 'of learning and piety ... whose influence has permeated the Anglican Communion' they serve as part of the spectrum of Anglican Divines (Booty, 1988: 174). In terms of social psychology (itself lying beyond our scope) such figures could be analyzed in terms of 'referent power' fostering problem-solving and helping to avoid 'a difficult, dominating ... orientation' to life (Fiske, 2004: 524).

Such 'influential figures' are often cited along with 'divine asides', two phenomena we see as related elements typical of Anglican spirituality. As mentioned in Chapter 1, such asides describe comments or questions posed almost 'in passing' within a conversation or brief exchange and which pinpoint an essentially profound issue, such as that of ordination. Teachers are, of course, familiar with the way students often recall things they once said but have long forgotten. These asides are similar, but often more powerful. They also reflect a certain style of informal Church of England discourse in which God is seldom the explicit topic of conversation but is assumed to underlie the spiritual life of the conversation partners. God is implicit. This is also exemplified in a phrase such as 'saying one's prayers', a condensed reference embracing much tacit information, shared values and anticipations. A typical example concerns Winnington-Ingram when in a youthful period of classical Victorian-Edwardian religious doubt – 'mental misery' – experienced prior to ordination. S.C. Carpenter, when Dean of Exeter, tells how the young man 'began to wonder. Was the Resurrection of Christ true? Is the whole thing a dream? How can we reconcile earthquakes with the love of God? ... He consulted an elder brother ... Ingram remained in the Christian fellowship. He did not give up saying his prayers and he did not give up going to Communion' (Carpenter, 1949: 13). 'Divine asides' and condensed expressions such as 'he did not give up saying his prayers' are particularly significant when the parties concerned are not involved in any formal context of explicit 'spiritual direction'. Similar examples both of passing consultations and more sustained encounters are associated with F.R. Barry, Oxford scholar, distinguished First World War chaplain, trainer of a generation of post-war clergy, Vicar of St Mary's, Oxford and a chaplain at Balliol, theological author, Canon of Westminster and Bishop of Southwell for half the duration of the period covered in our research (1941–63). He was 'much sought after by undergraduates for advice on their future careers', and 'after a few moments' talk it became plain that it was still possible to combine intellectual integrity with Christian belief' (West, 1980: 41).

When employed by an influential person, who in the Quaker tradition might be called a 'weighty Friend', these asides can be extremely telling and catalytic in provoking a thought or helping focus the unspoken feelings of the one addressed, especially during periods of decision-making. In the previous case study one might even identify the dream accusation – 'It was because of him that I didn't follow Christ' – as a negative form of such an 'aside'. One published example was recorded by Hugh Montefiore, later Suffragan Bishop of Kingston and Bishop of Birmingham. After his dramatic conversion to Christianity this schoolboy of a 'devout Anglo-Jewish family' received instruction from 'a kindly, learned, rather remote and academic personage who later became a bishop'. Though most of this instruction 'was aimed far too high and went right over' his head, Montefiore wrote: 'I can clearly remember, however, a casual remark which he made at the end of the course. "Well", he said, "you'll have to make up your mind which Church you should join. I don't think I need bother you with the differences between the Churches. It's clear that you ought to be a member of the Church of England."' Montefiore's mature reflection was one of deep gratitude for that vicar's 'casual remark'. Interestingly, however, he asked 'was it, on reflection, not quite so casual as it seemed at the time?' (Morgan, 1959: 117–18). And that is our point.

God, Character and Service

To speak of the dynamic relationship between influential individuals and spiritual asides affords a useful entry into a more formal sociological comment on the divine as a factor within our study. A frequent approach to 'God' in sociological studies is simply to record what people say about God. We wish to press that approach a little further and employ a scheme that helps show how the particular kind of belief that is held about God influences the way people understand themselves and relate to each other within a church. To do this we combine psychological and sociological ideas derived, respectively, from David Armstrong and Richard Sennett. In so doing the two disciplines practically merge, as they often do, and should, in complex studies of the human condition.[8]

Armstrong employs the notion of 'organizational object' to describe 'an implicit third' element 'in all the emotional exchanges of organizational life, however intra- and interpersonal, or intra- and inter-group such exchanges may appear' (Armstrong, 2004: 22–7). This 'implicit third' factor or 'organizational object' is 'a point of origin of … experience … which can elicit multiple responses': it concerns the tasks facing the organization, how goals are managed, as well as how the identity of persons and group in any given environment is resourced. In most organizations it would be feasible to identify the organizational object in relation to such a prime goal or primary task, as other psychologists would call it, as, for example, the educational fulfillment of students, the health and well-being of patients, the expansion of the company through satisfied shareholders or customers, or the maintenance of peace and order by the police. While many organizations engage in their primary task under the motivation of their organizational object – often expressed as a mission statement – the church conceives of itself as not so much possessing a mission statement but as called to or even 'being' a mission. In other words there is an explicit belief in a divine source: this means that the 'implicit third' factor of an ordinary secular company is potentially present in the church as an explicit source of motivation for the primary task. This is not to say that belief in God is like 'belief in' a company's product or even like 'belief that' a product is highly desirable. Rather, it is the underlying rationale for the life-direction of church members, not least its leaders: it is the basis, for example, of the 'spiritual aside' and for the potential significance of the influential leader.

While Armstrong's 'third' element may specify a secular organization's goal it may be conceived in church contexts as the point of engagement of the divine and the human and is clearly manifest in liturgy. Just how that divine effect might operate is a moot point within theology and, understandably, is quite opaque to sociological

---

8   Artificial distinctions between sociological and psychological interpretations of the human condition seldom foster understanding or truly represent how scholars actually work (see Moscovici, 1993: 1–23).

analysis. Its practical complexity is theologically framed in and through references to the Holy Spirit guiding or leading God's people into new ways, or of the leadership seeking to discern God's will. In individual terms it concerns the dynamic interplay between individuals' sense of self-identity in relation both to their private awareness of God and of their engagement with the church as an institution. As to its effect, this varies amongst different church groups as they might, for example, stress service to neighbor, the pursuit of justice, the evangelizing of the world, or simply the worship of God.

At one level that brief, psychological, analysis might suffice in relating church leaders to their divine source and to those they lead. But greater depth is possible if, for example, we draw from Sennett's analysis of human relationships in contexts of inequality, a valuable approach given that we are dealing with 'top' people living in and working through an essentially hierarchical organization but under an ideal 'organizational object' of love, service and humility.[9] Sennett's study *Respect*, subtitled 'The Formation of Character in an Age of Inequality' is partly autobiographical and partly theoretical: it probes ideas of power, identity, life-context and of a person's developing insight into the human condition. While his comments on old-boy networks and cultural capital obviously relate to our work with bishops it is his preoccupation with how people relate to each other despite their status differences that is important here. Drawing from previous work of sociologists Gerth and Mills on 'character' and psychologists Bowlby and Winnicott on 'autonomy', he explores ways of 'treating others with respect' (Sennett, [2003] 2004: 121). He understands 'character' as the way a person acts in relation to another, character concerns 'action' and the relational dimension of personality (2004: 53). But the problem is how to act? His answer depends upon a view of relationships in which the other person is, as it were, 'granted autonomy': and 'autonomy means accepting in others what one does not understand about them' (2004: 121, 262). His theme of respect is particularly germane for our analysis of bishops in the light of his prime question of 'how the strong can practice respect toward those destined to remain weak' (2004: 263). His answer lies in contexts of practice, with 'respect' understood less as a mental attitude or ideal value than as action. His experience as a musician underpinned this notion of performance and could be related to the liturgical and ministerial domain of the clergy.[10] His perspective increases in value still further if combined with our earlier use of Armstrong's 'third' element: the 'organisational object' that frames religious action. The granting of autonomy to others is, in more theological terms, to see them as discrete creatures of God and to possess, in that vision, a motivation for acting alongside them, as in worship or work, within the divine kingdom or community. This is enhanced when motivated by more recent Anglican ideas of 'fellowship' than was the case, for example when, 'well into the 1960s bishops and archdeacons frequently addressed the "inferior clergy" by their unadorned surnames' compared

---

9   Sometimes the essential hierarchy of church organization is overlooked, as Neil Burgess records in his study of curates and their vicars (1998: 41, 84).

10   Tensions between clergy and church musicians, for example, reflect, in part, 'absence of adequate discussion' (Rees, 1993: 183).

with recent trends when 'even the episcopate have adopted semi-informal titles such as "Bishop Bill"' (Burgess, 1998: 84).

These theoretical issues bring us to a second case study. As in the previous example this man was the son of the vicarage but this individual's movement towards ordination, his 'character' development towards others and his sense of the divine follow a different scheme of spirituality.

Case Study: Self-realization

This bishop progressed from parish priest, rural dean, archdeacon and suffragan to diocesan status. The roots of his spiritual career lay within home and public school. His housemaster set an example in daily Holy Communion and his pupil followed suit until university took him into more political involvements and, briefly after graduation, into teaching, but this was short-lived. He had sought to distance himself from the idea of ordination since his father was a priest and because his mother had rather wished ordination upon him. Referring to God he said he 'became convinced that He would get me in the end', so he thought: 'Why don't I face that one instead of just messing about and trying to find things of interest to do?'[11] He felt that he had 'sufficiently distanced' himself from his family expectation that ordination was now 'my own conviction and not something that I had been brought up to do ... after that I just felt that it was what I was meant to do'. Although he went to a recognizably Evangelical college he did not feel at home there.

The theological framework he felt characterized his ministry was that of 'the parish communion', having been influenced at theological college by 'the Parish and People movement' with its 'sort of twin things':the parish Eucharist and parish meeting. He sought not to be a 'party man' but 'a parish priest at heart' whose interest lay in the community, whether of his parish or diocese. His theological training had 'opened his eyes' to two elements, that of biblical criticism and 'the riches of the liturgy'. His subsequent commitment to saying the daily offices emerged from his appreciation of the fact that, 'to put it bluntly, if I didn't pray the offices, I found I didn't pray'. In terms of his own children this bishop had never sought to teach them the faith in any explicit way, he hoped 'that something would rub off on them', since, 'we don't sort of talk about faith a great deal'. As he also expressed it: 'I'm not a great proselytizer of anybody, really. Perhaps I fall short in that particular thing, but I try to set an example and offer some ... encouragement.'

This individual reflects the type of person whose relatively diffuse theology finds its manifestation in a combination of liturgy and community. For him it is easy not to be a 'party man' on churchmanship and, because of his own clerical-parental household and subsequent parochial experience he feels able to 'span the range from the council house to the castle'. He has been fully supported by his wife and felt

---

11   Here, perhaps, we encounter an echo of the Catholic poet Francis Thompson (1859–1907) and 'The Hound of Heaven', a poem that touched a certain Anglican chord in its description of God pursuing the fleeing believer: 'I fled Him down the nights and down the days; I fled Him down the arches of the years', and with a sense of 'those strong Feet that followed after' (1913: 51).

that his children had benefited as much as they had probably lost from having been vicarage children. Such case studies offer specific examples of the wider factors explored throughout this chapter in which we have begun to detail some of the factors motivating episcopal lives, framing bishops' ministries and influencing their family lives – all against demands of church and state. This has prepared us for the more extensive theoretical interpretation of the relationships of bishops to their managerial, pastoral and family commitments to which we now turn our attention.

Chapter 3

Changing Persons, Changing Roles

This chapter develops our previous theoretical interest in notions of spiritual capital and symbolic exchange in an analysis of bishops and their ecclesiastical work. In a broad sense our argument is that bishops *possess* spiritual capital but *are* gifts to church and society. While this reference to being 'gifts' is not a theological statement, but a sociological means of discussing the value transmitted within the key personnel of an ongoing institution or society, it is one readily accessible for theological comment and development. Here, however, our emphasis on capital and gift theories are intended to drive this chapter's consideration of bishops in a changing world of pastoral ideals, managerial goals and media-magnified crises.

The Church of England has been formed and reshaped by numerous critical events including the English Reformation, rural to urban industrial migrations, theological, liturgical and philosophical antagonisms,[1] two world wars, and the disestablishment of the Church in Wales.[2] The emergence of the welfare state, soon followed by the dramatic rise of the media in popularizing debates and transforming culture, especially youth culture, alongside a secular shift in attitudes followed by a growing individualism and consumerism in which 'choice' became a key word, all provided an increasingly open society whose developing professionalism – including managerialism – would influence established notions of vocation and the organizational patterns of church government. These changes affected bishops, their identity and work, as this chapter shows.

Numerous bishops exemplify concerns over society at the outset of our chosen period of study (1940–2000); we mention but three: Temple, Wickham and Henson. Archbishop William Temple (at York from 1929, and Canterbury 1942–44) hoped that the influence of a 'peculiar genius' for correlating opposing principles would witness the emergence of the intrinsic values lying behind 'communism and individualism' (Temple, 1963: 92). John Kent's telling comment on that particular anticipation was that Temple's view of Anglicanism as exemplifying that 'peculiar genius' within

---

1   Not all bishops resemble the indefatigable Bishop Barnes of Birmingham in acknowledging the secular nature of post-First World War Britain and the need for a bishop not simply to be 'an impartial administrator' but an opponent of doctrinal and liturgical obfuscation and a proponent of an episcopal teaching ministry embracing modern scientific thought to 'strengthen faith in Christ' (Barnes, 1927: xiv–xv).

2   With 1 April 1920 being its day of 'Disestablishment, Dismemberment, Disendowment', involving enormous political engagement and psychological strain on the part of the Welsh bishops, including the remarkable theological-political episode of Nonconformist Prime Minister Lloyd George, contrary to Prayer Book rubrics, presenting himself for Holy Communion at the period of the enthronement of the new – first – Archbishop of Wales at St Asaph (Owen, 1961: 434, 442).

the mid-twentieth century Church of England 'planning for freedom' was the result of his being tempted 'into the byways of Anglican romanticism' (Kent, 1992: 180). Far more realistic was E.R. Wickham's trenchant view of the Church of England rooted in his dedicated focus on the industrial revolution typified in Sheffield. His influential *Church and People in an Industrial City* (1957) remains a key text on the changes industrial life wrought upon British Christianity and post-war society. Prime needs were for the laity's work in embedded mission rather than evangelistic flurries, and for a Christian message grounded in God's justice 'slanted to the weaker' – itself a incisive precursor of the 'bias to the poor' that would emerge twenty years later (Wickham, 1957: 260). Above all he was aware that numerous reports, 'red-hot' topics or assemblies 'at Lambeth' caused 'hardly a ripple' in the church and 'none in the world'. For him 'the imposing role of Church leaders at national and local level and the deference still accorded to them in English life' gave the impression that 'the Church still exercised a formative influence in society' while, in fact, 'neither Church, State, nor the elite of society wished to expose so congenial an assumption' (1957: 240).

Whether in Archbishop Temple's romanticism or in the realism of industrial canon missioner and suffragan bishop Wickham, we encounter, in that post-war period, a deep questioning of church in society. This was part of the context within which the bishops in our study were formed and began their ministry, men who seem to belong to quite a different world from that in which, for example, individuals like Hensley Henson held sway. Paradoxical as he was, Henson, with his controversies over Virgin Birth and Resurrection remained avowedly for the establishment of the church and saw the bishop as 'more than a churchman', indeed, a 'national' figure (Chadwick, 1983: 147). From his politicized appointment to Hereford in 1918 – by Nonconformist Prime Minister Lloyd George and largely against archiepescopal desires – and subsequent translation to Durham (1920–39) Henson marked an end of a particular style of episcopacy even if his theological and political concerns would find echoes later in the century in men like bishops David Jenkins, David Sheppard and Peter Selby. One theme that grew in the second half of the twentieth century was that of secularization. Though not absent in ecclesiastical views of the unchurched masses of the nineteenth century, nor in reflections in the trenches of the First World War, secularization assumed a different significance in the realignment of social class, individualism, youth culture and forward-looking hopes that increasingly pervaded Britain from the later 1950s. One outcome was a concern over the rational control of institutions, whether of government, production or, indeed, of the church, within which the role of bishops increasingly grew in organizational significance with obvious consequences for issues of managerial and pastoral attitudes to ministry and leadership. This theme we take up here in terms of jural and mystical forms of authority, and in Chapter 4 as the distinction between mastery and mystery as forms of religious endeavor.

Managerialism

The latter third of the twentieth century witnessed large organizations developing managerial models driven by the desire for economy and organizational efficiency, pressured both by increased legislative demands and broad ethical expectations for the well-being of employees and the satisfied service of customer-clients. Life became increasingly demanding, often stressful, with obvious consequences for managers' health and family responsibilities. For the clergy the issue of work was additionally complex given the idea of vocation and not simply of work as a job with line-manager answerability. Even so, some clergy formed a kind of trade union,[3] while the courts even pondered 'God' as employer. The question of efficient servicing of customer needs, through increasingly streamlined organization serviced by company-minded personnel, was not so easily posed for the church for theological reasons and because of the long-standing and often counter-productive individualistic focus of ministry.[4] The nature of the 'customer' also differs quite considerably: changing dress fashions, for example, are not quite the same phenomenon as changing styles in religious adherence. The complex issue of reduced congregational attendance, for example, fueled the debate on secularization for several generations and shows no sign of abating. In this context it is interesting that one point of religious growth – The Alpha Course – focussing on small-group evangelistic teaching and discussion framed by mutual encouragement and influenced by Charismatic Christianity, did adopt its own copyright brand-style used extensively in public advertising.

While this is not the place for debating the secularization-sacralization theme and deciding upon which grand narrative to use to tell the story of twentieth century Episcopal life,[5] we cannot ignore the practical fact that the Church of England does not occupy the ground it did when the bishops in our sample were boys or even young men. Nor should we forget the theoretical feature of Max Weber's secularization thesis concerning the rise in rational control associated with a demystification of the world. As factory managers and bureaucratic officials sought rational means of regulating control and ensuring standardization and uniformity of operation, notions of caprice or spirit-power intervention were rendered redundant. However, there remain areas where rational procedures are inappropriate, as in personal and family life with ideas of commitment, romantic and self-sacrificial love and as, also, many might argue, in the church with its notion of vocation and service. The values involved in family and church can be identified as 'inalienable' and, as such, lying beyond the immediate scope of rational manipulation. Indeed, one may also suggest that post-industrial, service-based and person-oriented society may favor attitudes amenable to a resacralization of life as reflected in the post-1960s rise of the Charismatic Movement (Davies, 1985: 11).

---

3   A few clergy joined the Amicus trade union in the late 1990s.

4   Burgess exemplified hierarchy in the attitudes of some vicars to their curates (1998: 71–100).

5   Cox (2003): 201–17, raised the issue of the rhetorical power of secularization theory within historical and sociological accounts of religion in European society.

Essentially, we encounter two potential dynamics of the church, one as a formal bureaucracy the other as a community. In the former the church possesses identifiable tasks to be performed through limited resources of clerical personnel and money: rationality, efficiency of performance, and the managerial control by clergy answerable to their line manager with a job subject to regular quality control audit become prime concerns. The community model, by contrast, depicts the church as a family, a pilgrim people, or as the kingdom of God in which the Holy Spirit motivates, guides and leads into all truth: it is to be a place of love and self-sacrifice with leaders possessing a vocation rather than a profession. Indeed its central rite, the Eucharist, sometimes described as a sacred mystery, is a corporate event; its symbolic broken bread is not subject to portion-control, its altar is no cafeteria. How can such opposites co-exist and the bishop head both necessities?[6]

Manager-bishops?

The bishop's role has been variously identified with other dominant forms of authority such as the 'civil magistrate, feudal lord and tribal leader', and it has also been clearly seen that, 'in modern Western societies' it is easy 'for the bishop's authority to be modelled on that of the expert manager' (Norris, 1988: 308). One forceful theological-ethical criticism of the rise of this managerial model is that of Richard Roberts, for whom 'the *uncritical* incorporation of managerialism within the Church of England amounts to a betrayal' and actually 'endangers the "care of souls", that is the fostering of that delicate spiritual opportunity that constitutes the fabric of real human community, *koinonia*, itself' (Roberts, 2002: 164). Here the language of betrayal immediately suggests the theoretical appropriateness of symbolic-exchange theory given its emphasis upon the value of human relationships.

Roberts, a theologian with considerable grasp of sociological theory, focusses his critique upon Bishop Stephen Sykes and his theological account of the nature of Anglican thought and practice. Bluntly expressed, Roberts takes Sykes' view of episcopacy as reinforcing a managerial style during a period of potentially unstable social change The debate turns on the nature of power within church tradition and organization on the one hand and on the nature of God and divine revelation as perceived by insightful Christian leaders on the other: all within a church in which the people are much engaged with their faith and its expression through formal liturgies. Roberts sees Sykes as placing 'Christian identity … entirely and exclusively at the mercy of the informed virtuoso, the writer of Christian character, the Prince-Lord of the church' (Roberts, 2002: 158). This, he thinks, downplays the potential for evil in 'a theology that baulks at the prospect of a doctrine of "total depravity", the universal fallibility of *all* human agency'. Roberts thinks this involves the 'inevitability of the corrupt, obfuscatory manipulation of others through the management of power at the most fundamental and insidious level, that is in the construction of the self-consciousness of the other' (2002: 159). Part of the reason for Roberts' near damning critique lies in 'the theological invisibility of the laity … God's own proletariat. The

---

6   This problem relates to Bourdieu's analysis of transcendent and temporal interests (1984: 315–17).

people of God' (2002: 160), and in his radical distaste for the 'managerial revolution' which he sees, for example, as epitomized in the Turnbull Report of 1995.

Turnbull emphasized the importance of church members as the primary resource of the active church, reflecting wider society and secular institutions that speak of their workforce as their primary resource. The very phrase 'investors in people' not only heralded this emerging perspective but also became a mark of institutional competence often displayed as an 'award' on company premises and notepaper.[7] While, in analytical terms, it is important to distinguish between secular companies whose 'people' are its staff and the Church whose 'people' include both paid staff and participant membership there remains an appropriate comparison between a company's staff and the clergy as prime resources in organization.

In the theoretical terms of our study this phrase 'investors in people' is telling and begs caution, for while it explicitly invokes human capital theories for its rationale it also seeks to prize their symbolic worth as expressed in Turnbull's driving theological motif of 'gracious gift' used to describe the people of God (*Working as One Body*, 1995: 3). This is both judicious and potentially creative, since it integrates both a sense of a divine provision and the church's human membership. It also furnishes a valuable theological idiom to complement our own theoretical use of 'symbolic exchange' throughout this book. Still, Richard Roberts remained critical of the Turnbull Report, not least its suggestion that there should be a national executive core for the church: a suggestion that resulted in the establishment of the Archbishops' Council (Roberts, 2002: 169). Roberts was convinced that 'theology understood as a field of competitive forces' involves a 'struggle for power' and that, in a secular and pluralist world, the identity of the ministry has been increasingly magnified (2002: 117). Once that magnification is infused with a managerial spirit the laity is rendered relatively powerless: and that is the situation in which bishops become managers who have lost their sense of what the Church is because they have lost a sense of who the people of God are. This account of Roberts' views contrasts well with the descriptive models of episcopacy presented in Chapter 2, but it also demands some nuanced qualification concerning power in the light of the actual attitudes and experience we have found amongst those serving as bishops over much of the period covered by Roberts' analysis.

One area in which the Church may be interpreted as having come to 'accept the laity', or value its membership, during recent decades lies in the ordination of women to the priesthood. Inevitably entailed in that decision lies the question of consecrating women as bishops. Given that many of our bishops were in positions of power during the women's ordination debates we thought it useful to seek their current views on whether women should be made bishops. The results are shown in Table 3.1.

A majority of 70 per cent were in support, while 15 per cent were not in support and a similar number were unsure. To have nearly a third of these bishops not actively supporting the consecration of women priests as bishops adds an additional

---

7   'Investors in People' is explicitly raised in the Perry Report (*Working with the Spirit*, 2001: 3, 167).

and telling dimension to the theological uncertainty over the nature of episcopacy, an issue pursued in Chapter 4 over diocesan and suffragan bishops.

Table 3.1   Bishops' views on the consecration of women bishops

Response	Number	% (Adjusted)
Strongly support	30	50.0
Support	12	20.0
Don't know	9	15.0
Not support	6	10.0
Strongly oppose	3	5.0
Total	60	100

Jural and Mystical Authority

One means of achieving a different kind of perspective on manager and pastors is through the distinguished anthropologist Rodney Needham's notion of *diarchy* or *dual sovereignty*. He employed the terms 'jural authority' and 'mystical authority' to differentiate between 'political and religious, pragmatic and symbolic, or secular and sacred features' of human organization (Needham, 1980: 71). We take his jural authority to cover matters of law, established practice, the maintenance of discipline and of the fabric and organization of the church: it easily partners rational control and managerialism. Jural authority is not, however, an obvious or easy means of engaging with situations grounded in 'religious, symbolic and sacred' features. Here we encounter a slight problem of expression since the church clearly exists as a total 'religious' world that combines 'political and religious, pragmatic and symbolic, or secular and sacred features'. In practice, however, while matters of worship, devotion and spiritual care all do have jural elements to them they are, basically, much more firmly set in symbolically sacred ground better described in terms of mystical authority.

Rehearsing theoretical concerns raised in Chapter 1, we might say that in terms of 'gift-theory', the mystical form of authority may be seen as embracing the value of persons to each other as people and not as the more 'jural' actors in a legal world. In Cantwell Smith's (1963) terms, personal faith relates to mystical authority just as cumulative tradition does to jural authority.

From the 1960s the increasing scope of private life and religious diversity offered enlarged opportunities for personalized forms of what Paul Heelas (1996) has called 'self religions', in which mystical authority plays a significant part. The rise of Charismatic religion within churches also reflected a need for authenticity through individual-focussed religious resources and these, too, tend to be fostered by agents of mystical authority, sometimes leading to conflict with more jural concerns. Within church organization this distinction of jural and mystical authority is played out in one significant fashion between diocesan and suffragan bishops, as Chapter 4 shows, but it is no simple division of labor, especially in a period when the more authoritarian form of a bishop is also inclining more in the pastoral direction.

Directions and Dynamics

Informed by these jural and mystical elements of managerial-pastoral authority, by the gift-theory approach to the value of individuals in community, and by the faith-cumulative tradition dimensions of religion we take up again the topic of the two 'directions' of episcopal ministry – outward to the world and inward to the locality. From this perspective the centrifugal force highlights mission, the political economics of world poverty and justice, while the centripetal force emphasizes matters of church organization, liturgical reform, politics and pastoral care. Such forces raise interesting questions of ecumenism and inter-faith relations and help pinpoint episcopacy as a useful resource when viewed as a model of leadership open to changing demands. One issue concerns the way in which these episcopal directions and dynamics have been influenced by the pastoral factor. While it is relatively easy to speak of the local direction and the centripetal force as stressing the pastoral domain it is also worth considering the extent to which a 'pastoral' attitude of fostering and care becomes a value that pervades many kinds of activity.

This makes speaking of a 'pastoral turn' rather complex. Medhurst and Moyser, for example, stressed the way in which many bishops they studied came onto the bench 'following 'careers' spent as parish priests, rural deans, and archdeacons' (1988: 104). Such experience, they thought, had conferred a deep sense of 'grass-roots' pastoral needs upon these individuals. Of their diocesan bishops some three-quarters had held parochial incumbencies while, in our case, that number had risen to some 90 per cent, with all having held a curacy: this reinforces their thesis on the practical experiential base informing the pastoral shift. Here we should not ignore wider movements of thought that have, increasingly, fostered the needs of individuals as the twentieth century progressed. Theological concerns are also germane when understood as doctrinal creativity engaging with particular circumstances. And creativity is an important issue since we do not simply wish to speak of church 'responses' to changing times as simple effects of social causes. Sociologically speaking it is relatively easy to speak of cause and effect or, for example, of response to deprivation within religious groups. On that front, for example, Bryan Wilson argued in his influential 1966 study, *Religion in Secular Society*, that both ecumenism and increased interest in liturgical developments were responses of clergy whose wider social role was eroded in an increasingly secular world (Wilson, 1966: 154–65). Though he also mentions pastoral factors they are relegated very much to the background in order to focus more upon the way churches were being 'driven steadily back to the role of gratifying the demand for emotional expression, to the function of catering institutionally to emotional needs' (1966: 162). While the rise of the Charismatic Movement, largely after Wilson's study, might be seen in these terms it is not often interpreted in terms of pastoral needs though, doubtless, many such needs for such things as a sense of community or of personal expressiveness were present in the changing religious lives of its new adherents. More formally, both the *Faith in the City* and the *Faith in the Countryside* reports, for example, possessed strong theological motives directed to pastoral concern with several levels of national and local life. Similarly, David Sheppard's influential *Bias to the Poor* (1983) was rooted in a theological commitment to understanding and engaging in social welfare. A great deal of the church's concern with social responsibility can be approached in this way even if it is more obviously visible in the local diocese than in the nation at large. There are, however, key moments when events link local, regional and national concerns, as with disasters and tragedies of various kinds, as we see in Chapter 4: then the episcopal role becomes obviously pastoral and mirrors the local clerical role to a marked degree.

Our bishops, as Chapter 2 details, were far more prepared to agree very strongly that the pastoral care of the clergy (83 per cent) and the pastoral needs of the diocese (75 per cent) were of paramount importance to them than they were to emphasize the catholicity of the church (42 per cent), challenging the secular state on moral and political issues (18 per cent), or being the voice of moral leadership in society (18 per cent). In the light of that it is worth pondering the variety of meanings embraced by the idea of 'pastoral' attitudes since it tends to be interpreted by each bishop in the light of their own work. One, for example, spoke of 'partnership in the gospel', as one who 'shares' in a sense of 'corporateness' and as different from his own early clerical experience of the bishop 'as a remote figure'. Still, he noted the independence of many of the clergy, making it important for the bishop to judge when he was and was not needed. His desire was to 'motivate' people and help to 'focus a sense of direction'. Another and quite senior bishop thought that the three roles of 'theological teacher, role of unity and pastoral role … merge into each other'. He spoke of two main areas of pastoral work as basic to the parish priest as to the bishop except for the bishop's broader canvas. One was concern for his clergy, whom he thought had become 'much more dependent on the ministry of bishops' over the two decades of his ministry because of increasing demands made upon them. In so doing he was alert to the double hazard of people becoming dependent upon him and also of his own sense of enjoying having people as dependent. His focus, like that of some others, lay on 'giving people confidence': indeed, he spoke of 'using authority to set people free' to do what they had sought permission to do. His second point concerned pastoral opportunities with social elites of his diocese and with members of the House of Lords.

The fact that many respondents saw themselves primarily as pastors should not obscure the fact that the 'pastoral' element embraced numerous features. In some respects the element of 'vagueness' discussed in Chapter 2 over churchmanship resembles the 'pastoral' role here, each accounting for a generalized outlook and activity. As one put it: 'I've always regarded myself as a parish priest who found himself as a bishop … Being a bishop wasn't any great deal for me. Both my grandfathers were bishops – diocesan bishops – and I remember them both well.' Both the implicit and explicit assumptions of this response take the social status of bishop for granted in such a way that the pastoral dimension is allowed to take precedence with some ease. For many of our retired bishops their sense of success as bishops seemed to be evaluated in terms of whether they had been effective and observant pastors through having offered time and attention to their clergy and the parishes of their diocese.

New Pressures: Media and the Marginalization of Religion

If an inner-directed pastoral role came easily for most bishops, the challenge of the media prompting its own form of outward-directed action did not always do so. The rise of the mass media was amongst the most dramatic features of cultural change in the last third of the twentieth century, with political and religious life transformed, not least as modes of social deference changed. The center of gravity of opinion-making and of the arbitration of moral values, whether in Parliament or the synods of the church, could not ignore the media interviewer, producer of incisive documentaries, or broadsheet and tabloid journalists. Despite the fact that, from the 1960s these changes paralleled the now well-recorded demise of churchgoing in Britain and a decline in status of the national church, the media did not ignore ecclesiastical and religious topics and, periodically, bishops felt the pressure of media attention, not least in the two rather diverse contexts – one positive and one negative – of national distress and moral controversy.

One diocesan spoke of attendance at a disaster site as having become almost conventional, so much so that 'if a bishop doesn't turn up he's lacking in his job, and that's a pity because he can't do everything'. A more telling aspect of his observation was that the media had been responsible for making bishops into 'the people who count' at such a time precisely because, while there are prime national figures, there are not that many individuals who hold an appropriately high-status office at a regional level who can make an appropriate appearance. As he expressed it: 'Lords Lieutenant are not always articulate people.'

The appropriateness of association between bishops, crisis and the media is brought out clearly in this evaluation of the relative unavailability of persons invested with a suitable authority or presence at a regional level. It is an association that should not be passed over lightly for it brings our theoretical concern both with forms of 'capital' and with 'gift-theory' into sharp focus. The episcopal crisis-presence draws upon the cultural and spiritual capital embodied in a bishop as an 'establishment' figure in British society but who is definitely not a political figure. The nature of the Church of England also allows for bishops to make combined ethical and religious comment in an inclusive rather than an exclusive fashion, often in a way that embraces other denominational groups. Part of a bishop's spiritual capital underpinning these possibilities is derived from the public's widespread, and generally positive, experience of the Church of England especially in and through funerals, and to a lesser extent marriages and baptisms. His representative role depends, to a degree, on this grass-roots knowledge and broad public acceptance of 'the church'. But this 'capital' base is also complemented – in terms of symbolic exchange – by what is associated with traditions of faith embodied by bishops. Here we might speak of the 'depth' of human experience that comes to complement or enhance the 'mere' power of the establishment. What a bishop says about the importance of human life and people's response to its loss is framed by quite a different set of associations than is that of a politician. This is especially important in a media age in which news reporting depends largely upon 'expert' comment or else on critical interviewing of political figures in a blame-oriented culture, not least with what one of the authors has called 'offending deaths', in which mass popular reaction occurs to the death of individuals seen as innocent victims and where reparation is sought from authority figures who are, in some way, deemed responsible (Davies, 2001). Theoretically speaking we might, then, see the crisis-situated bishop as drawing both from his cultural-spiritual capital and from his embodying tradition. We might even explain that embodiment in terms of his 'being a gift' to society in the sense of being a person able to speak of values concerning the depth of human experience, of care, love, and of love's loss in a fashion that is not 'natural' for politicians or newsreaders. The irony of this situation in the period studied is that this role would not be as visible and influential without the media.

However, this collaborative atmosphere can easily transform itself into one of conflict, especially at the national level. One relatively high-profile diocesan starkly contrasted the local and national press, finding the local press 'always supportive', not least because 'they've got to live with you', while the national press 'had no commitment to the diocese ... they were simply like hyenas on the kill, coming in to snap at anything they could snap at', and with their own distinctive agendas. Indeed, he felt that one individual had 'suffered a great deal', and that by the end of the 1980s the national press could be 'pretty cruel'. It was during this period that the Church of England began organizing itself more efficiently in dealing with radio, television and the press through a Communications Committee, with some bishops receiving some media training. At least one who had been given 'some tuition' nevertheless 'felt weak' at it, 'seldom gave any interviews', and had been badly reported in one instance. He thought both that the media were sometimes 'very naughty' and that some bishops 'indulged' too much in media interviews.

This distinction between national and local press expresses something of the relationship between church and people over our period and echoes a degree of difference in identity and role amongst the bishops. Most bishops are only known regionally and their media ministry tended to be of a relatively non-controversial and more pastoral kind, reflecting the actual local work of the church. A few, by contrast, gained a high profile on the national level, largely in relation to what many viewed as controversial issues such as the ordination of women, homosexual clergy, or doctrinal issues debated by David Jenkins when Bishop of Durham and John Robinson as Bishop of Woolwich. Again, in the theoretical terms of capital and of gift theories, individual bishops can lose both some of their spiritual capital and their value as embodiments of the faith if people reckon they no longer uphold a proper value of life. Though the very idea of life as 'sacred' becomes contested in an increasingly secular public world, one depicted as risk-filled by the media themselves, yet it is still through media-covered ritual events, controlled largely by senior clergy, that British society largely copes with tragedy and broaches the question of the 'moral meaning of life'. And that moral significance is the precise key content of the gift-theory approach to human society.

It is often through such crisis-events that a sense of religiosity in Britain finds appropriate expression. This dispersed form of religion is neither doctrinally precise nor attendance-grounded, as the Doctrine Commission Report of the late 1970s fully acknowledged when it spoke of 'doctrine diffused' and placed strong emphasis upon 'corporate believing', subtitling itself 'The Corporate Nature of Faith' (*Believing in the Church*, 1981: 148, 286). That report is noteworthy because it appeared during the period of very active ministry of those in this study. In theoretical terms, while it shows the influence of aspects of sociology and anthropology, reflecting John Bowker's influence and ideas of that time, its use of the notion of 'corporate' factors falls upon the variety of groups comprising the church: whether core, more marginal members or theologians as such, the time was obviously not ripe for 'corporate' to stress the 'embodied' aspects of values. That is, perhaps, understandable given the doctrinal focus of an institutional concern. The decades since then have, in social and human sciences, and in theology too, increasingly interpreted 'corporate' in terms of embodiment. And that is important for understanding a significant part of a bishop's life and work, not least when he is present in the public arena of the media as a focus of regional-national significance combined with broad Christian ideas of the value of the individual, of caring relationships and of the ultimate meaningfulness of life.

Charisma

Here the sociological notion of charisma is useful because media images gain power from the degree of charisma inherent in the episcopal office. Max Weber developed the notion of charisma to refer to 'extraordinary powers', expressing a quality of authenticity allowing a leader to attract followers to some explanation of life (Weber, [1922] 1966: 2). One aspect of that quality of attraction – identified in successful politicians as the ability to establish 'in the minds of others a direct connection between themselves and the central values of society' (Bryman, 1992: 36) – mirrors the 'gift-element' applicable to bishops at times of difficulty. Bryman's stress on the relational nature of charisma, whether in terms of how people relate to an established office or a particular office holder or, more usually, to some combination of the two, was echoed in our biographical research capturing the interplay between ecclesiastical-social office and the force of individual personality (Bryman, 1992: 50–68). An associated factor concerns the context of episcopal action, especially if we bear in mind Talcott Parsons' observation that Weber's notion of 'charisma of office ... is identical with Durkheim's concept of the sacred' (Parsons, [1922] 1966: xxxiv). This sets bishops' liturgical roles within a sacred social order of things in which their precise individuality is relatively insignificant. Their media engagements, however, are not ritually conceptualized so that the charisma of office need not necessarily carry the day. The one context affords a protective sacred frame, the other potential secular exposure and, at that point, the individual's personal charisma becomes potentially decisive.

Charisma, Capital and Exchange

Bryman's relational approach to charisma also furnishes a valuable means of analyzing the themes of spiritual capital and gift-theory in relation to each other. This enhances our understanding of episcopal work and also contributes to the study of religion in general, where, at present, the notion of 'capital' is as popular as that of charisma is unfashionable.

While the notion of 'capital', like that of charisma, focusses on the product of relationships (whether economic, political, social, cultural or spiritual) it is essentially 'process-intensive' while charisma is 'person-intensive'. Together they describe the creative origin of social processes that result in the potential gain of advantage to the persons – leaders and followers – participating in the networks concerned. Each offers a way of understanding individuals and the networks in which their power of identity emerges and is employed. Bryman's account of charisma includes an emphasis upon 'a particular kind of relationship between leaders and followers which' – as he puts it – 'can be regarded as a form of exchange' and it is with respect to the precise nature of this 'form of exchange' within a charismatic relationship that we draw attention (Bryman, 1992: 68). It is an exchange that, potentially, fosters an increase both in the depth-worth of the individual and in the networked capacity of participants.

Other forms of leadership are also informative, especially the distinction between 'transforming' leadership and 'transactional' leadership[8]. Loosely speaking, the former may be equated with 'true' leadership and the latter with 'management' – a distinction of some relevance to Richard Roberts' criticism of the Church of England covered above. While it is relatively easy to use these sharp distinctions in abstract discussions or, indeed, in formal considerations of church organization, it is less easy to separate them in the actual life and work of individual bishops, not least when, as one leading bishop of his day put it, 'the Church doesn't teach you about leadership', and added that he had learnt 'most of my leadership' in the army, where he had been 'very well taught'. He had, however, gained some subsequent experience through the then newly established church-organized courses at St George's House, Windsor. Having said that, we do have cases of bishops who are easily aligned, and who align themselves, with the more visionary and the more routinely organized leadership types. And there is some evidence for intentional complementary balancing of types as insightful diocesans choose their suffragans but, for most, it seems that episcopal posts require some real degree of both transforming and transactional styles of operation. These brief comments on leadership, derived from management studies, need some theological complement given that the bishops understand their work to be part of a divine engagement and embody that ideal through such acts as daily prayer.

While management studies understand the relationship between managers and workers and their engagement with the ideals, goals and mission statements of their companies, they do not have to consider the idea of God as one to whom bishop-managers or worker-priests and their congregations relate. Even if a scholar wished to analyze the place of God in terms of people's attitude to God in an equivalent fashion to people's attitude to the dominant values of a company it would still be important to pay regard to the means by which those attitudes were fostered and expressed, in this case through prayer. Two cases will exemplify rather different aspects of prayer in relation to personal identity and to work.

One bishop, of a liberal catholic tradition and, influential in certain national church circles, spoke of the difference between his suffragan days when he met as part of a team, and of his diocesan status when he was much more on his own. His description was telling: 'For the first time in my entire ministry I prayed alone every

---

8   See Bryman (1992): 96, utilizing McGregor Burns' (1978) terminology.

single day.' He added: 'I think one is given grace to cope with that, and my whole prayer became more contemplative, I think, because of that. That was fine, it was marvellous. I wasn't looking back … thinking how marvellous it was in the team, of course I missed the team and companionship. As far as prayer was concerned I quite enjoyed that solitary life. And that has gone on ever since.' Here the emphasis was upon the role of prayer as much as a self-related meditation as upon any directedness to others or to his specific work. This not only reflected 'the first thing that [he] was told at theological college [and which he now recalled], "Prayer and teaching prayer, that is all"', but also the period of his earlier life when considering ordination. He spoke of this as a two-year period 'when the whole life of prayer meant more and more to me and more and more essential, and therefore there was that inner conviction as well', that is, as well as the encouragement he was receiving from two well-placed churchmen.

Another bishop, of Evangelical background, spoke of prayer as a matter of course and of how he asked his clergy for their prayer requests. His comments were emphatic: 'And they responded to that with enormous appreciation, and I actually did pray for them, I prayed a lot for the clergy, I kept them in my mind and in my prayers, I thought a lot about them. I really did go out of my way to do that.' This same individual had his own system of reference for his clergy and their families and endeavored to foster a sense of concern for and engagement with them that matched this practice of prayer that was, clearly, petitionary in nature and, in that sense, was outward-directed to the clergy.

Another contrast between commercial and episcopal leadership concerns ritual as a major point of contact between bishops, priests and the larger membership of their organization. It is here that symbolic-exchange theory is valuable in interpreting the complex practical reality of leadership and charisma in the Church of England. The nature of what the bishop does cannot be explained simply in the management-theory sense of wages paid for labour transacted in a market situation (McGregor Burns, 1978), but benefits from the more nuanced fashion of, for example, Maurice Godelier's (1999) development of Marcel Mauss's (1954) pioneering anthropological work. Godelier highlights the distinction between Mauss's 'threefold' obligation, in which 'alienable gifts' are given, received and given back again at a future date, and the 'fourth obligation' of 'inalienable' gifts that are given 'to the gods'. Our application of Godelier's scheme takes the inalienable category to describe the relationship between bishop and people that gives it a 'higher purpose' than would exist solely in a transactional form of leadership typified in a work-wages form of exchange. This inalienable mode of relationship can, indeed, bind 'leader and follower together in a mutual and continuing pursuit of a higher purpose' in a distinctive fashion (Bryman, 1992: 95, citing McGregor Burns, 1978: 20). And this is precisely where charisma of relationship becomes important as 'charisma of office' and 'personal charisma' interpenetrate (Bryman, 1992: 92, citing Etzioni, 1975: 5). The framing feature of this relationship that should not be sociologically or theologically ignored is the way in which leader and follower understand their mutuality in relation to God, since both gain their validity from what is believed about God within the church of which they are members.

This raises again the issue of the media because of the importance of context in and through which leader and follower usually interact. In one sense the 'leader-follower' language needs qualification within the Church of England since the interaction of bishop and people is through rather infrequent ritual events such as confirmation. These are highly symbolic acts with the bishop vested to denote both his 'high' office of ecclesiastical authority and his 'low' office of shepherd of the flock; his are the episcopal ring and pastoral staff. His key words are formally prescribed in liturgical form and his own added comment, perhaps in the form of a sermon, are very likely to follow suit. After the ritual event, in more of a reception or party mood, it is likely that the congregation will interact with him in a more informal social context but one in which his status remains a determining marker with him, for example, still wearing a purple cassock.

With the media, however, two rather different contexts tend to appear. The first, with which we began this immediate discussion, is that of crisis or catastrophe in which the bishop usually retains his charismatic potential as he acts in a pastoral relationship with those in difficulty, and in which his spiritual capital comes to the fore. The divine reference remains high as he seeks to bring a sense of meaning to complex contexts and the religious language used assumes that issues of 'prayer' are entirely germane.

The second media context, by sharp contrast, involves a bishop being interviewed because of some ecclesiastical, doctrinal or moral issue. This assumes a more inquisitorial than pastoral mode and the language of prayer, blessing, comment and generic goodwill gives way to question and answer, and the search for the controversial sound-bite that might catch the bishop out. One such bishop spoke of the press as 'setting us up', and of their 'private agendas', that were not in the church's favor. This latter context largely abandons the shared congregational assumption of a divine framework and the inalienable dimension of shared identity gives way, quite precisely, to what is up for debate and, in that sense, to what is alienable. And this is, potentially, seriously problematic for the church and the way it is accepted or rejected in society at large, as many already see, for example, in the case of the Roman Catholic Church and cases of sexual exploitation in parts of the USA and Ireland.

Another aspect of charisma and church authority comes to sharp focus in contexts of bishops' interviews because of the fact that in contemporary society the media themselves tend to be invested with a high degree of worth and, in the cases of several nationally known interviewers, one might even speak of their charisma. Along with particular sportspeople and musicians whose relationship with their fans is easily described in charismatic terms, these national figures enshrine the status of the media and can use that power either to boost the charismatic endowment of a bishop in the disaster situation or to decrease it in an interview over controversy. In theoretical terms, this kind of inherent 'charismatic' power and competition could also be described in terms of the capital and the 'gift' each brings to an interview situation.

While the dislike of a potential challenge to charisma might underlie the reason why some of our bishops were so cautious in relation to the media, some were also, perhaps, concerned with the way in which certain bishops became more evidently public figures through the media. Although largely expressed in suitably muted tones there was a degree of criticism of self-advertising bishops implied in what was said. Just how bishops relate to each other is not without its own form of critique as part of a person's self-image, of his own attitude towards ecclesiastical enhancement, and of a sense of proper Christian leadership. Such group-related forms of social identity have, of course, been widely studied in social psychology (Fiske, 2004: 475–95). Our purposes, however, are better met in terms of symbolic exchange applied here to the worth of episcopacy and to the potential abuse of its intrinsic giftedness by publicists acting outside ritual contexts.

Ecumenical, Inter-faith and Political Dimensions

Certainly, a bishop's spiritual career needs to embrace a breadth of interest given the established nature of the Church of England and the responsibilities of bishops in relating to other Christian denominations and religions beyond Christianity. While the former were more pressing in the 1960s–1980s, the latter assumed increasing importance from the 1980s to the year 2000. To consider this we explored the bishops' attitudes to other denominations, religions, to the nation and government at large, and to disestablishment.

To bridge our earlier consideration of detailed intra-church roles and these wider engagements with other groups we began with what might be regarded as a default position: how bishops saw the Church of England itself as a focus of their service. Some 80 per cent said that was principally the case, and 15 per cent partially so. This would surprise those who might assume that key leaders would inevitably see their own church as the complete focus of their service. Other questions developed this theme and helped explain it so that, for example, when asked if they saw their focus of service as that of 'all churches in Britain' (referring to non-Anglican denominations) 23 per cent said that was principally the case, and 60 per cent partially so. Only one bishop gave a completely negative answer to that question. In yet another question we asked their view of service to 'all of religious conscience'. Here a small 5 per cent did see that as their principal concern, while 47 per cent had it as a partial concern and a further 38 per cent as a peripheral concern.

These responses portray a spiritual career perceived as representing religious and moral positions of other churches and individuals as well as their parent denomination. But did they think they also represented people 'of other world religions'? Here we found a relatively equal division between the 48 per cent who said they did reckon themselves to have represented other religions and the 47 per cent who did not. Only a small 5 per cent gave no answer to that question. This is instructive information with representative bishops being in the House of Lords and since we often hear it said that many non-Anglican and non-Christian leaders support the fact of a state church and its representation in Parliament. Our information would seem to indicate a solid core of bishops prepared to support such groups. Amongst our respondents 38 per cent had, in fact, served in the Lords.

Indeed, when asked if they would support the inclusion of non-Anglicans and non-Christians as religious leaders alongside bishops in the House of Lords, we found the results presented as approximate percentages in Table 3.2.

Table 3.2   Bishops' views on inclusion in the House of Lords

Response	Non-Anglican Christian Leaders (%)	Non-Christian Religious Leaders (%)
Strongly support	50.0	30
Support	41.7	38.3
Don't know	1.7	10.0
Not support	5.0	18.3
None or complex	1.7	1.7
Total	100	100

The support for other Christian denominations is very high indeed, over 90 per cent, and represents the growth in ecumenical attitudes over the second half of the twentieth century. While the support for non-Christian religious leaders is also high (38 per cent support and 30 per cent strongly support) there was a sizable minority, nearly a third, that either did not know (10 per cent) or else would not support their inclusion (18 per cent).

As a final frame for bishops' perceived scope of action we posed three questions concerning their focus of service. The first concerned the British people at large: here 17 per cent thought their focus was principally 'at large', 48 per cent partially so, and 22 per cent as peripherally the case; only 3 per cent said it was 'not at all' the case. This gives a broad sense of their mixed perspective and highlights a kind of division of labor present amongst the bishops. It reflects, too, the distinction between many suffragan bishops whose work is often specifically dedicated to more local diocesan affairs, and those diocesans who have played some significant part in national affairs. The second question, on how their focus of service related to the British government itself, had none with this as their primary focus: a 15 per cent minority said it was partially so, 27 per cent peripherally the case but 42 per cent said they had no such focus on government. Finally, we asked if episcopal duties had fostered a different attitude towards the scope of ministry, and this met with a close division of opinion between 45 per cent who thought it had and 48 per cent who thought it had not.

We specifically explored political aspects of the bishops' lives and found that practically 90 per cent did not hold actual party membership. Amongst the 6 individuals who did, 4 were Labour and 2 Liberal Democrat. In terms of their personal histories the past was much the same except that three individuals had once been Conservative Party members but had given up membership. Sympathy towards a political party was interesting in that approximately 40 per cent identified themselves with the Labour Party in one or other of its 'Old' or 'New' guises. Approximately 22 per cent sympathized with the Liberal Democrats and 7 per cent with the Conservative Party. In terms of change of sympathetic allegiance over time, 55 per cent said they had changed their allegiance while 45 per cent had not. The shift will have been towards and between Labour and the Liberal Democrats. Certainly, these individuals reflect a church of the later twentieth century as not being the Tory Party at prayer, a shift that political scientist Dennis Kavanagh described in his analysis of Thatcherism (Kavanagh, 1987: 288). Their political outlook reflected the wider theological 'bias to the poor' and general notions of equality often more associated with Labour rather than the Tory ideology associated with the Thatcher era during which most of these bishops were in active ministry.

In terms of the status of the Church of England we looked at their attitude towards the idea of the disestablishment of the church at the time of their ordination and now that they were retired. This is an interesting issue since practically none of these bishops had personal memories of the issues surrounding the disestablishment of the Welsh church in the 1920s mentioned above. Table 3.3 shows the changes that had come about.

Table 3.3   Bishops' views on the disestablishment of the church

Response	*At Ordination (%)*	*In Retirement (%)*
Strongly in favor	1.7	1.7
In favor	1.7	11.7
Unsure	18.3	31.7
Against	53.3	43.3
Strongly against	21.7	10.0
Can't remember	1.7	-
No response	1.7	1.7
Total	100	100

The major trend over the course of their lives lies in a growth in uncertainty over the question (from 18 to 32 per cent), a decrease of strong opposition (from 22 to 10 per cent) and of opposition to disestablishment (from 53 to 43 per cent).

Identity, Character and Spiritual Career

One way of approaching both these shifting personal trends and the issue of the value of episcopal life is through the notion of identity. Itself a characteristic concept of many disciplines in the second half of the twentieth century and echoing ideas of character and personality so familiar to the later nineteenth and early twentieth century,[9] it still appears in some ecclesiastical reflections on contemporary leadership, as in Trevor Beeson's *The Bishops* (2002). He, rather like Richard Roberts, serves critical judgment upon the developing corporate character of church life and deplores the loss of character in individual leaders. This is no idle game, for the way in which a church conceives of leadership influences its entire mode of operation, involving both the general interplay between culture and religious values and the specific expectations of a leader's 'spiritual career'.

---

9   See Burkitt (1908: 28), Handley (1908: 16), and Jevons (1913).

One important way in which a religious group thinks of itself in relation to its wider world is through its ideal type of a leader. To know what it wants in its leaders is to see what it makes of relationships amongst the wider membership and of those in society at large. The Church of England seems to possess a cluster of values over leadership, some of which are contradictory. It wants 'godly' leaders who are wise and from the depth of their own spiritual resources and the 'giftedness' of tradition can speak of and foster the depth of human life. But it also wants efficient managers. Here there is no simplistic either/or divide but there are clusters of emphasis that do not run in parallel. Much depends upon the degree of control a central authority wields over the formation and/or the recruitment of leaders. One of the reasons why the Church of England remained moderately adaptable during the twentieth century was because of the later nineteenth-century theological and philosophical commitment to the notion of personality and the development of 'character' in and through personal piety and a variety of corporate commitments. These included both strong and weak church family backgrounds, a variety of churchmanship traditions and their associated colleges and parishes, and the experience of strong institutions such as school, college and military life. If 'character' and its underlying 'personality' lay at the heart of the individual life then 'service' was its framing social ethic. This outlook, rooted in a strong incarnational Christology and a growing sacramental theology, served as the basis for a spiritual career. Another form of spirituality was grounded in a theology of the Kingdom of God and service to the brotherhood of man. Yet another dwelt on the work of the Holy Spirit in helping to form the psychological dynamics of the faithful leader. While the nineteenth and twentieth centuries had more than one powerful model on which to draw when seeking to frame a spiritual career, that pool of potential orientations[10] became increasingly more shallow in the twentieth to twenty-first century transition as the background experience of increasing numbers of bishops became more uniform, a worry that was clearly detailed in the Perry Report (*Working with the Spirit*, 2001: 16–29).

Certainly, issues of identity are important when considering contemporary bishops and their 'spiritual career', a notion to which we now turn as a way of describing life in which hopes, aspirations and fears come to some degree of realization or frustration through their practical life in church organization. One important dimension of identity and spiritual career is that of ritual participation and, at this point, it is especially important not to create an artificial division between ritual and 'organization', even though our theoretical use of capital and symbolic-exchange theories might encourage it.

Ritual practice lies at the heart of most human religiosity and this is the case with the Church of England, whether in life-cycle events of very occasional attenders or the constant practice of the presence of Christ in personal devotion by core members. For many Anglican priests the Eucharist has come to be a focal rite in and through which their sense of piety and consequential ethics engages with and emerges from doctrinal ideas of the Incarnation. But the Eucharist is deeply embedded in the wider rites of the church, not only in a direct fashion with baptism, confirmation and ordination but also with the daily offices that are particularly significant for ordained

---

10   For 'pool of potential orientations' see Davies (2000): 247ff.

members. Nor should we forget marriages and funerals, through which clergy have the opportunity to practice their doctrine. Perhaps the very phrase – 'to practice doctrine' – may be permitted here to highlight the fact that much of what the church and clergy believe takes form through action.

Certainly, the interwoven activities of liturgy appear as one powerful stream of influence upon the bishops and it is telling that Stephen Sykes, bishop and theologian, stressed the importance of liturgy as a source of Anglican authority, not least because it is both the arena in which the people as well as the clergy are involved and in which the scriptures have a strong voice (Sykes, 1978: 131). This is an important element to add to Roberts' critique of Sykes sketched earlier because, for Sykes, liturgical reform and control of liturgical practice are basic to the Anglican expression of authority in relation to the Christian message. From a social scientific perspective what is interesting about liturgy, not least the Eucharist, is that many different theological ideas cluster around and run through the rites, allowing a variation of emphasis for each individual participant. Some may find sharp doctrinal motivation here while, for others, that 'vague' domain of insight can itself become a powerful force in an individual's life, as Chapter 2 suggested.

Conclusion

We began this chapter with Temple's romantic hope that a peculiar English genius might correlate opposing principles in the growth of freedom, and with Wickham's starker realism over Christianity's presence in an increasingly unchurched world. We have ended with a picture of continuing tensions in which correlation and conflict pervade the episcopal microcosm of growing inclusivity and pastorally inclined values, interpreted both through bishops' spiritual capital and embodied giftedness. From this tension we now move to another in the theological and organizational relationships between diocesan and suffragan bishops.

Chapter 4

Suffragan and Diocesan Bishops

The issue of power, its possession and use, is always problematic for groups claiming identity with Jesus of Nazareth. This is inevitably true for the Church of England, by law established, whose titular head is the monarch, whose bishops hold privileged social status but whose thought has come to be deeply pervaded by the doctrine of the incarnation. Anglican theology, much rooted in the idea of divine mercy, has increasingly spoken of divine love and, more latterly, of God's favor to the poor (Davies, 2005). While the tensions engendered by these considerations are numerous one lies at the heart of the church's own developing episcopal organization: the relationship between diocesan and suffragan bishops. This we now analyze through issues of vocation, episcopal appointment, career development, leadership needs, and the personal engagement of individual men of faith with the church as a social institution. Once more we employ notions of symbolic exchange to express an emphasis upon personal worth embedded in relationships and to complement ideas of spiritual capital.

Wanting the Real Man

An experienced non-episcopal dignitary, when discussing an impressive suffragan, commented: 'Still, they want the real man' – words that convey a readily perceived distinction between suffragan and diocesan bishops. His informal aside voiced that dissonant paradox engendered when theology and practice misalign, as formally expressed, for example, in Trevor Beeson's category of 'pastoral-manager', a notion invoked to account for suffragan–diocesan relationships. Setting the scene, Beeson notes how suffragans lapsed from the end of the sixteenth century until 1870 when Canterbury and Lincoln dioceses appointed 2, with 19 more across the country by 1900, some 40 by 1950, and with 66 suffragans by 2000 when they outnumbered the diocesan bishops (Beeson, 2002: 8). For Beeson, former Canon of Westminster Abbey, suffragans typify the pastoral pole of his pastoral-manager model, offering real opportunity for the pastorally minded person not wishing to bear ultimate managerial responsibility. He contrasts this position with that of the successful parish priest possessing considerable autonomy and who, as a suffragan, may find his secondary status difficult and may 'yearn for appointment to a diocese of his own' (2002: 8). Beeson sees the suffragan office as difficult in that it possesses freedom for pastoral opportunity amongst the clergy but lacks ultimate responsibility. He dislikes the suffragan scheme: 'The priest so chosen is not necessarily required to have outstanding intellectual gifts, wide vision or the ability to pioneer new expression of ministry and mission' (2002: 9). His ideal bishop is a 'pioneer visionary leader', leading the church into its difficult future. Beeson's political psychology of appointment reckons that, 'some diocesan bishops are careful not to choose suffragans more able than themselves', with the result that they are unlikely to bring 'insight or inspiration' into a diocese or the church at large. He readily cites Douglas Feaver (1914–1997), the strident former vicar of St Mary's, Nottingham and conservative Bishop of Peterborough, who refused suffragan help on the basis that they were 'no more than "consecrated nannies to look after the clergy"' (Beeson, 2002: 124).

But what of retired diocesan and suffragan bishops and their evaluation of episcopal work? In turning to their views, and as a theoretical introduction to their interviews, we draw attention to the way in which a research method may or may not resonate with the topic under analysis. Fixed questions, for example, can allow certain contradictions to be avoided. However, by employing semi-structured interviews one may hope to cover set topics in a relatively fixed way while acknowledging that individuals may take unpredictable paths, engage with complex issues and express the co-existence of contradiction. This reflects conversational language in which people easily make points that are mutually inconsistent or leave sentences half-completed while still indicating their preference through tone or expression. In our interviews some drew attention to the theological-organizational conflict, others alluded to it, ignored it completely or simply allowed the conversational format to take a topic elsewhere and thereby avoid the pressure to seek a logical resolution.

Written forms of communication, by contrast, tend to demand logical consistency or a fuller expression of preference. While writing may, however, press an author into making statements or arriving at decisions that are not demanded in ordinary discourse, it also allows a choice of topic that avoids problems caused by the interview situation. The Perry Report[1] on episcopacy provides some instructive examples, for instance in Bishop Michael Nazir-Ali's essay 'Towards a Theology of Choosing Bishops' which presents episcopal ministry both implicitly and explicitly in terms of an individual man who is the representative not only of worldwide and local Christianity but also of Christ himself (Nazir-Ali, 2001: 105). Since that report intentionally focussed on diocesan bishops it is understandable that Nazir-Ali made no mention of suffragans but, and this is our point, his constant reference to the singularity of the bishop in his various representative roles make it conceptually difficult to accommodate any suffragan within his discussion of episcopacy despite their prevalence. Simplicity is assured at the expense of practical diocesan episcopacy: it avoids the theological-organizational dissonance.

However, when our bishops were prompted to speak of diocesans and suffragans they frequently asserted or alluded to differences between them, often expressing some unease over the theological and managerial distinctions they felt it necessary to make. Doubtless, the enduring nature of English society's subtle and blatant markers of social differentiation expressed through rank-titles helped frame these comments while, sociologically speaking, this is accentuated by the relatively few positions of promoted dignity available to the professional clergy of the Church of England. In 1999, for example, only 4.5 per cent of all full-time diocesan clergy could be defined

---

1   *Working with the Spirit* (2001).

as dignitaries of the church. Numerically, of these 9,648 clergy there were 44 diocesan and 68 suffragan bishops, 120 archdeacons and, at cathedrals, some 43 deans and 160 residentiary canons.[2] Given that sharp divide in status it is not surprising that functional offices such as those of rural dean become valued and even the status of honorary canon is prized by many as a mark of recognition for long service or some other form of distinction. These statuses are frequently conferred through ritual performance, manifest in dress and reinforced by title. Church organization and architecture also complement each other and mark hierarchy with care taken over its order of precedence in processions and seating. Hierarchy, so regularly manifested, inevitably influences a group's outlook and may even imply a theological basis that does not, in any formal sense, exist. Here the complex interplay of organization, ideals and ethos is of particular significance within the church, as we have already seen in the previous chapter for issues of managerialism and as we now identify for the relation between the theology of episcopacy in relation to its organizational practice.

The Appointment of Bishops

The diocesan bishop stands as the legally appointed primary source of church authority within a specific diocese. Normally ordained by the Metropolitan (the Archbishop of Canterbury or York) and two or more other diocesan bishops, he has been 'selected' by the monarch from a name advanced by the Prime Minister who has already selected one of two names presented to the Prime Minister's office by the Crown Appointments Commission. Though the Crown Appointments Commission may express a preference for one name over another the Prime Minister is not obliged to take that name forward. Indeed, the Prime Minister may accept neither and ask for other names to be forwarded. Behind and before this process a great deal of work has been done by the local Diocesan Vacancy in See Committee as it draws up its own Statement of Needs of the diocese. It also appoints representatives to serve on the Crown Appointments Commission for that particular appointment. There also exist a Prime Minister's Secretary for Appointments and the Archbishops' Appointments Secretary, whose extensive networking in many church circles results in the appointment of a diocesan bishop. What is more, a great deal of secrecy has surrounded these appointments and, while the opening years of the twenty-first century mark a reconsideration of this appointment process, that world of secrecy certainly framed the lives of the bishops in this study.[3] In social and psychological terms, not to mention any theological issues that this might raise, it is interesting to note a firm expectation of secrecy amongst all concerned. This is evident in the Mellows Report, *Resourcing Bishops* (2001): 'On receipt of the Prime Minister's letter the candidate, if married, is permitted to discuss the approach with his wife. After meeting the Prime Minister's Appointments Secretary he can discuss the approach with his diocesan [bishop] as well as with his spiritual adviser or one close

---

2   Ibid.: 24.

3   Bishops in our survey include some appointed before and some after the official change in the appointments system, for which see Podmore (2000): 113–38.

personal friend' (*Resourcing Bishops*, 2001: 130). To this secrecy, and its potential symbolic significance for a bishop's spirituality, we will return; here we simply emphasize the wider significance of the Mellows Report, many aspects of which are related to our own research, though we only refer to more pressing overlaps throughout this book.

Against this background of intense consultation over diocesan bishops it is surprising to find that while suffragan bishops are chosen by the government-crown process from two names, those names are supplied by the diocesan himself without any necessary prior process of consultation. The significant implications of this for the church at large were taken up in the Perry Report's review of the Crown Appointments Commission which contrasted diocesan appointments between 1996 and 2000 with the appointments of the other diocesan bishops (still) in post in 2000, noting that 89 per cent of the 1996–2000 appointees had been suffragans compared with 56 per cent of those appointed earlier (*Working with the Spirit*, 2001: 16). In suggesting that perhaps 'safe choices' were being made and even that a certain 'cloning' occurred when diocesans nominated suffragans, the report echoes Beeson's criticism already noted above. The report worried over the fact that not all of these suffragans would be deemed suitable diocesans given that 'the roles of suffragan bishop and diocesan bishop are different in kind' (*Working with the Spirit*, 2001: 17). Accordingly the pool of candidates might not match the wide scope of diocesan ministry demanded in the country and its social and cultural life at large. While the report's numerous recommendations lie beyond our concern it is worth asking how some of our bishops reflected on the appointment of suffragans.

The clearest case of personal knowledge lay in the suffragan who had shared rooms at university with the diocesan bishop who nominated him. Their shared Oxbridge education extended to military experience though one was from a Grammar and one a Public School background: the suffragan described their relationship as 'a very good combination … [of] gentleman personality'. He commented on his appointment as something that 'could easily be regarded as the old boy network'. Certainly, while he saw their work as complementary, with his being more local and the diocesan's more national, he did not speak in managerial terms. Indeed, he thought that the 'greater emphasis upon management' was a development that had 'gone too far' in many professions and in the church. Tellingly, his criticism of the managerial ethic lay not in the need for 'high standards' but in the possibility of an individual engaging in managerial ventures and 'hiding in some cases from the costly business of personal contact'. He, himself, had hated but pursued the practice of hospital visiting expected of him as a curate. This person regarded himself as 'lucky' to have been a suffragan and not a diocesan because he did not want to have to 'make tough decisions about the clergy' or be the place where the ultimate 'buck stops'. For him the suffragan was 'quite a good chap' as far as others were concerned.

'It's the old-boy network absolutely, isn't it?' This was how another and well-known diocesan described how he had first become a suffragan, and thereby entered the episcopal lists. The details of preferment were rooted in private conversations between influential political, academic and ecclesiastical persons who sought, in a classic example of the British 'establishment', to bring about an appointment through personal nomination that, otherwise, would have not occurred because of other (and lesser) 'establishment' opinions to the contrary. All this was something he had only come to learn long after the event.

Similar and yet quite different was the suffragan whose initial path into ministry seemed entirely socially determined, in a passive sense, by a strong ecclesiastical family background and, more actively, through that typically Anglican form of 'direction' (already encountered in Chapter 1 with another bishop) in which his Oxbridge college chaplain asked him: 'When are you going to decide to be ordained, because if you don't decide to be ordained soon, there won't be a place for you at [a named theological college]?' At that time he did not even know where that theological college was. However, he decided to go, and in due course became a committed priest. He saw his move into episcopacy as making good managerial sense since it followed directly from his appropriate and extensive parish experience. As might be anticipated he much enjoyed his work, it suited him very well, not least because he was an Area Bishop, with a clear role in a system that 'was totally devolved', and in which 'everybody knew who you were'. He saw this sense of identity and discrete responsibility as 'an enormous advantage from a suffragan's point of view'. He added that he knew 'quite a large number who have been quite desperately unhappy as suffragans, because they were simply Episcopal curates'.

Diocesan–Suffragan Paradoxical Dissonance

Such varied responses to the theology and practice of episcopacy demand some consideration. Theologically, episcopacy has come to be a focal concept of Anglican identity, often endued with images of apostolic succession by some and with a biblical legitimation of pastoral oversight by others. Its relatively uncertain status, however, is reflected in the Perry Report's observation that in none of the current three main stages of nomination, election and consecration is the diocesan bishop given 'authority to continue the mission entrusted to the Church' (*Working with the Spirit*, 2001: 10). One might have thought such a key concept would possess an inevitable pride of place in the ritual making of a bishop. Be that as it may, bishops act as though it is given and do so in a hierarchical fashion when it comes to the diocesan–suffragan relationship where theological rationales of episcopacy sometimes conflict with issues of authority and responsibility. As a former suffragan and diocesan bishop, one particularly well informed on the issue, expressed it:

> There is a distinction … [the suffragan] is the assistant to the diocesan bishop, but a bishop is a bishop is a bishop. The episcopacy is one and there is no different theology of episcopacy when you talk about suffragans or diocesans. I believe that it is one of the faults of the church, or some people in the church, because they do see that difference. Including some diocesan bishops I have heard talking. I see no difference whatever: there is a difference in role and responsibility [but] that is not a theological difference, and that is not a difference in the nature of the ministry at all.

This bishop, after asserting that he felt 'quite strongly about this', then explained his view of the relationship between these bishops in a clear theological fashion: 'The relationship between suffragan and diocesan bishop is absolutely a core relationship, theologically, because it is a sign of the complex unity, it is related to the theology of the body of Christ.' His emphasis was on the fact that 'the unity is not a single organ. Theological unity is not simple unity, it is a complex unity.' Indeed, his basic view was that 'episcopacy is the focus of unity in the diocese that includes bishops'. Here the bishop was engaging in a form of theological shorthand that sought to use the idea of a close relationship between diocesan and suffragan bishops as a model of and for the unity of numerous diverse elements present in any Christian community following the Pauline image of the body with its many parts (I Corinthians 12:12–30). These issues were explicitly pursued in the Mellows Report (*Resourcing Bishops*, 2001: 24) in terms of the alternative models of either one bishop per diocese to maintain simplicity or more than one bishop as a symbol of episcopacy's essential complexity.

One feature of the church as such a 'body' lies in its degree of relative plasticity in response to emerging situations rather than pro-activity driven by a prior theological rationale. One of the best examples of its responsive 'complex unity' is that of 'flying bishops', already mentioned in Chapters 2 and 3, but important here as suffragans who operate by request of diocesans across a series of dioceses. As Peter Beesley emphasized, not all parishes seeking the oversight of such a person appreciate that their diocesan bishop 'retains his jurisdiction over a parish that does not regard itself as being in communion with him' (Beesley, 2001: 232). These bishops are exceptions to the geographical nature of a bishop's diocesan ministry and emerged in the 1990s following the Episcopal Ministry Act of Synod of 1993 that allowed individual parishes, through their Parochial Church Council, to seek alternative episcopal oversight in the light of disagreement between that parish and its diocesan bishop over the question of the ordination of women. The Act created this office of Provincial Episcopal Visitor. This status is, in fact, one of suffragan bishop with two for the Province of Canterbury – designated as the Bishops of Ebbsfleet and Richborough, and one for York – the Bishop of Beverley. These individuals came to be known as 'flying bishops' precisely because their brief was to serve over very wide areas. These exceptions not only prove the rule of geographically aligned bishops and the subordinate status of suffragans but also indicate the managerial usefulness of purpose-focussed suffragans. Here we see the church drawing from a flexibility of its managerial structure and the pragmatism of its theology to accommodate internal difference and sustain its 'complex unity'.

Another example of institutional response lies in 'area bishops': suffragans whose diocesan bishops have legally delegated specific powers to them in contexts where the diocese has, itself, been organized into geographical areas by means of the Dioceses Measure 1978. These were represented in our interviewed bishops with one describing the area bishops of one diocesan as 'colleagues and rivals', each wanting his area 'to be the best', and another offering quite a different view, seeing his work as very self-fulfilled given the degree of freedom he had in which to operate and given his appreciative view of the strength of his organizing diocesan bishop.[4]

---

4 An interesting example of an Assistant Bishop in relationship to 'flying bishops', churchmanship and the open attitudes of bishops is that of the Revd Sandy Miller, former

While these cases exemplify how episcopacy responds to organizational necessity there are always instances where that 'complex unity' is poorly reflected, as with one bishop who overheard a fellow diocesan recently say to his suffragan: 'when I'm not in the diocese you are me, when I'm there you are nothing'. He commented by saying that this was 'not a very theologically or personally sound way of putting it, but I think that is what has been the view of suffragan bishops in some cases'. Despite his critical view this bishop, who had himself been both a suffragan and diocesan, went on to speak of a 'certain inevitability' of difficulty over the diocesan–suffragan relationship 'because you have got this difficult thing of a two-headed monster, if I can put it like that, and people need to know where they are in the scheme of things'. His talk of 'the scheme of things' was, primarily, a reference to the authority structure of diocesan organization for he thought it vital that once,

> portfolios are clear ... the person appointed has the freedom to develop [it] without somebody breathing down his neck all the time – I think that's about as clear as you can get it actually, because it is anomalous, it is anomalous.

His strong emphasis on the anomaly is telling, and is not removed even when he seems to move to a sense of its resolution by citing the Act of Synod and exemplifying this by reference to Area Bishops. Indeed his very conversational expression, caught here in the transcribed text, is awkward, reflecting the difficulties he has in moving on from talking of anomaly: 'Now where there are Area Bishops I think other arrangements are possible, but they seem – however clearly that's delineated – there still seems to be quite a lot of difficulty about who makes the decisions and who doesn't'. He then added as a postscript, as though this had to be said as a follow-on from this obvious hierarchical scheme of decision-making:

> One PS. Yes, but the person is still a bishop in his own right and if ... I mean ... that is recognised in the Act of Synod, so there is the possibility of suffragans being elected, and they are fully bishops, and if one of them is appointed to chair a General Synod committee ... his life isn't wholly determined by his diocesan in that sense, at all, because he's part of the corporate episcopate of the Church as a whole, and has responsibilities arising out of that.

What is clear from this relatively unclear statement is that there is a real dissonance between the organizational status difference of diocesan and suffragan on the one hand and their apparent theological similarity on the other. The suffragan is responsible to the diocesan in organizational terms but the two are equal in theological understanding of status consequent upon their consecration as bishops. Perhaps the

---

vicar of Holy Trinity, Brompton, and much associated with the charismatic evangelicalism for which this church is famous. For various technical reasons he was consecrated bishop in Uganda, by request of Canterbury and London, to serve under the jurisdiction of the Bishop of London. Interviewed on the BBC's *Sunday Programme*, 12 February 2006, he was asked whether he was going to be a 'flying bishop for the evangelicals'. He replied that that was certainly not the case because, as he replied to the interviewer, 'I'm a no-labels man, as you know.'

best summary is to set alongside one another the two expressions: 'complex unity', and 'two-headed monster'.

Another bishop, who had also been both a suffragan and diocesan bishop, talked of dramatic changes having come about over expectations of suffragan bishops since his 'clerical youth' when 'suffragan bishops tended to be sort of older clergymen, many of whom for financial reasons, were incumbents and housed in the better vicarages, and were – if I can put it crudely – an extra pair of purple gloves to help when the bishop was away'. He saw subsequent changes in 'synodical arrangement' as ensuring that suffragans 'have a position in their own right', but such changes were not without their own difficulties as far as the question of responsibility was concerned, in that there remained a distinction between the suffragan who is intrinsically better as second in command than as the prime decision-maker. For him a suffragan was particularly useful when given a distinctive brief to develop a particular aspect of diocesan organization: in other words, a suffragan with a delegated task but answerable ultimately to the diocesan. In terms of relatively recent history it is interesting to see how the recruitment of diocesans from suffragans has developed. In 1984, for example, 24 out of the 43 diocesan bishops (56 per cent) had been translated from a suffragan post (Medhurst and Moyser, 1988: 105). This had changed to approximately 90 per cent of those who were nominated to diocesan sees between 1996 and 2000. Despite that there was still a trend whereby the highest fliers were often promoted directly to a prestigious see, as with Coggan, Runcie, Habgood, Jenkins and Carey. Indeed, of the 14 who occupied an archiepiscopal office during the twentieth century, only one, Cosmo Gordon Lang, had ever held a suffragan's post, as Bishop of Stepney, but that was to follow Dr Winnington-Ingram just translated to London's prime see.

Episcopal Career Development

So far, we have considered the mutual coherence and incoherence between ideology and action as far as the relationship between suffragan and diocesan bishops is concerned. Something similar must now be accounted for in the case of bishops as we distinguish between 'career' and 'vocation'. Priests, and by extension bishops, probably more than any other group now defined as professional, present a testing problem for sociological analysis given the way they themselves evaluate their lives and work.[5]

Sociologically, this topic is rooted in Weber's consideration of vocation in social life. He approached social phenomena through the idea of the ideal type, an abstract construct ordering the complexity of actual life by summarizing a topic's basic features in a rationally coherent fashion.[6] One of Weber's ideal types is particularly valuable for our study of bishops, that of 'inner-worldly asceticism', because it is

---

5   See, for example, Davies, Watkins and Winter (1991: 96) for the relationship between a sense of vocation and issues such as leisure or being 'off duty'.

6   See Käsler (1988): 183–4, on Weber's work. Similar configurations have been widespread in theological descriptions. William Law's *Serious Call* (1906) is replete with descriptions of typical forms of religious piety in Julius, Leo and Eusebius. Kierkegaard also

closely aligned with his description of the notion of 'vocation' (Weber, 1966: 167–83).

While recognizing that the idea of a vocation – as a sense of living in response to a divine calling – had long existed within religions, Weber saw the Reformation, especially in its more Calvinistic variety, as producing a distinctive form of living. Weber is best known, and most frequently criticized, for developing this perspective in relation to economic activity in his 'Protestant Ethic' thesis in which a rational and controlled form of human endeavor in husbanding one's resources led to capital growth and worldly wealth. That wealth was then taken by believers as a sign of divine blessing and, indirectly as it were, an indication that they were counted amongst God's elect. This was a considerable advantage, and no small relief, to their spirituality since the formal doctrine of their religion, grounded in divine predestination, divided all people into the saved or the damned in lists of destiny that were not accessible to humans. Although Weber, who spoke of such inner-worldly ascetics as religious virtuosi, had Protestant laity in mind, it is also possible to hold this ideal type in mind when considering the episcopal virtuoso in the Church of England. For here is a person operating within a kind of 'social class system' who is encouraged to think of his status as involving a divine call to serve the wider world through a particular institution 'by means of rational ethical conduct': 'the order of the world ... becomes for him a vocation which he must fulfill rationally' (Weber, 1966: 167). In this we encounter an anticipation of later theories of capital as we view a church as a human institution needing to manage its material, cultural and spiritual resources.

Among further features Weber had in mind when developing his ideal type of 'inner-worldly ascetic' was the management of, or control over, excessive emotion, passion or revenge when thinking of others and of the grand scheme of divine grace, as well as a general control of eroticism in relation to the necessity of family life and the production of children. While the proper use of power is enjoined for the good order of society, its enjoyment and misuse is forbidden. This account is useful when considering the varied complexity of bishops' lives, including family life, but its real import concerns ideas of mastery in relation to a religious life. Ultimately, as Talcott Parsons (1966: li) made very clear, Weber's approach to religion involves a fundamental distinction between persons set upon a path of mastery, pursued by those he calls ascetics, and persons who become resigned to life's contexts, pursued by those he deems to be mystics. The question for us is how such high levels of generalization may apply to the detailed complexity of our bishops' lives. Although we have already approached this problem in Chapter 3 in terms of both jural-mystical forms of authority and managerialism and leadership, we rehearse it here because of the subtle issue of authority that emerges between diocesan and suffragan bishops. What is certain is that bishops at large, and most especially diocesan bishops, are by virtue of their office engaged in a form of mastery through their managerial control over what is, in effect, an institution whose goal is that of salvation. The nature of this institution is such that one is able to speak of its need for management just as one

---

deploys the device to good effect as, for example, in 'The Unhappiest Man' or 'The First Love' and so on (1959: 217ff).

can speak of it as a community in relation to the divine, in which context 'mastery' becomes a problematic notion. This complexity is reflected in what the bishops said in discussion over the notion of vocation as opposed to career.

One very well-known and strong-minded diocesan saw 'career' as quite the wrong language for describing his life – 'the vocation which God put upon me' – in which he had experienced the sense of a divine calling in a very distinctive fashion. His self-reflection spoke of the feeling of pressure from God; indeed, he spoke of not having wanted to be a clergyman but did not think he 'could face himself' if he had not become one. This individual had not been brought up within a Christian and churchgoing family and, for him, Christian status involved a clear conversion into the faith.

However, another, a relatively scholarly and quiet bishop, found it perfectly possible to 'use the language of calling' and could see his life 'as such'. Still, in more practical terms he saw the path of his life more simply in terms of 'what happened'. Appropriately, perhaps, he described himself as not being a 'card-carrying Catholic, nor Liberal, not a card-carrying anything'. Tellingly, for him 'God and religion was a very natural thing, as natural as breathing' and his life has been 'broadly secure'. Appropriately, this individual had been brought up in the church as part of his natural family and community life.

As already indicated, the likelihood of any individual priest becoming one of the 42 diocesan or 68 suffragan bishops is limited. Expressing this, one of our former diocesan bishops reflected on what we are calling career development by referring to himself and to those for whom he had been responsible by speaking of his generation (embracing most bishops in this study) as being 'brought up not to be ambitious, ambition was a sin almost'. He then made two other kinds of comment, one concerning himself – that he had 'never applied for a job' in his life' – and another concerning some 'senior clergy who were very clearly wondering about their future'. By considering these comments, respectively, under the headings of 'institution and humility' and 'institution, ambition and fear', we can elucidate some of the complex personal dynamics as well as explore some technical themes operating between bishops and other clergy in their relation to the church and to each other.

Institution and Humility

As to the first comment, this bishop is not the only one to speak of never having applied for a job. While the nature of the episcopal appointments system would, in any case, have made application impossible there may well be more to this self-reflective statement than at first appears. Many social contexts reveal intimate alignments between values and organization and that is as true for the church as for many other institutions. The idea of episcopacy held by the bishop just mentioned matched his experience of entering episcopal office.

The very process of his invitation to office was, symbolically speaking, entirely consonant with the notion of priestly life as a vocation and not as a career. He was 'called' to be a bishop. One might even speak of this as a 'call within a calling'.

Ordination to priesthood itself – the basic 'calling' – is often described as a divine calling expressed both bureaucratically through the church's selection procedures and liturgically through the rite of ordination. This affirms the individual's sense of vocation and legitimates it ecclesiastically. Consecration as bishop – the call within the calling – takes this process further and, in a manner of speaking, deepens the very notion of 'calling' in and through its secretive process. Indeed, this notion of secrecy merits attention because it is not without sociological significance in relation to religious ideas. Rather than simply assuming that secrecy serves a utilitarian bureaucratic function it is worth considering secretive processes of selection in relation to theological ideas of the divine call. For individuals who believe in a personal God, and who see the church as something in which God has an interest and through which the divine will is, in part at least, enacted, those beliefs may be reinforced as and when they receive this further call – 'a bolt from the blue', as one bishop called it.

For the kind of bishop who had never applied for a job and for whom the call to episcopacy was a surprise, the combined processes of original selection for priesthood and later invitation to episcopacy express well the theological and spiritual sense of vocation to a way of life related to a divine reality. And such a divine element runs counter to any sense of ambition, a theme developed below. First, however, it is worth developing this issue of vocation in relation to that of humility, reflecting what one of the authors has, elsewhere, analyzed in terms of the 'humility response', a theoretical hypothesis relating to our discussion of jural and mystical forms of authority in chapter three (Davies, 2004b: 97–105).

When a society or some institution recognizes the worth of one of its members and marks that recognition in some honor or advancement it is frequently the case that the individual speaks of feeling a sense of humble gratitude rather than of inflated pride. In this process the individual is not only affirmed by his peers and superiors but he, himself, almost inevitably, and by the very fact of accepting the proffered honor, reinforces his sense of the worth of the institution and of those who have so generously recognized him. In such attitudes we see a distinctive example of symbolic exchange with its stress upon the value inherent in the attitudes and relations of appreciation of people to each other. This response is of some considerable importance for the nature of bonding between appointed leaders and the groups appointing them. It is this very 'bonding value' of relationships that participates in the symbolic-exchange model of social life: as Godbout suggests, such 'bonding value is the symbolic value that relates to the gift, to whatever circulates in the guise of a gift' (Godbout with Caillé, 1998: 174–5). In terms of this chapter the gift is consecration. Such a gift assumes particular significance for religious groups in which the doctrine or history validating its existence is also part of the ideological rationale underpinning the personal identity of its members, especially of those who are so committed that they are appointed to leadership positions. Something can be gained by utilizing this notion within a sociology of the Church of England when considering its primary leadership in the bishops and its secondary leadership in the remainder of the clergy. Accordingly, we might suggest that, concerning their sense of self and their mutual relationship, the secretly appointed diocesan bishop gains a sense of honored gratitude, as one admitted to a small senior hierarchy, which leads to his reaffirmation of the church's nature and purpose. The secretive processes that bring about a priestly elevation to episcopacy serve to accentuate the 'mystical' qualities of that to which he has been called. Here the nature of the institution's social organization is intimately aligned with the experience, one might even say with the religious experience, of the appointed individual. Indeed, religious organizations would not survive if their key personnel did not possess some sense of deep commitment to the institution's actual mode of operation. Churches, in particular, need a sensed correlation between theological validation of organization and the experience of their leaders. The degree to which this alignment functions at different levels of the organization is, itself, an important factor in the overall success of a church.

This assessment directly touches the theme of humility within a sociological appreciation of religious leadership, despite the fact that 'humility' is rarely discussed in British society at large, neither in the press nor in the life of most organizations. Indeed, humility would seldom count as a strongly positive attribute within the *curriculum vitae* of most secular job applicants, though this is not quite the case as far as the church and indeed some other religious groups are concerned. The reason for this is evident in humility's ambiguous position within religious groups where it is likely to appear either as a joke or as a serious description of a particular individual. To refer to someone's 'book on humility' is to offer a jesting, light-hearted contrast between a person's intrinsic sense of pomposity and the contrastingly absent but favored attribute of humility. It allows for an easy acceptance of the frailty of people, but of people within an organization or group that aspires to higher and greater things: even to divine things. And this is where the second, and serious, reference to humility arises, in that it is important for a church to possess genuine humility – or some quality that brings humility into some kind of cluster with ideas of holiness or godliness – in at least a few of its actual members. The institution's claim upon divine legitimation must, at some point, be manifest, not least in an embodied form if it is to have any sense of being a place in which the divine is encountered.

Because we cannot assume that the notion of humility is immediately intelligible to all, we take it here to refer to an attribute of a person who, while open to engaged relationships with other members of society is, in some appreciable way, fulfilled within themselves and, apparently, not set upon a path of ambitious achievement in and through those relationships. Our discussion of the 'humility response' relates only in part to this condition, dealing with an episode in a person's life in which they can abandon any actual ambitious achievement, at least for a period, while society's gaze is upon them. This is not to say that such a person may not go on to be, or may resume, a highly ambitious attitude in terms of what they achieve while in office.

Nevertheless, in religious contexts, and in theological terms, humility becomes, for believers, one embodied sign that divine grace has, in some way, been effective upon an individual's life. This brings a sense both of vitality and veracity to the church's message. It is, at the individual level, what a thriving congregation is at the organizational profile of church life, a sign of divine life. In more theological terms it might even be better to say that such humility is a symbol of that divine life, in that it participates in that which it represents, and it is that which prompts people to speak of 'godly' or 'holy' people.

This is not to say that the Church of England is over-provided with bishops or priests who embody humility. Beeson's bishops' book, for example, contains but few references to humble bishops, and these tend to be found within his broad category of 'the pastors', as with the former Quaker Edward Woods, Bishop of Lichfield (1937–53) with his 'engaging simplicity and humility', or Launcelot Fleming (Portsmouth 1949–59 and Norwich 1959–71), a 'shy and humble man' (Beeson, 2002: 91, 95). Still, this attribute is found as a partial characteristic in the life of some and, it would be true to say that more than a few of the bishops interviewed for this study disclosed aspects of it. It is likely to be the case that it is within pastoral contexts that humility may be encountered more than in publicly staged events. It may well be a feature of self that is disclosed or becomes apparent within the more interpersonal moments of relationships. Still, it must also be said that some bishops, as with some priests, have, in the past, displayed a considerable degree of assertive self-advertisement, and have operated within a state church context that provided ample opportunity for pompous display. However, both secularization and bureaucratization increasingly hinder such performance, as lower public support for official religion along with an increasing standardization of the types called to episcopal office narrow the bishop's public stage.

The Call: From Personal Piety to Structured Obedience

At this point it is worth introducing one account of how this issue of a personal religious disposition can, theoretically, relate to the structured organization of the church. It is one in which a form of humility – grounded in a sense of personal spiritual obedience to God – becomes integrated into a sense of obedience to the voice of God as spoken through church leaders.

This bishop had been a diocesan of a significant see. As with a number of others, his early religious life was moderately churchgoing until deeply influenced by an evangelical conversion and an awareness that set him on his way 'bursting with confidence and a joy that God had accepted' him. A Christian-minded schoolteacher, an earnest curate and an influential and inspiring Oxbridge chaplain-tutor all played their part as far as his ultimate ordination was concerned. Encouraged to attend a selection conference, he was deeply moved when he was 'strongly recommended' for training. This 'strong' recommendation long influenced his life and, during our interview, he stressed that such a 'strong recommendation' was relatively rare, adding: 'I've never told anyone that, but they did.' Such a disclosure by a retired man looking back on his life is significant in that many people probably keep some of the key moments of their life quite secret, and disclose them – if at all – at a moment when the truth of their self-reflection demands it, and when the relationship with the partner in conversation allows it to occur.

This individual gained a great deal of formal success in academia and in another professional world, as well as in the church. Though he had devoted a great deal of youthful and young-adult energy to pondering just what to do with his life, when it came to the issue of vocation he expressly said that he found the word itself 'a mealy-mouthed religious word which I eschew'. For him it was 'conversion' leading into 'commitment' irrespective of occupation that really counted. In and through a diverse ministry he came to accept and to relate to the part played by other Anglican traditions. Given his experience and success it is not surprising that the thought of being invited to be a bishop had crossed his mind, indeed a very specific bishopric whose vacancy was unlikely for some considerable time. But then, quite unexpectedly, letters arrived from the Prime Minister and her ecclesiastical Secretary. Almost as a form of testimony recalling a significant life event he now gave the actual date when the letters arrived by the same post. Then he described how: 'I got the letter from Margaret Thatcher, it made me ill. Oh yes ... I was very distressed and I couldn't sleep that night.'[7] The immediate effect was all the more problematic because of the instructions to men at that time of invitation not to discuss the issue with anyone other than the Archbishop or his own diocesan bishop. 'It was not being able to talk to anyone about it ... dealing with this secret that was very, very hard. ... I was having palpitations at night, I was quite sure they were going to take me away in white coats.' As for his early response: 'my guts told me to say no, but that was fear'. This person, who described himself as essentially an optimist, who sought to ground his ministry 'on the principle of affection', had some difficulty with the idea of potential failure. He could only think of 'being bishop of such and such a diocese ... as beyond his reach ... a quantum leap is the word in my mind'. But as the conversation with the archbishop turned to focus on the role of a bishop as a 'vicar of vicars' then he could see himself in the post.

Our interview also opened another window upon this bishop's perception and interpretation of his own theological understanding in an account of a letter from the archbishop that thanked him 'for your obedience'. He pondered this and thought 'that's what it is'. He went on to say: 'What I had begun to appreciate, which doesn't go with evangelical theology very well, is that the voice of the bishop can be the voice of God and the call of the Church is a bit more important than your inner stirrings.' Still, he had difficulties, for example, with the words in the rite of Consecration of Bishops – 'Do you feel called to be a bishop in the Church of God?' – because all he wanted to say was: 'No, no, I never felt called to be a bishop in the Church of God, it's the last thing that I thought I would be. I felt called to serve God, oh yes, but not to be a bishop.' It was here that the dawning sense of obedience and of the voice of God spoken through the church came to engage with his personal religiosity. Later in his life, when established as a bishop, similar feelings resurged when still higher-profile appointments seemed possible and which he certainly did not feel were his niche: 'I would have had the agonizing decision of feeling that it wasn't the job I would choose but I know something in me would lead me to say that I've got to say "yes" because I'm obedient.' This example is particularly instructive in that the individual's early evangelical identity is, in some ways, maintained while

---

7   A generation earlier, Lloyd George's 1917 letter had, similarly, kept Hensley Henson 'awake most of the night' when offering him the See of Hereford. Motives doubtless differed, given Henson's current engagement in doctrinal disputation over the Virgin Birth and Resurrection and his affirmation to Archbishop Davidson: 'I shrink from the episcopate with a kind of terror.' Though, as Chadwick comments, 'that was not at all to say that he did not want to be a bishop' (Chadwick, 1983: 135).

also significantly transformed. It highlights the complex process by which a person's formative religious experience, and its shaping theology, developed in and through subsequent events experienced through that institution.

Institution, Ambition and Fear

That same evangelical bishop also helps us pinpoint two other issues relating to high office: the fear of failure and rejection on the one hand, and fear of ambition and what it might do to the self on the other. While it might seem strange that we address ambition along with the issue of fear, we do so believing that ambition involves at least the double dynamic of a desired success of the self in a particular social world balanced by a degree of awareness of potential failure. Another way of looking at this would be even more psychological and focus on the balance between acceptance and rejection on the part of one's favored constituency, but that would take us into psychological fields beyond our level of competence. Still, we think that some consideration must be paid to the inner reflections of these men as they pondered major changes in their life. Here it is this bishop's actual words that highlight his fear of failure. Before the event he was 'terrified of being a bishop' because the job was an 'exposed' one with 'so many expectations on your shoulders [that] you can't afford to have a day off … The prospect of being a failure, which I thought was more than likely, was a daunting factor.' Indeed, we have already seen how the letter of invitation made him ill. Part of this potential failure lay in the way his fellow evangelicals might react given their view of bishops that he expressed in this way:

> Most of my folk, I suppose the evangelical constituency, didn't really have a lot of time for bishops, they regarded them as a necessary … not as a necessary evil … but as a necessary feature of the structure … just a necessary intrusion on the important work that was in the parishes … I think most of them were more concerned that when someone became a bishop they lost their identity, and particularly – the magic word – their cutting edge. In fact I think this was my fear more than anything else.

Running through this fear of failure and rejection was a kind of fear of ambition itself, though it was not put in those words. What is evident is a sense of a potential contradiction of the deep motives upholding this person's sense of identity. To be 'of any use to God at all I'd got to be the same [Christian and surname] … I always had been'. This individual was, of course, aware of ambition and, in fact, contrasted himself with some others: 'I had not hobnobbed with bishops in the way some people have, and always aspiring to be bishops.' What was more problematic for him was not the desire for a future identity as bishop but not to lose his established identity as a committed Christian with the 'cutting edge' so easily identifiable in the evangelical world. As it turned out, this communal support of individual identity was retained and, when he became a bishop, he found that 'everybody was quite astonishingly supportive'. It is possible that his sense of surprise is misplaced in that his acceptance might well reflect the period of evangelical ascendancy in the church. What is interesting is the way in which this individual went on to interpret his evangelical identity, as it developed in and through episcopacy, in a way that allows us to see how the formal organization of the church intimately extends into British social organization at large.

> I had to learn, over time, to relate to people outside in the county and in the diocese but, in fact, that was the part of the job I enjoyed almost more than anything else because there I was meeting the coalface, and was able to go there simply because I was the bishop. Whatever the kind of invitation I accepted by return of post. I regarded it as so important and enjoyed it very much … As far as my own view is concerned I've woven that in and it was a lot to do with fear and inadequacy and wondering whether if a person who was fairly 'low' … no I was never low church … I've always been high church I say … I've always had a high regard for the doctrine of the church, I'd always moved in evangelical circles and I wondered how that would go down in a diocese like [X].

Here, then, was a man 'starting so under-confidently' who had his 'confidence built' as he saw that 'people wanted me to succeed and cared for me as a person and not just a bishop', this support was, increasingly, from a wide constituency. So it is that his evangelical theology still with some echoes of an 'outsider–insider' reference is qualified by a word-play on 'high church' albeit interpreted doctrinally not ritually, and whose constituency of support and acceptance moves out from a narrower evangelicalism into the wider church and that social world in which the bishop does not simply represent the church but is, rather, a given part of a certain social nexus.

It is that status-aware world that is desired by some other aspirant clergy and returns us to the above bishop whose second observation concerned the desire of some senior clergy for advancement within the church. He spoke of the way in which he could 'recognize pretty soon what was niggling in their mind', and would get them to come and talk to him 'about the future'. In conversation with them he would often speak of the appointment process, of how there were many on the list of clergy who were potential bishops in their area with the implication that, given the limited number of available posts, 'the mathematical changes of being appointed were slim'. This is a most telling set of observations for it set the theological sense of vocation against the pragmatic facts of organization to engender a sense of realism.

Whether or not it was an appropriate evaluation of potential resources, however, might be questioned especially if we compare it with the view of another bishop, a suffragan from 'a highly ecclesiastical family' with a wide sense of church organization and operation. Reflecting on a long episcopal ministry he not only spoke of the importance of the 'old boy network', where much was achieved 'in bishops' meetings', but also reckoned that there were seldom more than 'half a dozen real high flyers' to choose from at any one time. After them, he thought one could choose from a wide group of 'the rest'. His formula for this select group was 'a really good mind allied to a deep faith'. By this he was not, essentially, focussing entirely on the academic achievements of a person, indeed he felt that 'very, very few academics in fact probably make good bishops', and mentioned some by name who had, he felt, 'found it tough going'. For him, the good mind and deep faith also needed to be 'streetwise'. As for himself, he was happy to admit a degree of what we are considering as ambition: 'There was a time when I wondered whether I would become a diocesan bishop or not, and I was a bit annoyed not to have been asked.' But he went on to say that he 'gradually realized that if I had been asked I

1. The Rt Revd Edward Henry Bickersteth, Bishop of Exeter (1885–1900).

2. His son, the Rt Revd Samuel Bickersteth, Residentiary Canon of Canterbury Cathedral (1916–36) and Chaplain to King George V (1916–37).

3. His grandson, the Revd Canon Edward Monier Bickersteth, Secretary of the Jerusalem and the East Mission (1915–35).

4. His great-grandson, the Rt Revd John Bickersteth, Bishop of Bath & Wells (1975–87), his wife, Rosemary, and their youngest son, Sam, outside the Bishop's Palace in Wells.

5. The Rt Revd Robert Bickersteth, Bishop of Ripon (1857–84).

The Tasks of a Bishop

1. To accept responsibility & oversight
   i) For the promotion of mission/evangelism
   ii) For the maintenance of the faith
   iii) For the ordering of ministry

2. To identify & communicate vision
   [Vision Keeper]

3. To make appointments consistent
   with vision

4. To create atmosphere
   i) morale
   ii) holiness
   iii) passion for souls

5. To clear up the messes

6. To engage as a Xn leader in public affairs

6.   'The tasks of a bishop', as noted by one of our respondents while he was in office during the 1990s.

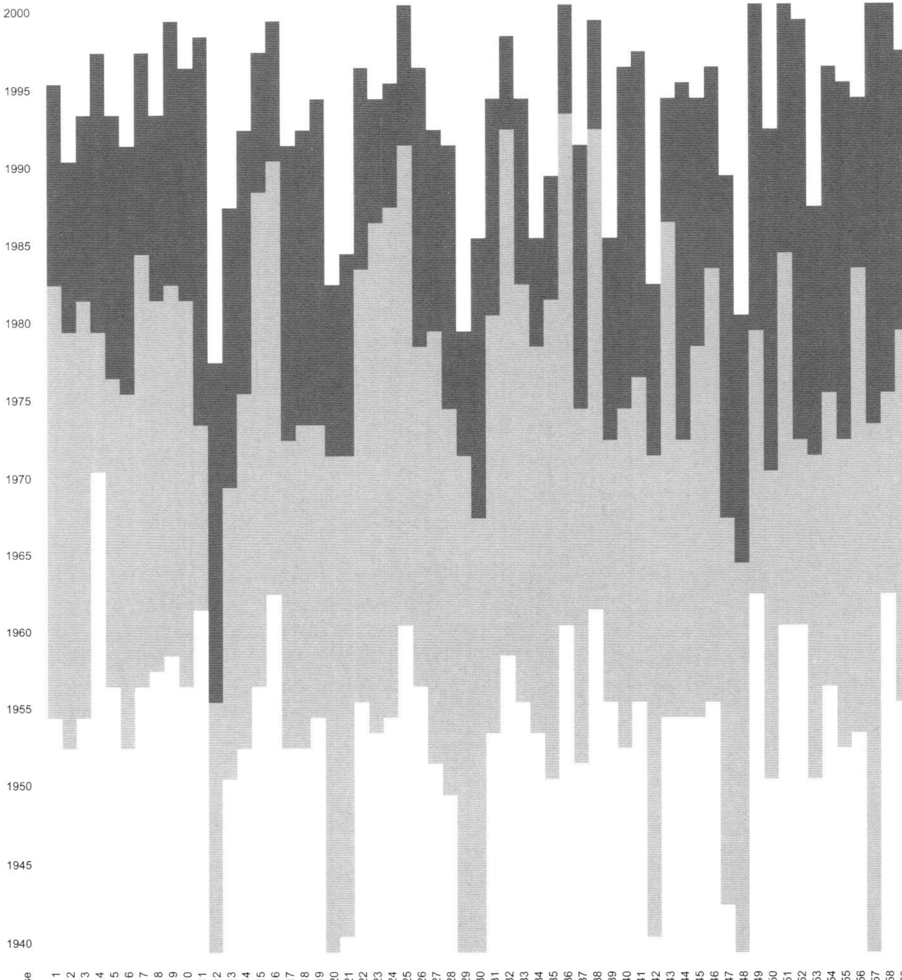

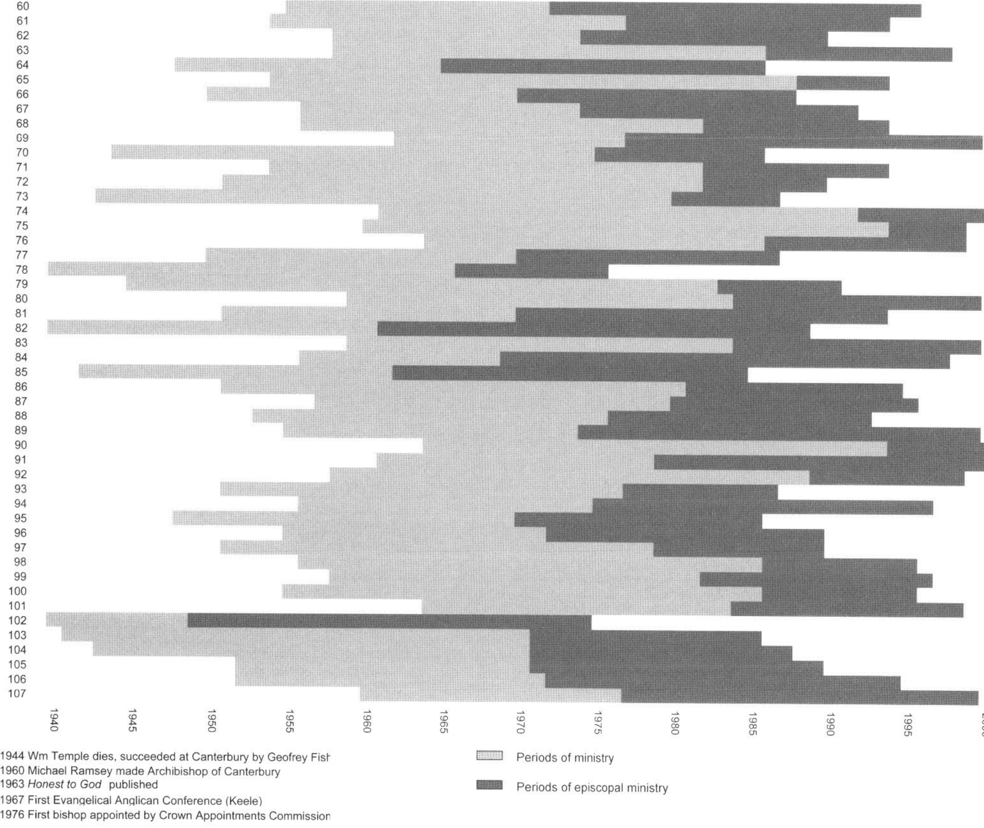

7.   Bishops' timeline.

8.   Auckland Castle, residence of the Bishop of Durham.

would probably have accepted, and that would have been disastrous'. His reasons for potential disaster lay in self-appraisal and recognition of 'weaknesses' that included viewing committees as 'anathema', so much so that he vowed never to sit on General Synod. Comparing himself with one well-known diocesan bishop – 'a very tough man and a very strong man' – he though that he, himself, would 'keel over' under any comparable social pressure, most especially that of the media. As far as ordination itself was concerned this man, from an established public school background and a highly ecclesiastical family, said: 'I'm absolutely hopeless with my hands. In the end I came to the conclusion that I had to be ordained because there wasn't anything else I could do. It was the only thing I was good for.'

Against that self-reflection it would be easy to typify this individual's priesthood in terms of family tradition, and view his choice as a negative necessity. But that would ignore the part played by his subsequent experience in post, under the influence of priestly life and within the wider ecclesiastical context. Indeed, on the negative side, we find someone who can describe himself as a 'not very holy' student who, despite family background, knew so little about aspects of Christianity and other churches that he had never come across the idea of a religious 'testimony' and had not encountered the terms 'evangelical' or 'Anglo-Catholic'. His choice of ordination, while still at university, was even influenced by his desire to give up his present academic subject for something else: 'What really attracted me about ordination was [that] this gave me a cast-iron excuse to give up Classics, which I was fed up with … and read Theology instead … and I absolutely adored it.' This echoes comments in Chapter 2 on the role of Oxford and Cambridge in clerical education.

Once this individual had been ordained and gained some experience, especially as a priest, he came to know 'that this is what God wanted me for … specifically to be a parish priest'. The personal practice and experience began to engender something new in him. When he did become a suffragan bishop he felt that he was simply immersed in work with practically no appropriate training. Indeed, he noted with some irony that the only advice received from his diocesan when he asked for some in respect of confirmation services, and only days after his consecration, was to 'stay clear of the sausage rolls at the bun-fight after the service'.

This apparently simple case, combined with the previous example of the evangelical ordinand, returns us to our earlier sociological discussion of Max Weber and to the relationship between values and action in defining the nature of any particular institution's goal, ethos and ethical sense. Where a company needs to grow within a competitive market it will value successful achievement of set goals and will promote individuals capable of effecting ongoing development. It will often be future-orientated and hire or fire personnel as appropriate. While the well-being of individual workers is desired, especially in so far as it enhances the company's performance, it is hardly an ultimate goal. Against such considerations the Church of England raises profound issues since, from one perspective, it is an institution which needs an effective professional personnel to ensure its future existence. But, essentially, its personnel exist as those possessing a vocation to serve God in and through people who both are and are not paying customers. In practical terms it is impossible to speak of the church's nature without referring to its self-claimed goal as involving both human and divine referents. Similarly, it is impossible to speak of the career or vocation of bishops or priests without considering how their own sense of achievement, success or failure engages both with the work opportunities provided by the church as an institution and with their sense of relatedness to God.

Conclusion: Gift-motifs and Episcopacy

To embrace these complexities we return, once more, to the theoretical gift motif of symbolic exchange already invoked in relation to the 'honor' of episcopacy and now employed to analyze these diocesan and suffragan cases. For each of these their appointment manifests a confidence placed in the appointee: from an anonymous committee to the diocesan, and from a known diocesan for the suffragan. Now, if it is the case that '"To have confidence in someone" is the permanent founding act of any society that operates through the act of the gift', then these appointments can be understood as all the more important foundational elements within a church that, theologically, views its very existence as a divine gift (Godbout with Caillé, 1998: 190). In fact these very processes of episcopal appointment furnish a dramatically clear example of Godbout's general description of the gift-motif process as possessing 'the depth and the multiple levels of the state apparatus, but … is a network with all the density of personal ties and their historical weight' (1998: 202).

Here the importance of informal relationships is crucial to appointment and subsequent work, for: 'Any network of affinities owes something to the gift' (Godbout with Caillé, 1998: 81). And the ordination of a suffragan is a 'gift' in a most profound sense, for it not only marks a personal relationship but also grounds it in a religious belief of how God acts in the world through the church. It entails a certain institutional risk depending upon just how the appointee will perform. These risks are embedded in commitments of several types, especially of the nominating bishop and of the responding suffragan in his consecration vows. Furthermore, it is a means in and through which the diocesan bishop's identity – part of the meaning of his life – is enhanced by the bringing of another person into a bond of divine service. In Godbout's terms such an ordination would represent a traditional gift more than a modern gift on the basis that the former reinforces a person's 'individuation *within* society' rather than serving to 'individualize that person *from* society' (1998: 146, original emphasis). He also highlights the importance of 'birth, engendering … the appearance of life, the source of everything' as foundational to the traditional gift. This is especially germane, for example, in connection with Anglican episcopal consecration with its strong focus upon the Holy Spirit and the divine gift-giving to the original apostles. The central use of the ninth-century hymn *Veni Creator Spiritus* is significant here in Durham's Bishop Cosin's well-known translation – 'Come Holy Ghost our souls inspire'. This was included in the 1662 *Book of Common Prayer* and continues in use. It dwells both upon the inspiring and illuminating power of the Holy Spirit – likened to the fire-like image of the first giving of the Spirit at the Day of Pentecost as portrayed in the Acts of the Apostles – and upon the imparting of the sevenfold divine gifts.[8] It also concludes in a strong desire for interpersonal engagements:

> Teach us to know the Father, Son,
> And Thee of both, to be but One,
> That through the ages all along,
> This may be our endless song:
> Praise to thy Eternal merit,
> Father, Son and Holy Spirit.

As a hymn in itself and, even more, as a hymn within the ritual of the consecration liturgy focussed upon the imposition of hands by the consecrating archbishops and bishops it marks as clearly as any form might an 'individuation *within* society' of the man being consecrated bishop. In relation to both capital and gift theories this ritual focus is inescapably foundational for the bishop, whether diocesan or suffragan. In capital terms his pre-existing networks become visible and his spiritual capital is validated and raised in and through the gathered, consecrating, bishops. In terms of reciprocity, the inalienable gift of the Holy Spirit is formally granted him as he is called by the church community into new responsibilities within the corporate body.

In many respects this rite is paradigmatic for symbolic exchange theory and shows quite starkly the Christian ecclesiastical rooting in both tradition and community. The past and the present cohere in a person who kneels for others to lay episcopal hands upon his head, a clear example of the process by which core values become embodied. It also heralds a contradiction of modernity in which the 'imponderables of personal relationships' are avoided whenever possible – for here they are paramount (Godbout with Caillé, 1998: 162, citing Simmel). Godbout reflects the thought of many when talking of the division between impersonal mercantile contracts and personal bonds of social relationships as poles marking the dynamics of contemporary life. He even speaks of the 'difficulty of thinking of them together' (1998: 162). This is precisely why the management debate in Chapter 3 evoked such powerful emotions and also the reason for the dissonance between 'senior' and 'junior' bishops in this chapter. In the church the ponderables of individuals are important, but so is the institutional need to respond to more mercantile demands.

---

8   A key feature of the Acts of the Apostles involves transformations of traditional Jewish ideas of ritual purity in a sense of sincerity towards the Holy Spirit expressed in and through attitudes towards money (Davies, 2004a).

Chapter 5

The Place of Clergy Wives:
A 'Shared Ministry'?

In her novel *The Rector's Wife*, Joanna Trollope rehearses the image of the oppressed clergy wife, passively accepting her position as a dutiful servant to her husband and the parish, while harboring secret desires to break free from her mundane existence. Tellingly named, Anna Bouverie is liberated by getting a job in the local supermarket, earning her own money and consequently achieving a sense of self-worth. We are alerted not only to the rather limited life of the clergy wife, but also to the opportunities for escape and fulfillment offered by the world outside. Trollope's treatment is colored by the rise of feminism and its impact on wider cultural norms, and illustrates a shift in attitudes that poses a challenge to the place of women within the clerical household as traditionally conceived. Clergy wives, in particular, have been faced with a growing number of women seeking, securing and often maintaining a professional career in place of, or alongside, responsibilities as a mother.[1]

Having considered the ministerial careers of bishops, this chapter now examines its impact on their wives. This involves family and church contexts, the evolution of prominent cultural stereotypes and the acceptance or rejection of these stereotypes by the women in question. A major concern is with how clergy wives have responded to expectations imposed upon them by their husband's ecclesiastical position. As Michael Hinton's historical study of Anglican parochial ministry puts it: 'The spiritual hallmark of clerical marriages down the centuries has been the *identification* of the wife with her husband's ministry' (Hinton, 1994: 48; our emphasis). As we shall see, some clergy wives have found room within the social world surrounding their husband's ministry to affirm a positive sense of identity of their own and find significant fulfillment, sometimes understood in terms of a personal vocation. Others have pursued a life independent of their husband's ministry, and the church has begun to accept and adapt to this accommodation to wider cultural trends. As the wives of bishops during the later twentieth century, many women in our study may be seen as trail-blazers setting a standard for future clergy wives, though a significant number sustain the ideal of a supportive role, focussed on pastoral care and integrated into their husband's ministry.

In this chapter we examine patterns of life choice and commitment among the wives within our study, paying particular attention to how notions of professional and religious identity are related and to how they generate feelings of personal

---

1   In Britain generally, in 1989, 36 per cent of women went out to work while their children were under school age. The figure rose to 42 per cent in 1994, and to 48 per cent in 2002 (Park et al., 2003: 163).

fulfillment. An underlying concern with how expressions of identity are constrained or facilitated by the peculiar situation in which clergy wives find themselves, including the nature of the clergy home itself, will be explored in Chapter 6.

Clergy Wives: Image and Reality

The popularity of marriage among Anglican clergy meant from the outset that our research would have to deal with clergy wives as a significant factor. Of the 107 retired bishops in our study, only 13 have never been married and incomplete records prevent us from accounting for the remaining one; 94 have been married, and of these, only 5 have never had children. Of the married, 9 have married a second time (following the death of their first wife) while 10 have been bereaved and not married again; 18 have never had children. In short, the vast majority have lived their clerical lives as married clergymen, 89 conducting their ministry alongside women who have at once been wives, mothers and, in some sense or another, ministerial partners.

Of the 43 bishops' wives who took part in our questionnaire survey, 35 per cent were daughters of professional men, 19 per cent were the daughters of clergymen, and at least one was the daughter of a bishop.[2] All attended church during their childhood, and for the majority of 79 per cent this was an Anglican church.[3] For 86 per cent this was at least a weekly commitment, and 56 per cent backed this up with Sunday School.[4] Consequently, a small number were prepared by their prior experiences for the peculiar domestic arrangements associated with clerical life, and many more were acculturated into the conventions of the Church of England, including ideas about the status of women. Some went on intentionally to embody these ideas, while others remained determined not to commit what they saw as the mistakes made by their own mothers. As such, prior experience of the 'clerical household' can be either a schooling for later conformity or a foundation for rebellion. A significant number of these women (36 per cent) also went to university and apparently drew from their higher education in creating opportunities which would elevate them above the constraints of the previous generation. This makes the issue of their own status as clergy wives even more interesting, raising the question of whether clerical life – and later episcopal privilege – acts as a constraint or springboard for female upward mobility. Did being married to a clergyman create opportunities or impose limitations?

---

2   Comparable figures were found for our bishops, with 42 per cent the sons of professionals, and 22 per cent the sons of clergy.

3   This compares with a figure of 93 per cent for their husbands. Only 4 out of 60 bishops had attended a non-Anglican church during their childhood, while this applied to 9 out of 43 of their wives. While this generation of senior clergy have not generally strayed from an Anglican commitment which goes back to their childhood, they have not all felt the need to always select their life partner from this tradition (although we have to allow for the possibility that, in some cases, wives may have moved into the Church of England in early adulthood, before meeting their future husbands).

4   These represent comparable levels of childhood piety to our bishops, although more of the wives were Sunday School attendees (56 per cent compared to 43 per cent).

Wives of Anglican clergy are socially in a rather distinctive position, and have been for some time. The domestic situation of the Roman Catholic priest is, of course, entirely different since celibacy involves no new nuclear family. Nonconformist ministers, by contrast, have included women among their number for a good many years, with full clergy rights accorded to Methodist women from 1956. Therefore, while there is a role-expectation attached to the wives of male clergy, the lack of such a clear gender distinction in ministry may be expected to create fewer tensions than within the Anglican world. Within the Orthodox tradition, the situation is different again, with the priest's wife attributed a specific title – that of *Presbytera* in the Greek Orthodox Church. This expresses the theological sense that a wife to some degree participates in her husband's priestly status. The Orthodox situation is comparable to the Anglican in embodying ministerial expectations of the clergy wife while maintaining a clear distinction between gender roles.[5] For the Anglican clergy wife, however, the role is informal and unwritten, maintained by the cultural expectations of church and society. In this sense it is an identity with a high expectation of conformity set alongside a lack of any official status.[6]

Recent changes have, however, seen an increasing tendency to recognize the contribution that women make to the life of the church. The decision to allow the ordination of women in 1992 was the culmination of a long process whereby women had increasingly occupied positions of leadership, whether as members of General Synod, as deaconesses, parish workers or lay readers. In more evangelical congregations women had been leading non-Eucharistic Sunday worship and prayers. This process has, for some, gradually undermined the belief that certain ministerial roles are the preserve of men, a belief that effectively reinforced existing gender divisions in the broader society and raised the question of the position of women within the church as a whole. A perception that the church is lagging behind its surrounding culture has generated a feeling of dissonance and frustration on the part of many within its ranks, especially when women outnumber men in British churches 2 to 1.[7]

Amongst these changes, an ambiguous movement has emerged from among the evangelical contingent, which has exerted a growing influence over Anglican beliefs and styles of ministry over the past forty years. British evangelicals, while often in favor of women taking active roles in church life, have nevertheless tended to adopt a view of women based on the complementarity of the sexes.[8] This view claims that men and women have distinctive kinds of gifts to offer the church, with 'leadership' – designated as 'headship' in some circles – often viewed as a gift and responsibility

---

5   This role is perceived as a defined and coherent vocational identity, as demonstrated in *Presbytera: The Life, Mission, and Service of the Priest's Wife* by Presbytera Athanasia Papademetriou, a guidebook for women married to Orthodox priests.

6   Since 1992, in the Church of England context, we have been able to speak also of clergy husbands, although our specific generational focus puts that issue beyond our purview here.

7   Recent figures suggest that women make up between 61 and 65 per cent of the English churches (Churches Information for Mission, 2001: 9; Wraight, 2001: 21).

8   For a discussion of the debate about complementarianism in the USA, see Gallagher (2003), especially 57–8.

particular to men. Within the context of clerical life, this strand of theology has fed into an understanding of 'shared ministry', the notion that the wife of the clergyman has a specially defined role to play within the context of her husband's ministry. This trend has gained momentum through the strong evangelical tradition of recognizing the validity of women's work in the church, often formalized in special roles and organizational structures.[9] These roles, while diverse, are most often centered on ideas of support and encouragement, pastoral assistance, entertainment, hospitality, and a Christian mission to women and children. They are therefore very much in keeping with what some would call traditional gender roles, albeit with the added factor that this constellation of responsibilities is accorded validity by virtue of Christian teaching. Given that the latter half of the twentieth century bore witness to the ascendancy of the evangelical movement within British Christianity, it is not surprising to find a persistent tension throughout the church when it comes to the position of women.

Moreover, these factors exist alongside a period of changing trends in marriage and family life among Anglican clergy, with – from the 1960s – an increasing proportion choosing to marry after or just before ordination. This resembled trends in the general population, and marked a shift away from a clerical experience distinguished by bachelorhood in early adult life. This had implications not least for clerical training, which became transformed for many from being a 'total experience' during which ordinands were 'wholly immersed' in the life of their college to being a much more partial experience, allowing clergy to devote more time to marriage and family life (Towler and Coxon, 1979: 77–8). As we shall see, the careers of the clergy in this study spanned this time of change, and an investigation into their family lives suggests some significant and persistent tensions between church and family commitments.

From Clergy Wives to Bishops' Wives

The women in our study are distinguished by their transition from clergy to bishop's wives, and while there are important continuities between these two positions, a significant difference lies in a change in social identity, expectations of others and associated power and authority. This is a complex phenomenon, not least because the status accorded to the bishop's wife is, as with the role of the vicar's wife, learnt through experience rather than inscribed in official documents or imparted through ritual. Though never formally taught nor legally prescribed, it nevertheless comes with a set of narrowly defined and keenly held expectations on the part of the church hierarchy, civic dignitaries, diocesan bureaucracy, parochial clergy and local parishes. This curious dissonance between official and popular role definitions has already been commented on in Chapter 3 with reference to the position of the bishop

---

9   David Bebbington traces this tradition back to the nineteenth century, referring to authors who argue that, paradoxically, 'Evangelical religion, despite its emphasis on the domestic role of women, was more important than feminism in enlarging this sphere during the nineteenth century. In the churches women of all classes found much to satisfy their aspirations' (Bebbington, 1989: 129).

himself. The episcopal job description effectively emerges through an ongoing and locally specific negotiation between church and people; so too in the case of bishops' wives, though less formally. Such negotiations between church and people mean that status is not simply ascribed to a passive recipient; indeed, the bishops' wives we spoke to had learnt to embody this status through positions of influence offered to them. That is, it is a status that has consequences in practice.

But this is not to suggest that the bishop's wife enjoys a life of indulgent privilege. Her status is frequently accompanied by responsibilities that both reflect and exaggerate the heavy but unpaid workload of parish priest's wife. While many will be aware of the pressures of public office that bishops often have to face, they may overlook the impact this office has on his wife and children. The expectations of public commitment and personal piety expected of the bishop are mirrored in similar expectations of his family, and these are often felt most keenly by their wives, who shoulder the responsibility of maintaining a public face that is in conformity with the heavy professional burden placed on her husband. Grace Sheppard wrote of these in her autobiographical *An Aspect of Fear* (1989), in which she reflects on the daunting transition her family made in 1969, when David Sheppard moved from being the Warden of the Mayflower Family Centre in working-class Canning Town to succeeding Dr John Robinson as Bishop of Woolwich:

> … the reality of the situation dawned on me. It would mean moving again, after all this time. We would be much more in the public view and I would be a bishop's wife, whatever that might mean. He would have to wear grand robes, to process in formal church services, and I would have to sit in the front row and be smartly dressed. … We would belong to one hundred and fifty parishes instead of one, and David would be out, travelling a lot. It would mean leaving our East London friends, and that felt like dying a little. There was a lot to think about. (Sheppard, 1989: 18–19)

Although her book is primarily about her personal experiences of anxiety and how she overcame them, she also writes of the 'enforced isolation' many bishops' wives feel as their husbands are thrown into a ministerial schedule that leaves them alone and unsupported (1989: 20). Indeed, many of the women in our study commented on similar difficulties, made worse by the fact that they were now expected to take on a much larger portfolio of tasks and responsibilities. One of our interviewees attempted a list of the jobs she was expected to perform, including 'management of staff, house, gardens, estate, cook, housekeeper, caterer, cleaner, hostess, consort to services, events, opener of things, speaking, voluntary work and then at the end, wife and mother. And then at the very end, my own job, if there's any time left for that.'

This is neither an exhaustive nor definitive list, and the tasks incumbent upon the bishop's wife will vary according to numerous factors, not least the size and structure of the bishop's residence. While present-day bishops can expect more professional assistance in the upkeep of the bishop's palace, those in our study held posts when the bulk of the domestic responsibilities were left to the bishop's wife. This is a significant workload given the size of some residences. Bishop's Lodge in Liverpool, for example, sits in two and a half acres of garden, playing host to parties of two thousand people during the Sheppards' residence (Sheppard, 2002: 149–50). The women we spoke to also emphasized the expectation that they would provide or at least organize the catering and hospitality for large functions, a daunting prospect even for those with experience in large and active parishes.[10] Hospitality is also a variable factor, with the wives of diocesan bishops bearing this responsibility on a more frequent basis given the ecclesiastical, civic and political circles in which diocesan bishops move. While suffragan bishops are also likely to attend such official functions, the extent to which they and their wives will be expected to host high-profile dinner parties varies, depending in large part on the roles delegated to them by their diocesan superiors.

The wives of bishops are often drawn into some kind of 'shared ministry', a powerful and influential shaping factor in the formation of the role of the bishop as well as his wife. But it is not one that is shared across the episcopate or indeed, among clergy of all persuasions within the Church of England. Indeed, one of the bishops we interviewed was most skeptical about the notion that the wives of bishops might have any kind of active ministry at all. He compared the responsibilities of the clergyman with those of a medical practitioner, commenting that we wouldn't go and see the doctor's wife if we were ill, would we? His comments, reflecting more than a more catholic churchmanship, affirm a professionalized understanding of Anglican ministry, one subject to academic and pastoral training and official accountability. This example of skepticism demonstrates how emerging conceptions of the cleric's role can impact upon understandings of gender difference, and of the role – if any – of the bishop's wife.

Mapping Patterns of Vocation and Identity

In many cases the social position of the women in our study was transformed when their husband moved from clerical to episcopal status. While a good number had seen their husbands rise through such intermediate roles as archdeacon, rural dean or positions at theological colleges, many had spent the largest period of their 'working' adult lives as the wife of a parochial clergyman, an existence bringing with it a peculiar blurring of boundaries between the spheres of work, religion and family life. For clergy wives this arrangement appeared as a mixed blessing: for some, a vision of integrated harmony in which the ideals of Christian charity and family are lived out through the routines of domestic life; for others, a high pressure environment in which time and space for family intimacy and personal fulfillment are perpetually set aside in deference to the demands of the parish. Most, inevitably, recall an experience that combines both sentiments.

But the experience of the bishop's wife is quite different in at least one crucial respect – that of the domestic residence. As discussed in Chapter 2, the bishop's palace differs from the vicarage in the way in which it is conceived and managed as a place of ministerial work. Typically, the palace houses the offices of the bishop's

---

10   Leslie Paul found that, during the 1960s, many parochial clergy were housed in large vicarages with large gardens, the maintenance of which put significant pressures on them and their families (1964: 131). If this was the case with parochial clergy of that period (and many of our bishops would have been in this position during the 1960s), we might imagine the pressures of maintaining an episcopal residence.

chaplain and secretary, from which day-to-day business is arranged, and the bishop's study, in which many important meetings will be held. It is also often the venue for frequent social functions, and thus a place through which many unfamiliar figures will pass on a regular basis. And yet the invasion of the bishop's family's domestic space is less likely to be as profound or as frequent as in a vicarage. This is so for four related reasons. First, the palace is larger, sometimes much larger, and thus can accommodate greater privacy alongside public ministerial use. Second, there are staff – at least a secretary, chaplain and chauffeur – to relieve some duties from the wife. Third, there is often a chapel,[11] in which ritual and prayer functions take place which might otherwise occur within the domestic sphere of the vicarage. And fourth, the bishop is required to perform fewer of his pastoral responsibilities within his own residence because his flock is so widespread that he often has to travel to them.

While there are variations from this pattern, it is pervasive enough for us to use it as the foundation for further analysis. Most importantly, it demands a revision of our model of the blurring of the spheres of work, religion and family life characteristic of vicarage life. Simply stated, the day-to-day ministerial work of the bishop is less likely to intrude into the day-to-day family life of his wife and children than that of a parochial clergyman. This transforms the experience of the domestic sphere and reconfigures public and private space. It also has important consequences for the bishop's wife, who now finds herself with a greater degree of space and opportunity to embody an occupational or vocational role distinguishable from that of her husband. Her children are also more likely to have left home and/or be financially independent at this time, a factor enhancing a sense of regained freedom to realise goals and renew professional ambitions. Indeed, many of the wives within our study said that they felt most fulfilled after retirement, when even more freedom allows for the pursuit of these personal and professional goals.

Both as clergy and bishops' wives, the women within this study appeared to negotiate their status in relation to two ways of dealing with their domestic and ecclesiastical position, summarized here as 'shared ministry' and the independent career. These are not to be seen as alternative (and certainly not mutually exclusive) life options, but available traditions in which they find meaning for their lives.

Shared Ministry

In commenting on marriages amongst parochial clergy, Michael Hinton argues that, in the eyes of the church, 'The ideal has been complementarity and close union, together with dedication to a common task' (Hinton, 1994: 46). This 'ideal' reflects the perspective of many women within our study, whose understanding of their position amounts to what has been called 'shared ministry', the notion that a married Christian couple engage in ministry together, sharing responsibilities and pooling resources. In some circles it is an understanding shaped by the evangelical tradition that wives should submit to their husbands, which among clergy is extended into a

---

11   This varies, in part in relation to the age of the bishop's residence: diocesan bishops are more likely to have their own domestic chapel than suffragans, who are often housed in more modest properties.

duty to submit to the needs of the husband's formal vocation as well. According to this understanding, the 'clergy wife' is as much a part of her husband's ministerial identity as this artificial title suggests. Her responsibilities are utterly defined by his position.

Most of the wives within our study found themselves conforming to this model at some point and to some degree, especially during periods in parochial ministry. The expectations that parishes had of the vicar's wife tended to focus on a local ministry to women and children, channeled through institutions like the Mothers' Union or Sunday School, with additional responsibilities associated with caring and catering at parish functions. Even those not setting out to conform to such roles found themselves adopting them in part because they were relatively easily accommodated into family responsibilities, not least childrearing. Many of the pastoral responsibilities associated with the clergy wife are easily accomplished within the vicarage, especially if the wife assumes a role as counselor to the troubled or feeder of the needy. Naturally, this transforms the character of the clergy home. As one bishop's son commented: 'the parish down-and-outs would turn up and my mum would always be there with a cup of tea and a slice of cake and a shoulder to cry on. It was almost a waiting room, you know, go and see the vicar's wife first' before seeing the vicar. The provision of pastoral care within the vicarage creates roles for the wife that are, by their nature, highly consonant with her roles as wife and mother; in this way the adoption of traditional gender roles within the clerical home generates domestic conditions ideally suited to the 'shared ministry' model.

Yet while the adoption of domestic and pastoral responsibilities by the clergy wife can to a degree be understood as a consequence of circumstance, many appear to make sense of their role in much more decisive terms, indicating a more consciously applied role. As one wife commented: 'I decided from the outset that my husband's vocation was what I wanted to be involved in.' Another affirmed this decision as part of her generational identity, considering herself 'part of the "final" generation that believed "my vocation is to support you in your vocation"!' Another suggested her role was important to her sense of identity: 'My "job" was being a bishop's wife – though unwaged. I had a strong sense of vocation to that role.'

This use of the language of vocation is telling, and reflects the fact that many of the women we spoke to resisted the idea that they merely adopted a supportive role in deference to their husband's position. While their role was a supportive one, it was not seen as submissive but rather as making an active contribution to the church in itself. Some had actually formalized their role, one acting as her husband's secretary when he was archdeacon for twelve years, another serving as her husband's paid secretary during his tenure as a suffragan bishop. While these may be interpreted cynically as compensatory mechanisms, empty gestures intended to bring a sense of autonomy to a genuinely disempowered position, this would be to discount the views of the actual women in question. One said she had 'always felt' she had been 'a working partner in [her husband's] ministry'. In responding to a question about whether her career path would have been different had she not been a clergyman's wife, one woman said that her career would have probably been 'less satisfying – I might not have been thrust into working with people who are both needy and very interesting (both in Africa and in UK)'. Another pointed out opportunities to establish ecclesiastical and social action initiatives that would not have been available to her without her husband's position. We also asked wives if they felt their commitment to their 'job' amounted to a sense of vocation. Here, 58 per cent said yes, and yet only 28 per cent claimed they had pursued a career independent of their husband's ministry, so we can assume that almost half of this 58 per cent are referring to something other than paid employment outside of a church context. Our interviews suggest that this work is most likely encompassed within the broad category of 'civic and pastoral responsibility related to the husband's role'.

There is a very real sense in which the experience of 'shared ministry' generates a sense of purpose and personal responsibility among these women. An interesting question is whether this apparent sense of empowerment is a consequence of having been a bishop's wife, that is, do the opportunities arising from that position create the conditions for a more defined, meaningful identity? This has to do with the broader question of capital – social, cultural and symbolic – and will be revisited later in the chapter.

One further comment worth making here relates to social networks. Repeatedly in our interviews and in questionnaire returns we were faced with comments about groups of clergy wives who would regularly meet in order to exchange stories, ideas, and generally to offer one another support. These networks were organized, and appear to have been greatly valued by the women within them, not least as a source of comradeship and a means of exchanging advice based on past experience. For women new to their status as a 'clergy wife', such meetings can begin to remedy feelings of isolation and alienation through conversations with more experienced peers, not to mention their value as a means of building friendships among others living a similar lifestyle. For the wives of bishops these networks have been arguably even more significant, and for two main reasons. First, they have served as in-house training in the new responsibilities expected of the bishop's wife, responsibilities that in scale and kind are quite unlike those expected of wives of the vicar. As one commented:

> I found that really useful … being able to get together with other bishops' wives and sort of thrashing out really how they related to the church commissioners, what it was possible to squeeze out of them or not squeeze out of them, how to … cook for thousands instead of five, you know, all that kind of thing, and just have a laugh, quite honestly.

In this way networks of bishops' wives, gathered together at meetings on a national or at least inter-diocesan scale, served as a context in which women could learn the skills necessary for them to manage their new responsibilities. The second reason for appreciating these networks relates to their capacity to create and nurture roles that carry status within the church. What is interesting about this phenomenon is how arrangements reflect the male church hierarchy. One woman, who had been a suffragan bishop's wife, had been approached by her diocesan's wife who felt her role – and that of the other suffragan bishop's wife in the diocese – was to care for the 'clergy wives' of the diocese. They consequently organized a series of events for this purpose, alongside the wives of two archdeacons. This pattern of mirroring male responsibility in a female hierarchy of pastoral care is replicated in other very similar accounts from across the Church of England. They portray bishops' wives as assuming positions of patronage that potentially reinforce notions of gender difference embedded in the 'shared ministry' model. More importantly, they also allow the status of the bishop's wife to be an empowered one, one with a pastoral remit, a concrete set of responsibilities and embedded in a clearly defined hierarchy. Offering guidance to others through organized networks lends credence to a sense of pastoral identity and provides a focus for ministry. In this respect, through the transition to episcopal status, the 'shared ministry' can become a specialist concern as wives focus on the specific pastoral and professional needs of other women in a similar position to their own.

However, this phenomenon also raises some interesting issues related to power, with interviews revealing how a mirroring of the husband's status can provoke tensions between wives. Certain episodes exposed how the status of the husband is assumed within struggles to achieve a position of dominance and autonomy. What is the place of the suffragan bishop's wife, for example, when the diocesan bishop's wife is also present at ceremonies or public functions? Who takes precedence, and on what grounds? The fact that this can even be an issue illustrates how the social life surrounding the bishop and his wife is often one characterized by experiences of being status conscious. Moreover, for the suffragan and his family the lack of clear guidelines only serves to exacerbate an enduring experience of frustration and potential alienation. The anomaly of the suffragan bishop is not restricted to the experience of the male who holds the title.

Many wives embraced their role as an unpaid pastor, viewing it as a natural responsibility given both their husband's position and the obvious empathy they felt with clergy wives and their predicament. Their new status – while in some sense vicariously ascribed – merely reflected advantages of personal experience aligned with the conveniences of being located within the church hierarchy. However, other bishops' wives explicitly rejected this role, perceiving associations of domesticity and a submissive willingness to be defined purely in terms of their husband's status. These women were more likely to affirm their own professional identities, seeing themselves as supportive of yet occupationally independent of their husbands.

Others expressed interest in pursuing a professional life apart from the church but had simply set their role as wife and mother above these ambitions, reflecting what they saw as the cultural expectations of the time. When asked whether she would have pursued a different career path had she not been a clergyman's wife, one responded: 'I would have been a career woman! I married in the days when women were not expected to have jobs after marriage.' But while cultural norms were a barrier for some, for others the problem was simply one of time: with their husband working long hours and parish obligations intruding into domestic life, clergy wives have often found themselves automatically adopting a traditional, home-based role and have found this sapping most of their energy. One woman was sanguine about her time living in a vicarage, having enjoyed the experience and found it fulfilling, but she adds: 'I couldn't organize four children, and have a job. Some people can and I respect them for it, admire [them] for it … but I couldn't do it.' That so many of these women, when faced with family responsibilities, prioritized them over and above their own professional ambitions is perhaps unsurprising for this generation:

when asked about their attitudes to the family, 47 per cent agreed or agreed strongly that family life generally suffers when the mother has a full-time job.[12]

Other wives appeared to embrace a traditional gender role, but alongside a fairly cynical attitude towards the expectations they found people typically projected onto the 'clergy wife'. One suffragan's wife had pursued no career of her own, had very little experience in paid work, no vocational training and did not see a career as very important to her sense of identity. She had raised two children, mostly in rural areas, and had adopted a fairly traditional set of roles, and yet, according to her son, whom we interviewed, remained utterly resistant to the traditional image of the 'clergy wife':

> She wanted to be her own person and yes, she provided the coffee and biscuits ... and she did the flower arranging at church and she did all the things that you'd expect from that point of view, but I think certainly in [dad's parish] the locals expected her to run the mother's union and the young wives and all these sort of things, and she sort of said no. I'll come, but ... my husband's the vicar, but not me. So I'm not 'Mrs Vicar', I'm my husband's wife if you like, and I'll support him 110 per cent, but that doesn't mean that I'm gonna run all your things that the previous vicar's wife might have run ... She's not in any way, shape or form a typical vicar's wife ...

The stereotype of the 'vicar's wife' – gleefully captured in the 'Mrs Vicar' expression – is evident in both this woman's response to rural parochial life and in her son's reflections. The quotation illustrates how this stereotype is invoked as a way of challenging the expectations imposed, especially when one's efforts are inevitably compared, favorably or unfavorably, with the wife of the previous incumbent. In this sense expectations are built around a common image centered on a selfless, deferential, homely figure, serving the parish through involvement in ancillary activities usually focussed on women, children or tasks associated with a Victorian image of both, but are filtered and interpreted with reference to previous exemplars. Tim Jenkins makes a similar comment about expectations which are imposed upon rural clergy. In his anthropological study of Comberton, Cambridgeshire, he observes that the local parson is often unfavorably compared by villagers with a litany of former incumbents, falling short of his proper role in maintaining a traditional social and moral order. This order is inevitably idealized, and characterized in terms of a close-knit social cohesion with the clergyman at the center of village life (Jenkins, 1999: 62). Similarly, whether previous 'Mrs Vicars' have genuinely done a better job is irrelevant; what is important is that they play an important role in shaping the identity to which the new clergyman's wife is expected to conform. Who effectively defines this role and sustains expectations associated with it is an interesting question related to the politics of parish life. What is perhaps more interesting about this case is that it illustrates how, within this generation, the stereotype of the clergy wife is being challenged, even among women who do not pursue an independent career of their own. What we are witnessing here is not simply a choice between two options,

------

12   To put this in context, the British Social Attitudes Survey reported 34 per cent of women responding positively to this question in 2002, following a 5 per cent drop since the late 1980s (Park et al., 2003: 167).

but a gradual shift in attitudes and a detachment of the role of the 'non-paid curate' from the clergy wife as a wife and mother. Perhaps as clergy wives now become even more resistant to traditional roles we will see even more evidence of the separation of domestic from ministerial concerns. Should this occur, then what is at stake is not just the nature of clerical marriage but the structure of the clergy home, and therefore of parochial ministry itself.

The Independent Career

While a good proportion of the women in our study had been content to adopt a supportive role, assisting their husband's ministry, and others had developed this 'shared ministry' further into a vocation of their own, there remained a contingent who sought fulfillment beyond the world of the Church of England. For some this meant an independent professional career, and there is every indication that this is a growing trend among the wives of clergymen. Publishing the results of a survey in 1964, Leslie Paul found that 1 in 7 incumbents' wives were going out to do paid work to augment their family income (Paul, 1964: 131). One couple we spoke to told us about a survey they had administered during the late 1980s to all the clergy wives within their diocese, aimed at eliciting information about the support they might need. It revealed at least 75 per cent of wives engaged in paid work, and we might expect figures to be rather higher now, for changes were already in motion during the careers of the bishops featured in our study. On an episcopal level it is fair to say that Rosalind Runcie, wife of Robert Runcie, former Archbishop of Canterbury, emerged as a significant focus of change. During the 1970s and 1980s, when her husband was in office, she openly pursued an independent life, with a non-ecclesiastical social existence and her own career as a pianist and piano teacher. In interviews Mrs Runcie was recalled as a source of empowerment for some, who, inspired by her example, felt able to pursue professional and personal goals quite separate from their husbands' ministry.[13] Others were more equivocal, affirming her right to an independent career but none the less remaining supportive of a more traditional understanding of the clergy wife – active, with a definite and important role within the context of her husband's work as a clergyman. While this stance still existed, it was not affirmed without qualification by any of these women as the only desirable option for all clergy wives. The notion that the wife of the clergyman *ought always* to defer any professional ambition in favor of voluntarily supporting her husband in the parish has simply ceased to be normative.

Most of the wives in our study were born around the 1920s, educated in the 1930s and 1940s, and were less influenced by feminism and cultural changes associated with gender equality than the contemporary generation of clergy wives. And yet they represent a generational sample that is atypical in several respects, not least when it comes to professional training and educational mobility. The privileged origins of bishops are mirrored in their wives, with 58 per cent of our return sample

---

13   In Humphrey Carpenter's biography of Robert Runcie, Mrs. Runcie is reported as reflecting on her independent attitude as inspiring to other clergy wives. As she commented: 'the other clergy wives said "you've freed us"' (Carpenter, 1996: 177).

attending a private or independent school. Perhaps more significantly, 35 per cent took a university degree, and this at a time when women's participation in higher education was the preserve of a select few – roughly 0.2 per cent of the relevant age group, compared to 0.8 per cent of men of a university age.[14] Some 91 per cent had received training for a variety of professions, including school teaching (35 per cent), secretarial work and nursing (both 12 per cent), psychotherapy and social work (both 5 per cent). In addition to possessing unusually high levels of cultural capital for women of their generation, several of these women were also the daughters of female professionals, women who – working as doctors, teachers or, in one case, a musician, during the early 1900s – would have been pioneers among their sex and quite probably strong professional role models for their daughters. This continued on to the next generation, as with the case of the daughter of a suffragan bishop who had been inspired by her mother, one of the only working mothers in an industrial northern town in the 1950s, who had resisted ecclesiastical and cultural norms in order to provide for her family. She had effectively provided her daughter with a vocational role model:

> She was probably the only mother working … she was certainly the only vicar's wife working. Very rare in the fifties, 'cos my brother and I were at private schools, don't forget, got to pay for it somehow, on a stipend that wasn't very big … Mum was a teacher – no other real choice. You become a nurse, a secretary or a teacher. That was it. Never wanted to do anything else, never thought of doing anything else. [I] enjoyed going with Mum when I went, so I was like her, natural thing, that's why I did it.

The number of women within our study who actually pursued full-time professional careers beyond their husband's ministry amounts to a significant minority. When asked if they had pursued a career wholly separate from their husband's ministry, 72 per cent said no, 28 per cent said yes. However, we need to be cautious about these figures, aware that this question might be interpreted differently by different respondents. For example, one woman affirmed she had pursued a career that has been wholly separate from her husband's ministry, stating her profession as 'a committed Christian'. Here a sense of personal ministry has merged into a sense of vocation, something this respondent also affirmed she had, so that Christian identity is seen as a professional occupation. It may be that this conception is influenced by the fact that the husband has made a career of Christian ministry. In this case it is also a product of a particular evangelical ethic, to do with living out the Gospel through practical effort in all areas of one's life. Note also that a far greater proportion surveyed claimed experience of paid work than said their career was wholly separate from their husband's ministry, suggesting a reluctance to detach themselves from their husband's clerical work even when pursuing a career. As one respondent put it: 'I simply believe that my commitment to teaching was

---

14   Given a lack of available statistics, the figures cited here apply to the nearest available cohort to our population, that of the 1934/35 academic year (Dyhouse, 1995: 249), compared with the number of men and women of university age in Britain at that time, figures taken from the archives of the Office of National Statistics. A lack of precise fit between the two data sets means these figures are at best approximate.

 Bishops, Wives and Children

part of my commitment to shared ministry.' According to this understanding, shared ministry and an independent career are not alternative options, but complementary dimensions to a single vocation.

It is also significant that the 28 per cent who claimed an independent career were not the same women who were university graduates. There is no simple correlation between education and a tendency to resist the 'shared ministry' model; cultural capital acquired early in life can be put to use in a variety of ways, including through channels not inconsistent with a supportive role defined by the husband's profession. Those who have pursued independent paid careers have tended to gravitate towards the caring and public service professions, most prominently teaching, medicine, psychotherapy and social work. Only 14 per cent had gained any experience working in business and commerce, while 49 per cent had worked as teachers at some point. Several had retained jobs until the responsibilities of motherhood changed their priorities, and from that point on the 'shared ministry' arrangement seems to have emerged. Others gave up their careers upon marriage, following what they perceived as cultural expectations of the time; as one put it: 'I gave up my job as a teacher when I married him ... because that's what we did in those days.' Significantly, many bishops' wives had renewed their professional ambitions later in life, some returning to earlier careers in teaching and social work, others finding fresh avenues in publishing or broadcasting. Grace Sheppard has produced two books in recent years, addressing pastoral concerns arising from her own experiences, while Ann 'Steve' Henshall – wife of Michael Henshall, former Bishop of Warrington – has combined writing with radio broadcasting. In many of these cases, women have found themselves drawing from their experiences as the wives of bishops as a resource which opens up new professional opportunities. Both Sheppard and Henshall publish on the stresses of clergy life, their aim in part to offer support and guidance to other women who share their experiences. Others drew more directly from the skills developed when working alongside their husband in parish life, as with this woman, who even wonders whether her skills could have led to ordained ministry:

> Parish life made me aware of [the] need to train in marital therapy and gave me experience of the potential of group work, these being the two main paths I followed. The whole experience of getting things to happen (playgroups, crèches, home groups etc.) probably gave me skills as an initiator and something of a pioneer which came into play in [our diocese] especially in my professional work. However, if he had not been a bishop I might well have sought to be ordained, or would have taken up more career opportunities as a psychotherapist.

The idea of having one's own career was clearly important to many of the women in our study, but the fact that our results suggest a sense of 'vocation' (embraced by the majority) is interpreted very broadly indicates that we need to adopt an open perspective on what comments about careers and career fulfillment might mean. Clearly, for many, fulfillment outside the world of the Church of England has been achieved through voluntary work. We asked whether, apart from the church, wives had any experience of long-term voluntary work, and a large majority of 79 per cent answered in the affirmative. It seems that a sense of vocation was extended into flows of social capital outside of traditional ecclesiastical circles. This work has taken a variety of forms, including pastoral care (bereavement support, hospice work, Samaritans), civic duty (Citizens Advice Bureau, Scouting), civil rights (Black Sash – South Africa, Tradecraft), and politics (one had been an independent parish counselor). Several had held senior positions in local civic life, one holding the position of Deputy Lieutenant of the County, and at least five bishops had wives who had been local magistrates. This is aside from numerous roles of influence within the Church of England, such as Diocesan President, being a pastoral selector for ACCM,[15] and contributing to the work of the chaplaincy team at the local prison. Voluntary work, while often viewed as ancillary and perhaps reflective of a traditionalist view of conjugal roles within the clergy family, may actually create empowered roles for these women. Within this context the 'independent career' of bishops' wives needs to be understood as following a variety of different, sometimes unconventional routes. While many have sought fulfillment outside of the context of their husband's ministry and beyond the organizational structures of the Church of England, they have done so at various times in their lives, and through a range of available channels.

Conclusion: Bishops' Wives and Spiritual Capital

According to Bourdieu's analysis of the social mores surrounding matters of taste, people will be attracted to practices that make best use of the particular kinds of the capital they possess (Bourdieu, 1984: 128–9). Aligning Bourdieu's argument with our own treatment of capital, it is reasonable to assume that people seek opportunities to express the capital they possess as a means of enhancing their sense of identity. Those with particular combinations of capital – cultural, social, symbolic, economic, spiritual – will also tend to adopt particular styles of expression. Such an analysis of bishop's wives sheds light on the complex negotiation of power and status that characterizes their position and also allows us to advance our model for understanding the development of Christian tradition through the clergy family.

In considering the wives of Anglican bishops, a key observation relates to their possession of significant *symbolic capital*. That is, they enjoy status and respect that is ascribed to them because of their position, rather than because of their achievements, experiences or material affluence. Moreover, this status is enjoyed as a direct consequence of their husband's official title and position within the hierarchy of the Church of England. We might say the status of the 'bishop's wife' as 'bishop's wife' is one that is ascribed by association, and is a consequence of their husband's ecclesiastical rank. This is not to suggest that these wives do not deserve the respect, affection and admiration they are often accorded. Nevertheless, though their contribution to the diocese is often substantial and enduring, the fact remains that their status is not earned as such, but ascribed. Indeed, the fact that bishops' wives are expected to 'not rock the boat', as one put it, suggests that significant demands are attached to that role. In other words, it exists as a symbolic title apart

---

15 Advisory Council for the Church's Ministry.

from its holder, and thus is associated with a complex series of responsibilities and privileges implicit in the assumptions of observers and associated colleagues.

And yet she is also equipped with a wealth of experience and knowledge based on her previous experience as the wife of a vicar, archdeacon, rural dean or principal of a theological college. (This is not to mention the pre-existing cultural capital associated with social class and educational opportunities documented earlier.) This has involved extensive negotiation with church authorities, experience of parish life, including the demands on the vicarage as a center of pastoral care, and the embodiment of various roles consonant with and complementary to her husband's position, roles such as organizer, carer, pastor, advisor, treasurer, administrator, comforter, caterer, hostess and general co-minister. The experience of being a clergy wife, and perhaps especially a bishop's wife, comes with pressures and anxieties, and may even lead to the wife feeling absorbed into her husband's role to a degree that leaves her without any sense of identity herself. As one expressed it:

> ... I would always feel a little bit bemused when perhaps somebody from No. 10 would come to stay with us, and have a bit of a chat with [my husband] and then would politely turn to me and say to me, two questions: how are the family? And how are the clergy wives? And that's how we are perceived: either as mother or as clergy wife. And that can be quite difficult over a period of time unless you carve your own identity so that [it] is absolutely clear to people who can't be expected to know any better. But I remember feeling very bolshy at times ... thinking, I do wish you could ask me something else! Perhaps about me!

Clergy wives whose center of gravity is the home arguably find a need to sustain distance from their husbands in order to achieve a sense of distinctive identity. Clerical life blurs the boundaries between home, work and religion, and for the wife whose existence is centered around the home, her quest for a sense of her own purpose and sphere of significance can be frustrated by the roles imposed upon her by her husband's clerical status (Richmond, Rayburn and Rogers, 1985: 84). What is to be the zone of self-engagement for the wife – motherhood, a professional career, voluntary work? Clearly, it is impossible to pursue a vocation entirely separate from the husband's unless their career is completely non-ecclesiastical, and this is an option only pursued by a minority. Moreover, for these women, their lives have often been so bound up with their husband's ministry in the past that their ambitions become one and the same, the dominant perception being of a single, shared ministry. It is not insignificant that our survey found that almost twice as many wives said they played an integral part in their husband's ministry than did their husbands in answering the same question. In other words there was a strong perception of an integrated, shared ministry among the wives that was not matched by the same understanding by the bishops.[16]

And yet, if it is important to these women that their ministry is shared, it is also important that it retain some autonomy and gain momentum apart from their

---

16 Thirty-five per cent of the wives felt they played an integral role in their husband's ministry; when asked what role they felt their wives played in their ministry, only 18 per cent of the bishops answered in the same way.

husbands' efforts. Certainly, elevation to the status of bishop's wife appears to generate some further opportunities, so that being a pastor to clergy wives, pursuing voluntary work from the platform of ecclesiastical experience or a professional career on the basis of this experience become positive vocational opportunities. While they may not always be seen as part of their husband's ministry by all of these women, they proceed very much from advantages generated by the experience of being a clergyman/bishop's wife. In other words, if a sense of losing one's identity is a possible negative dimension of occupying this status, then the social and cultural capital generated within the context of previous pastoral experience often equips them to pursue other avenues of fulfillment, especially once their husband is a bishop. In this sense the bishop's ministry is very much shared, but shared in so far as the spiritual capital generated by and within it is drawn from in empowering his wife in her own pursuit of vocational fulfillment. This is not to suggest that the vocational identities of these wives are entirely dependent on their husbands, precisely because the pool of experiences from which they both draw is not restricted to the bishop's theological prowess, pastoral skill or ecclesiastical contacts. Rather, it is a capital that has its locus in a context to which they both contribute and in relation to which their identities are most radically defined. This locus is the clerical home, to which we next turn our attention.

Chapter 6

Growing Up Clerical

The experience of growing up as the child of a clergyman is peculiar in many respects; growing up the child of a bishop is, if anything, even more peculiar. British society has borne witness to the increasing marginalization of the Church of England during the twentieth century, and the authority of its leaders has been eroded, yet bishops remain in the House of Lords, carry grandiose titles, officiate over public ceremony and occupy networks of civic hierarchy that remain the preserve of the privileged and the focus of limited but not insignificant regional power. But apart from their fathers being members of the social and spiritual elite, 'episcopal children' are also subject to a set of domestic arrangements that can be traced back to the conditions associated with parochial ministry. Indeed, it is these arrangements that characterize one of the formative experiences earlier identified as central to this study.

To some extent the pressures felt within the clergy household are a product of the trials and tribulations that are experienced as part of childhood in any generation. Resentment towards figures of authority, including parents, feelings of constraint and alienation during adolescence that breed yearnings for freedom and individuality, a thirst for rebellion when faced with unwelcome moral or religious expectations of conformity – all are widespread characteristics of growing up in western post-industrial cultures. In addition to this, the clergy child's difficulties with their father's public profile may also be found among children of local policemen, teachers, GPs – all of whom have a prominent and active presence in the immediate community. And yet the 'clerical home' presents a set of distinctive challenges and experiences that are not found elsewhere and are likely to shape the familial context – both home and role divisions within it – to an extent that we can expect processes surrounding socialization to be profoundly affected.

In this respect our study is built upon an unfashionable assumption: that the family is a significant factor in shaping values adopted and maintained in adulthood. More specifically, that the experience of being raised within a particular kind of family both bequeaths individuals a certain collection of resources, and that life values emerge in dialogue with these resources. As argued in Chapter 1, one way of conceiving these resources is with reference to the idea of spiritual capital as gift, encapsulating the generation and formulation of resources within an ecclesiastical context but acknowledging that such capital may be transformed and deployed in different contexts over time. To assume that the family is a *persistently* important factor in shaping value formation throughout the life-course is contentious, especially amidst narratives of late or post-modernity that emphasize fragmentation, creativity and the sovereign individual, reflexively shaping his or her own destiny independent of traditional social institutions such as education, social class or family background (Giddens, 1991). The concerns of the individual – not the family – have been given center stage, and yet recent studies have appealed to empirical evidence that challenges this orthodoxy. In the USA, for example, Bengtson, Biblarz and Roberts (2002) have drawn from the longest-running longitudinal study of families in the world, examining continuity and divergence in values among members of several generational cohorts, including the baby-boomers and Generation X. Contrary to the post-modern narrative, their findings suggest that the family remains an important influence over people's values, that the values learnt within the family during childhood often persist in some form throughout life. The family remains an important shaper of social values that has an enduring influence on educational and occupational aspirations, achievements and social values (Hout, 1984). Similar evidence has been gathered in the UK by Furlong and Cartmel (1997), who found that – against hyper-modernist theorists such as Ulrick Beck (1992) and Anthony Giddens (1991), who take late modernity to be characterized by unpredictability and the negotiation of risks on an individual level – young people's life opportunities are still largely shaped by their location within social structures, including gender and the social class status they inherit from their family background.[1]

However, it is not our chief aim to compare the impact of clergy with non-clergy families. Rather, we appeal to the recognized importance of family in shaping social values as a foundation for an analysis of how being raised within a clergy household generates experiences which are later drawn from in adult life and incorporated into the narrative construction of identity. Using the theoretical terms discussed in Chapter 1, we aim to describe the locus for the generation of spiritual capital and embodiment of values and examine their distinguishing features before looking at qualitative data gathered from clergy offspring as adults to see how they reflect on such endowments in relation to their current professional and religious identities.

Accordingly, this chapter examines the nature of the clergy household as described by the children of bishops, bypassing the numerous cultural stereotypes and instead building on empirical evidence. In addressing this upbringing, one significant factor relates to the ideas, teachings and experiences of the 'formative years', which we take to be between the ages of 5 and 18, when they would have been more consciously aware of the impact their father's occupation had on their home life. Conscious awareness is important here because we are addressing the ways in which childhood experiences are consciously drawn from within the meaning-making processes undertaken in adulthood.

In some respects the characteristics of a clerical household are not wildly different from the domestic situation of many non-clerical families living in late twentieth-century Britain. The clergy of our study have enjoyed apparently stable marriages, most have more than one child,[2] and most – though not all – have wives who have willingly adopted fairly traditional roles focussed on maintaining the home and raising the children. Other characteristics are more unusual, though not particular

---

1   National survey data also paint a robust picture of family life in contemporary Britain, with a majority maintaining high and regular contact, and depending more on extended families for support than on friendship networks (Park et al., 2002: 204–5).

2   Among the 89 bishops who have had families, the mean average is 3.1 children per family.

to clerical families, such as their tendency to have moved the family between geographical areas several times with the father's job. This is perhaps a function of the upwardly mobile status of the clergy of our study, who have climbed the rungs of the ecclesiastical hierarchy, perhaps occupying jobs as rural dean, archdeacon, or principal of a theological college along the way to becoming a bishop. Most of these changes would have required a move to a new neighborhood, perhaps a completely different region of England (or beyond), and such upheaval has left a lasting impression on many of their children, whose childhood experiences are colored by memories of cultural change and new challenges, but sometimes by a resentment at being uprooted, with the fracture of friendships, schooling and local connections that this often brings.

A more distinctive feature of clerical upbringing relates to an ambiguous social class status. While benefiting from tied housing, clergy salaries, relative to general standards of the time, were low.[3] Many told stories of 'just getting by', especially when in parochial ministry, and clergy children recalled financial limitations often preventing them from enjoying the consumer luxuries of their peers. For example, one bishop recalled that, of all of the people his children knew, his was the last family to have a television. Even as bishop, with all of the almost aristocratic connotations of this position, these clergy were not well paid, and their children were well aware of their family's financial limitations. And yet their father – as a vicar, archdeacon or bishop – enjoyed a certain high status, especially within the local community. This was manifest in a variety of ways, from a traditionalist deference expressed by passing local residents to invitations to elaborate functions alongside senior public figures like MPs or local counselors, chief constables and business leaders. Clergy children were aware that their father moved in influential circles, and carried significant authority at a local, regional or even national level. Given the middle- or upper-middle-class backgrounds of most of the clergy and clergy wives in this study, the culture of family life was also colored by intellectual family discussion, middle-class etiquette and the nurturing of high educational and career aspirations among the children. Hence, these clergy children were exposed to a mixture of sometimes conflicting ideas and values during their upbringing and, in terms of the sociology of knowledge, these were not always supported by the conventional social structures we associate with them. Education (cultural capital) was unaccompanied by wealth (economic capital); public status (symbolic capital) was maintained, but within a social context that harbored an increasingly skeptical attitude towards religious hierarchy, the grounds upon which this status is founded. Such ambiguity demands careful treatment and generates interesting questions about the kinds of social values instilled and embodied within the clerical household.

---

3   Neil Burgess comments that during the 1960s, when a large number of our bishops were in parochial ministry, some curates were reported as living below supplementary benefit level (Burgess, 1998: 102). Leslie Paul's data from the early 1960s reveal that, while most incumbent clergy of that time earned above average industrial earnings, there was an astonishing range of annual stipends, with clergy at the lowest end of the scale – probably working in rural dioceses – earning less than the average salary of male industrial workers at that time (Paul, 1964: 127; 308–9).

The most distinctive aspects of their upbringing relate to the father's pastoral responsibilities, and 78 per cent spent some of their formative years living in a vicarage. This is highly significant for any understanding of how clergy children draw from their background in making sense of their current identities, for these experiences become a long-term focus of value formation. As we shall see, the children of clergymen express their core values in part by negotiating with the childhood experiences of religion, family and the church that shaped their outlook early in life. Because these experiences carry profound and enduring consequences, we divide the central section of this chapter into three distinctive facets of the 'clergy upbringing': the clergy household as an ideological household, the home as public space, and experiences of public exposure outside of the home framed by the father's status. Together, these three dimensions shed light on a more general trend related to the imposition of inflated expectations on to clergy children. All are rooted in the cultural identity of the clergyman, but find their most explicit and socially significant expression in the clergy child's experience of being raised within a vicarage.

However, vicarage life does not exhaust the issue; for some 47 per cent of our sample,[4] these formative years overlapped with their father's tenure as a bishop. It is difficult to say what precise difference this makes to the experience of home life. Some difficulties – such as the invasion of private family space – appear to be exacerbated in some cases but alleviated in others, much depending on the size of the bishop's residence and the bishop's management of his work space *vis-à-vis* the previous vicarage. Intrusion into the home is sometimes perpetuated in the episcopal residence because of the emphasis on increased pastoral responsibilities in recent decades. Positive advantages, such as those related to social and cultural capital, are often enhanced by the transition to episcopal status, with fresh social networks opening up new opportunities. However, no clear trends attributable across the population can be argued and we offer only tentative suggestions on an 'episcopal' experience of family nurture in an additional section.

The Ideological Household

Childrearing norms change over time, with the late twentieth century shifting in emphasis from obedience to autonomy, from expecting children to conform to their parents' rules and expectations to an acknowledgement that allowing them a greater freedom might actually encourage a more healthy maturation (Bengtson, Biblarz and Roberts, 2002: 43). And yet such changes are neither simple nor experienced in the same way by all, and the ways parents embody them may, in large part, be shaped by whether or not they see parenting as demanding an expression of their ideological convictions. While we may expect all parents to act upon some set of values, these are not always explicit or formally articulated. What we have with clergy families, however, is something quite distinctive: a family led by a father whose life is meant to be an embodiment and expression of a religious tradition, at once leader by instruction as well as by example, and whose formal religious vows

---

4   Of which 33 per cent overlap with our 'vicarage' group mentioned above.

include his family's lifestyle. He is frequently engaged in teaching the values he is expected to embody, and this expectation is heightened in parochial ministry by the priest's geographical proximity and frequent contact with those who look to him for guidance. The clergyman is made constantly aware of the values by which he works and lives, and may therefore be expected to organize his family life with them clearly in mind. Consequently, the process of childrearing may be described as in part an ideological process, although the clergyman's orientation to family life may lead him to express his values in a variety of ways. Some of the clergy we spoke to had clearly made an effort to minimize the explicit use of theological language in the home, in part so as not to add to their children's sense of being under pressure to conform or maintain an unrealistic religious or moral integrity. Others made a more obvious effort to integrate all spheres of their lives into a concerted attempt to affirm and advance a particular theology. Their attempt to embody their tradition was effectively extended into a desire to express it corporately through the lives of their immediate family.

In the twenty-first century we might expect there to be a more obvious balance between conjugal roles, between the power of both husband *and* wife to shape family life, and this would also apply to clerical families. But the imbalance described above, and illustrated in cases described in the previous chapter, has to be understood in light of the changing understandings of gender roles emerging during the 1950s through to the 1980s, and if many women tended to occupy a more traditional, supportive domestic role during this period, clergy wives were even more likely to do so. As such, while they played a crucial role in sustaining the clerical household and the pastoral care and hospitality expected of the vicarage, our clergy wives appear to have generally deferred to their husband in many respects, including his ideological framework. This many of them came to share, and see as their duty to support and advance, as in the 'shared ministry' model discussed in Chapter 5, further illustrating how family life is organized around an attempt to negotiate a set of values which are inextricably bound up in the clergyman's professional identity.

Aside from the complex implications associated with the blurring of boundaries between family life and vocational duty, this distinctive feature raises the question of how the clergyman's ideology is manifest in the family context. We are concerned with how clergymen express what Bourdieu calls 'knowledgeable mastery', that is, specialist theological knowledge, within their everyday family lives. The time lag between experience and reportage is significant here, for our impressions are built on narratives of the clergy home constructed by bishops, wives and children many years after the process of raising the children. For the older and younger generations there is arguably a temptation to coalesce memories into meaningful forms and perhaps, in doing so, build up what Charlotte Linde (1993) calls 'coherence systems'. One way in which narratives acquire a sense of meaningfulness is when the narrator appeals to pre-existing schools of thought or bodies of knowledge. Within our context we might expect elderly bishops to appeal to the theological traditions they have embraced in interpreting their family life. Indeed, some of them will have played an active part in the construction of these theological traditions, both as influential authors and leading churchmen. What was interesting in listening to our tape-recorded interviews was hearing how the wives and children of bishops also sometimes appealed to the same sets of ideas, thinkers, concepts and explanations, illustrating how, if these ideological tools are present in the expressed outlook of the clergyman, they also find their way into the discursive life of his family. In such ways is spiritual capital absorbed as theological literacy.

And yet to describe such ideological resources as 'theological' is arguably misleading, for the bodies of knowledge and values to which these clergy refer embrace social, political and ethical concerns, some of which have a more obvious theological root than others. David Sheppard's *Bias to the Poor* (1983) owed a great deal to liberation theology, and in turn to Marxist economics, just as John Robinson's *Honest to God* (1963) drew from philosophical and sociological insights of its time as much as, for example, Paul Tillich's theology. Moreover, such movements gain their currency from their relationship to the age in which they are expressed and taken up. The values of the 'parish and people' movement – which exerted a strong influence over some of our bishops – cannot be detached from the cultural and geographical idiosyncrasies of mid twentieth-century Anglican Britain. The more recent popularity of contemplative spirituality cannot be appreciated apart from the therapeutic overtones of clinical theology, the interest in inner healing filtered through the wider cultural influence of the human potential movement, and perhaps the feminization of the clergy driven by the rising influence of women in the church. The emerging clusters of ideas, values and associated practices are complex and multi-referential, and they are a distinctive product of the 1940–2000 period. This complexity allows them to be appropriated by clergy children in a variety of different ways, and we will explore in later chapters how political, ethical and theological concerns – bound together here – may be separated out and reconceived as part of an attempt to achieve meaning in adult life.

This notion of clergy being an embodiment of an ideology is especially important for the individuals within this study because their upwardly mobile status means they are more likely to be theologically, ethically and politically articulate. Indeed, while a pastoral model of episcopal responsibility had become dominant by the end of the twentieth century, many of our bishops were also aware of the need for members of the episcopate to be theologically competent, following in the footsteps of individuals they had known and learnt from, like Michael Ramsey, John V. Taylor and Stephen Sykes. While many felt their generation had fallen short of this ideal, they had nevertheless made a concerted effort to incorporate theological study into their vocation, and into an ongoing process of ministerial development.

Some of the most striking examples of how bishops' ideological convictions radically shaped their children's early experiences illustrate the significance of theologico-political convictions. This is perhaps to be expected, as the practical implications of a leftist or liberation theology are more easily imagined and realized in concrete domestic terms than the implications of a perspective grounded in, say, clinical theology, parish and people, or the radical theology of John Robinson. Moreover, an effort to live out the principles of a leftist theology is likely to be experienced as unusual by clergy children, given that these ideas were, during their childhood, far from the cultural and political norm. A life lived in this way is a life publicly identifiable as distinctive and, in some respects, counter-cultural. One bishop, when in parochial ministry, expressed his conviction that he ought to live amongst the working-class members of his parish by waiving his right to a tied house, which was in a more salubrious area, and instead purchased a Georgian residence within the heart of the community. Paradoxically, and as recounted by his daughter, this marked them out as a family more keenly, as they were the only people living in their own house; all of the other parishioners lived 'on the estate'. An effort to overcome class differences served only to heighten an awareness of them, and such tensions were recalled as most uncomfortable by the clergy children we spoke to. They generated for them a thoroughly ambivalent status: both clearly middle-class in terms of parental background and education, and yet with little money and with aspirations to live amongst and thereby understand the working-class culture of the locality. While such aspirations are to be applauded as a genuinely sympathetic and socially engaged attempt to live out an incarnational theology, they also have serious implications for clergy children, who may experience feelings of alienation, isolation and confusion as they struggle to find a sense of identity in this ambiguous situation.

Such political and theological persuasions were also recalled as having a direct influence on which schools clergy children attended. One respondent recalled that, despite consistently under-achieving and having a miserable experience at the local comprehensive, her parents refused to send her to a private school because of their political convictions. As she put it: 'it would have been fee-paying and that wasn't in the script'. Their leftist beliefs committed them to the welfare state and to the socialist value of quality education for all, rather than just for those with the wealth to pay for it, although their daughter now interprets this cynically as a social experiment, in which she was the suffering party. She also finds this difficult to reconcile with her father's distinctively middle-class background, which included attendance at a prestigious public school which, from one perspective, bequeathed to him the cultural capital essential to his later ecclesiastical achievements. This displays a paradoxical rejection of the foundations of cultural capital – 'he drew a line under his background' – while on another level it reveals a thoroughgoing pursuit of ministerial ambition dependent upon these resources.

Another respondent recalled how her father's Christian Socialism shaped his distinctive outlook on family and parish life, which were practically merged so that 'we felt part of an extended family'. She describes her father's vocation as self-sacrificial and dutiful, with a strong emphasis upon sharing common resources among the community, but comments that 'vocation, duty and ideals [were] being put into practice … possibly at the expense of the nuclear family'. Here, the presence of an ideology shaping practice effectively drew attention away from the immediate needs of the domestic household in favor of a more communal model, and radically shaped the experience of family life. Tellingly, both examples cited above are of clergy offspring who subsequently sent their own children to private schools and who found a need to live a religious and family life markedly at odds with their own childhood.

In practical terms the ideological convictions of bishops appear to have been manifest in family life through four different routes. First, and most obviously, there is the explicit teaching of values to the children in the home, either in occasional conversations, moments of chastisement or more focussed moments of principled guidance. Given the time lag between our interviews and the experiences to which they refer we do not have a great deal of evidence about this, presumably because, unless childrearing practices are ritualized or attached to unique occasions of significance, they are often not readily recalled from memory.[5] Second, there is the maintenance of Christian devotional practices in the home, such as grace at family meals, family prayers, and Bible stories at bed-time. The efforts of some bishops to separate their work from family life extended to abstaining from these elementary rituals, while others attached a great deal of importance to them, adding multiple service attendance and even occasional communion services in the home. One respondent emphasized the formative experience of living in a house where formal prayer was a regular practice; theirs was a 'Christian praying home, not just the vicar's house'.

Third, the bishop's beliefs and values were channeled into the home through regular discussion of theological and ethical issues. Here, the father's knowledge and commitment to open debate may generate opportunities for his children to question and explore his ideas and values, an experience that was often invoked as empowering. One daughter spoke of regular Sunday lunch discussions, when she and her siblings would rip 'apart dad's sermon'. Another related intellectual empowerment to the parochial context, saying they 'enjoyed the opportunity to question [their] own religious/humanitarian beliefs'. In this respect the introduction of an ideological component into the clerical family was not about the imposition of rules and conventions to which the children were expected to conform. Rather, the clergyman's enthusiasm for theological discussion fostered the development of debating skills, wider knowledge and personal confidence. When he allowed his own work or sermons to be part of the discussion, then he also subverted any authoritarian aspect of his own role, arguably facilitating a healthy rectifying balance to the sometimes unquestioning deference of parishioners. The clergy family here becomes a site for the generation of valuable cultural capital, which may be drawn from later in life if the context allows it. One telling case was recounted by a bishop's son who recalled home life as a context in which people talked to him on an equal level, as a conversation partner in an open and sincere discussion. However, this caused problems when he entered the more tightly controlled environment of public school, where his desire to challenge and question ideas was interpreted as insolence. The tension between intellectual empowerment and institutional control represents, it seems, a paradox for the lives of bishops' children as well as bishops themselves.

Fourth, and perhaps most importantly, the ideology embraced by the clergyman is expressed and affirmed in the pastoral care of his parishioners within the clerical home. Not only does the father embody his tradition but his interactions with others also represent and advance it, presenting to his children the all pervasiveness of their father's convictions and the fact that such expressions of a practical theology have a proper place within the domestic sphere. To this important characteristic of 'growing up clerical' we now turn.

---

5   Perhaps more significant here, in terms of explicit religious instruction, is Sunday School (Gill, 1999: 92), and 69 per cent of our population of clergy children said they had been regular attendees.

The Home as Public Space

When asked what it was like being raised the son or daughter of a clergyman most of our respondents mentioned the peculiarities of living in a home that was in many respects a public space. Their comments focussed on the fact of intrusion, specifically on the fact that their family space was used for the pastoral care of outsiders. One had herself gone on to marry a clergyman and found herself reflecting with some concern on the experiences of her own children. Her reservations about the consequences of a vicarage upbringing were profound, commenting that she 'hated the fact that my parents always seemed to *belong* to other people first *before* our family' (original emphasis). This was a common criticism, grounded in a feeling of coming second to the needs of the parish or diocese. One respondent offered a comparison with how clergy function in the present day, and with what parishioners have come to expect of their minister:

> ... if the phone had gone at any point in my childhood, my father would have been there for that person, whatever else was happening in the family. And yet ... if I phoned the minister [now], I'd probably get an answering machine. I'm sure he would respond, but Dad would have been there for everybody. And that's not necessarily the best thing for the family, is it? Though it's wonderful for the congregation.

Another respondent extended this criticism to their mother, who had been central to the pastoral care dispensed within the home. They enjoyed living in a house that was often occupied by a variety of people, but recalled 'feeling a bit put out that "yet again" there was someone with a problem talking to my mum, when I wanted to talk to her'. Professional pressures have practical implications and the demands of work in the vicarage may mean that clergy find it difficult to find time for their families, to take proper holidays or enjoy leisure pursuits apart from church responsibilities. Pressures of work may also mean that clergy are too tired for these things, and while necessary periods of rest may be required in order for them to fulfill professional obligations, it is easy to see why clergy children might perceive this as neglect.

In these cases the 'public' nature of the vicarage is associated with the needs of parishioners, given priority over the needs of the family; the parish intrudes into what the child sees as family space. More profoundly, it is a space in which the pastoral care of the vicar is visibly and tangibly dispensed, but to those in need who are outside of the family. A sense of feeling excluded from parental intimacy is likely to be exacerbated by the fact that the father's attention is not only visibly diverted away from family needs, but that this attention is devoted to a duty of care that is often close in kind to that expected within the familial context. The roles performed by the clergyman – teacher, comforter, advisor, consoler, helper, mediator – have obvious overlaps with the roles commonly associated with parenthood, and while such processes refer, strictly speaking, to 'professional' relationships, the nature of parochial ministry means that the relationship between pastor and parishioner is not simply one of practitioner/client. Behavioral boundaries marking out professional from platonic or familial interaction are far less clear here than they would be with, for example, patients and doctors or teachers and pupils. The nature of the minister's work arguably demands a degree of warmth and personal concern that challenges professional distance, but in doing this it renders ambiguous the boundaries between family relationships and relationships with parishioners. As such, we might expect clergy children to react with concern and perhaps confusion when such relationships are conducted within their family homes.

For some this experience was replicated – but on a larger scale – after their father became a bishop. The marginalization of 'family space', even within a sizeable residence, was recalled by one respondent as a source of much disdain, leading to a description of the 'family home' as a 'public building', devoted first and foremost to the day-to-day running of the diocese. She described the bishop's residence as an 'enormous house', but focusses her description on the fact that 'it had an office, it had a chaplain's study, and my father's study, you know, the phone was going all the time … there was no private area apart from my own room'. She even recalled how the designated 'family room' was transformed into a 'waiting room' when clergy were visiting, this enhancing her perception that the business of the church took precedence over family life.

In this case the experience of being intruded upon led to feelings of resentment projected onto the church and its personnel, who were associated with the cause of the situation. But it was the lack of privacy that was felt most profoundly, a lack of personal space, which is reflected upon by some as frustrating a quest for identity, explored in more detail later on. The intrusion of outsiders and outside influences – all associated with or connected to the church – led to a feeling of being smothered, which in turn triggers in some a yearning for escape. The same respondent goes on:

> I spent a lot of time out of the house in order not to be in this environment, which I really didn't like…There was no privacy. There was no opportunity just to relax and be yourself … I was always on show, always... And I loved being in ordinary homes, where kids played and watched TV and people sat around having tea and chatted, you know, just ordinary stuff. Particularly when I was seventeen and I met the next boyfriend … and his family were absolutely wonderful to me. I still keep in touch with them now, and I used to like being there. I felt that the level of conversation was somehow a bit more authentic, it was more real. There wasn't a sense of everything being good and everything being nice, it was 'this is the real world, we can be critical, we can talk about things that aren't very nice'.

The respondent views the church as penetrating every aspect of her home life to the point where she searches for an alternative family context in which to find space to be herself. Part of the pressures from which she sought refuge have to do with an evangelical discourse expressed by her parents, which she appropriates as idealistic and detached from the 'real world'. She associates this both with her mother and father, and with the home life they created around them, and found it stifling and alienating, an obstacle which was blocking any authentic exploration of life on her part. The extent of her negative feelings drove her to seek out a surrogate family, which took on such significance in her life that she keeps in touch with them now.

While this example is rather extreme, it highlights trends which are not atypical. When asked to identify the distinctive challenges of being brought up in a clergy household, another interviewee emphasized:

> Adjusting to the fact that the house isn't a straightforward private home. So adjusting to a lot of visitors to the house. And then, asserting my self. I think a vicarage child has some need to find themselves apart from a vicarage identity. I can certainly remember it being said, through my childhood, that vicars' sons were either the best or the worst of people. There were clearly expectations around but also, I think, some sort of dynamic at work in which you need to find yourself in relation to this quite strong formative experience. You need to know where you lie.

This individual had gone on to become a parochial clergyman himself, with children of his own, so is especially aware of the realities of being raised in a vicarage from the perspective of child and parent. He reflects on a 'strong formative experience' and focusses on the search for identity in a context that is somehow a constraining influence that blocks or frustrates a sense of personal autonomy. This has less to do with social intrusion, and appeals to a more general experience of being raised in an environment pervaded with 'public' processes. The ontological quest for identity is made sense of against the background of the vicar's life and work, built around a series of expectations, processes and responsibilities that draw in the regular participation of outsiders. In this sense the time and space of the parochial clergyman are 'owned' by people external to his immediate family, and this obstructs the quest for individuality and independence of purpose on the part of the clergy child.

And yet not all bishops' children described the invasion of home life in negative terms. Indeed, for some, the hospitality and pastoral care offered to outsiders was remembered fondly and appropriated as a strong and positive source of moral education. Having an 'open house' is in some cases incorporated into a positive image of healthy family life, a paradigm to be emulated or at least an ideal towards which one might strive. One interviewee recalled: 'the house was a constant stream of people. The front door seemed to be always open …'. He told us stories of how the vicarage was a place of refuge for those in need, that his mother used to make tea and marmalade sandwiches for the homeless, and would offer a kind ear to those waiting to see the vicar. Most significantly, he remembered these experiences positively as an education about the world and a source of great moral example. It taught him the importance of providing for the less fortunate, and became the foundational experience upon which later social skills would be built and practiced at work. Moreover, living in a house in which many strange individuals were often visiting appears to have generated for many a sense of learning how to interact comfortably with a wide range of people. One bishop's daughter found that she 'became able to just talk to anybody, it didn't really matter whether the person who had just arrived for tea was an MP or a missionary from Africa or some poor soul who was struggling and suffering and we had them for a meal'.

Some mentioned the advantages of having a father whose work was based at home, so that he is, for example, potentially more available to contribute to family life, do the school run, help with dinner or simply be there when needed. While some emphasized that, while their father was in the house, his preoccupation with work meant that he was 'never truly there', others affirmed a positive view, their father's occupation allowing them more opportunity to be integrated into family life, an opportunity some had clearly used to the positive advantage of the children. As one individual poignantly commented: '[my father] was always around, so I suppose I grew up fully aware that I had two parents ...'. In cases such as this the home was not seen as invaded but enhanced as a consequence of the vicar's work. This is especially striking when set within a historical context in which changes in parental practice and employment patterns meant that such an arrangement was becoming increasingly rare. Here, as in many other respects, the clergy family appears as a distinctive exception to a dominant cultural trend.

Overall, however, the sense that the father was present and available during childhood was affirmed only by a minority of respondents. Most concur with the notion, expressed emphatically by one interviewee, that 'my mother has ... had a much greater impact, I think, on growing up. I mean, she was always there, she didn't work ... she was the one who gave us ... emotional support ...'. In our questionnaire we asked bishops' children who had been the most important person in their personal development. We left this an open question, and answers varied, from those who cited family members to those who highlighted the importance of spiritual mentors or inspirational teachers. But it is significant to note that while 36 per cent named their father, 47 per cent pinpointed their mother. Thus, while some clergy had clearly attempted to integrate parochial and family responsibilities to a degree that was recalled positively by their children, more have emerged from family contexts in which the mother has played the central role. In this respect, while the father's presence is clear and dominant in so far as his work shaped family life, the emotional and familial processes associated with the care and nurture of his children appear to have fallen to the clergy wife.

Exposure and the Public Gaze

Aside from the clergy home, clergy children also have to deal with their father's profile within their locality; they are easily identifiable and many have expectations of them. Clergy also share with local politicians a persistent call from members of the public to intervene in affairs as a matter of principle. The local populace often feel their vicar is both representative and advocate, and while it is easy to overstate this status in a post-Christian culture, it is not insignificant, especially in rural areas or where the media help constitute an arena of opinion. Moreover, when the bishops in our study were in parochial ministry – during the 1950s and 1960s – the local standing of the vicar was less in question than it is now, and their family lives would have been familiar to many within the parish.

This exposure was sometimes intensified by clergy who made a point of making their priestly role explicit to the local community, sometimes to the embarrassment of their children. As one bishop's son put it: 'he wore a cassock all the time ... your identity as a vicarage family was both very, very clear: not negative, but also quite exposed ... our house was not an obviously private house'. Another respondent recalled how, when receiving lifts from friends, she would ask to be dropped off a block away as she was embarrassed by where she was living. She talked of the difficulty in having parents who did not conform as this marked her out as different in the local community, an experience that was both uncomfortable and potentially alienating. Such exposure was, for some, exacerbated upon their father's elevation to the episcopate as his status was then even more public, and even more unusual.

Such public standing has obvious consequences for the children of parochial clergy, not least that they are often easily identifiable as the vicar's children and are consequently associated with their father's status. In this respect clergy children can be seen as involuntary actors on a public stage,[6] behaving in the knowledge that their performance is being measured against certain role expectations. Many bishops' children had an experience of exposure that highlighted social class difference: for example, those who grew up in working-class parishes recalled how their father was viewed as separate from other local people, and that this difference was projected in turn on to his family. Education, wealth and religious piety all inform the socially constructed image of the local clergyman during the 1950s and 1960s, and together form an identity that is both socially other and religiously elevated. The consequences of this status vary by locality, although respondents mentioned reactions from local people that ranged from a sense of alienation and distance, deference to authority, amused mockery and wary suspicion, and all were in some measure applied to the clergyman's wife and children as well as to the clergyman himself. Consequently, some reported a sense of isolation from their local communities, a feeling often exacerbated by the frequent house moves that accompanied changes in their father's professional position.

Feelings of exposure in the local community also intensified pressures to conform to norms of respectability. One interviewee recalled stories of his youth, during a time when his father was a vicar in a working-class area of London. He remembered times when his mother would walk into shops and local residents would change their conversations accordingly, keen not to say anything untoward in the presence of the vicar's wife. One bishop's son reminisced about his childhood, remembering his capacity for rebelliousness, but recalled that a disincentive had been 'the realization that my dad had a ... serious social standing in the community and anything that I did would influence that standing'. His knowledge that bad behavior would be noted by local people and have a detrimental effect on his father's reputation was enough for him to curb his behavior, thus illustrating how associations of moral integrity attached to a clerical status may impose themselves upon clergy children and influence their conduct. This pressure is especially acute when the father is working within a close-knit or sparsely populated area in which the local elite are more widely known and recognized. One woman recalled her experience living in the town in which her father was based as the diocesan bishop, and commented that it was always 'difficult to hide', that she had a public profile that most people do not have to live with. While many enjoyed their father's status in the wider community and church, and embraced the social capital that was generated by this, the exposure that it brought was for some both oppressive and stifling.

Indeed, such status had an ambiguous effect on the way in which clergy children were dealt with in institutional contexts, particularly church and school. Several cited their father's involvement in their local school, for example, as a prominent aspect

---

6   A perspective developed in Chapter 7 with reference to the work of Erving Goffman (1959).

of their childhood experience. Clergy were governors, took occasional assemblies or even taught lessons, and if their involvement did not stretch this far their status in the local community might generate invitations to speak at functions and participate in school events. Several felt they had been given high-status roles in school simply because their father was the local vicar or bishop. Such positive discrimination is invariably experienced as embarrassing in the long term, as it highlights a spurious ascription of social capital – children wish to be recognized for their own merits rather than for their father's – and because it further marks them out as different among their peers, possibly incurring some vilification from jealous pupils. However, reverse discrimination was also possible, with one daughter telling us how, as her church had been bombed during the war, a new building was built and the Princess Royal had come to lay the new foundation stone. She recalled not being allowed to carry the brownie flag 'because it would have been seen as favoritism'. One bishop's son was ambivalent, describing seeing his father at school with a 'mixture of embarrassment and pride'.

Inflated Expectations

The issue of public exposure highlights the oft-cited problem of clergy children feeling that they are expected to behave in a certain way, usually with a high expectation of social conformity, educational achievement, moral integrity and religious piety. Hardy suggests that these experiences mark clergy children for life, that such expectations persist into adulthood, and that the lives of clergy offspring are evaluated in light of the expectation that they be 'outstanding achievers' (Hardy, 2001: 546). These expectations arise from multiple sources, including the local (and in some cases wider) community, the parish congregation and from within the clergy family itself (McCown and Sharma, 1992). It is worth noting that we are dealing with clergy who were upwardly mobile high achievers for their generation and who are likely to have served as strong, perhaps imposing, role models for their children. But interestingly, when we spoke to bishops' children about the expectations imposed upon them they rarely mentioned their parents as actively pressing this imposition. More frequently, expectations were communicated by subtle suggestion or cultural absorption, clergy children picking up a sense that others were judging them according to different rules to other children. When these expectations were expressed within an institutionalized context, as at school, they may be expected to be more enduring, and clergy children were often held accountable to their stereotype even by their peers. Indeed, some commented that both staff and students were complicit in sustaining a common image of the clergy child, unfairly using their father's status as a moral yardstick with which to chastise and taunt them. When asked what kind of expectations he thought people had of him as the son of a clergyman, one respondent emphasized being in frequent adult company at an early age, and that this generated expectations of behavioral conformity replicated at school, where his father's status was well known.

Another, who was made head boy of his cathedral choir school (he suspects because of his father's position), linked his father's standing among the school staff with expectations placed on him as a pupil. He comments that 'all the teachers knew dad' and refers to a definite 'level of responsibility' that was expected of him. In a very real sense, then, clergy children share in their father's dual status, in being expected to embody an ideal and be human (Burton, 1999), although in the child's experience this expectation is invoked less as a professional aspiration and more as a cynical labeling tool, recalled as inappropriate, unfair and in some cases having lasting damaging effects.

There are also implications arising from one's status as a moral exemplar. As one daughter of a bishop commented, if you do not behave according to the high expectations of others there is a feeling that 'you're not only letting your parents down, you might be letting ... the whole community down'. There is a sense of representing a collective, of guarding an image, and the notion of respectability is manifest in the pressure to conform and preserve the image of the clergy family as orderly, separate and morally upstanding. Also important is how the local nexus of relationships becomes the meaning-making context, a factor that brings notions of hierarchy (colored by social class and ecclesiastical difference) to the fore. That is, while the projection of otherness onto the clergy family may have associations of class privilege, local status and spirituality, it also comes with expectations that these qualities be reflected in appropriate behavior. One respondent compared his family's status in the local area to that of the royal family, commenting that they would have benefited from 'someone to manage our PR. The impact was one of conformity to status, [our having a] separate entity within the village.'

It is a well-known fact that congregations often expect the clergyman's family to be an exemplary model: morally upstanding, reliable, devout, functional and content – an example of Christian life (Rowatt, 2001: 523). We might venture to say that the transition to episcopal status intensifies this pressure, as the bishop's family is regarded as a desirable model by other more junior clergy who look to their bishop for pastoral guidance through lifestyle as well as verbal advice. But it is worth reflecting on the fact that clergy are aware of these pressures as well, and some appear to actively arrange their family lives so as to minimize their negative impact upon their children's upbringing. As one bishop put it: 'it's difficult enough to be a clergy child anyway – all the expectations that people throw at you, if your parents are going to back them up ... [you'd have a] hell of a life ahead'. One of the cases we examined is particularly illuminating in this respect and highlights the ways in which the clergy household may be organized not just in deference to external pressures but in critical response to them. It also highlights how these factors may interact with other pertinent forces which exert their influence over the clergyman and his family.

'Sarah' is the daughter of a clergyman who became a suffragan bishop. She is the eldest of two daughters, and both her and her sister, while acknowledging their father's absence due to ministerial responsibilities, have fond memories of their childhood. Sarah describes her father as being quite 'detached from his job' and as a consequence they did not feel pressures to behave in a particularly moral way. She contrasts this with other clergy children she has encountered, who had negative experiences, emphasizing how 'most of our friends, unless they were church friends, they didn't even know that dad was a vicar'. When we asked Sarah why her parents had made such an effort to create a welcome and pressure-free family life she referred to the fact that her mother had been a clergy child herself and had exerted a firm influence over family life. Most importantly, she had been determined her daughters were not going to experience the same unhealthy repressed life that she had. While she had gone back on her vow never to marry a clergyman, she raised her own daughters in light of her own experience of being raised in the shadow of her father. Sarah suggests that this instilled in her mother high expectations associated with the maternal role, while also demanding a commitment to her husband's ministry that prevented her from fulfilling these responsibilities to her satisfaction. This paradoxical experience had, according to her daughter, led to a preoccupation with guilt and a determination that her daughters not acquire the same principles.

The resulting low-pressure, laid-back family life was also influenced by Sarah's father's liberal Anglicanism (in our questionnaire he described himself as an 'affirming catholic' with a background in 'prayer book catholicism') and her experience of Christianity during childhood was not at all associated with the doctrinaire, authoritarian or dictatorial. Neither daughter was ever made to go to church during the teenage years, and their home life was noticeably void of any theological discourse which might have marked it out as a space dedicated to their father's ministerial vocation. To Sarah, he:

> seemed quite normal, but wearing funny clothes, he didn't preach at us … other people that we know, whose parents [were religious] … had [a] much more religious home life than us. I mean, we said grace, but that was about it. We … never kind of talked about you know, Jesus … God did not come into conversation at all … It was my dad's job, and it was very separate actually …

So a separation of home life from ministerial vocation appears to have been not only possible but desirable among some clergy. Of course, the extent to which this is perceived as a separation rather than a subtle expression of a kind of incarnational theology depends on who is interpreting the situation, and some of our clergy may well opt for the latter understanding. However, what is important for this chapter is the fact that clergy children perceived a separation and that the narrative expression of this reveals some interesting inter-generational correlations, particularly to do with the clergy upbringing of the mother. Previous experience of living in a home dedicated to clerical ministry may have a tempering influence over the way in which one raises one's own children in a similar context. This tendency was also apparent in the recollections of some clergy children who were younger siblings, like one whose parents had always made it clear that they had no expectations of him with respect to religious belief. He explained this with reference to the experience of his elder brothers and sisters, at least two or three of whom had rejected the church entirely. His parents' attitude, it seems, had changed in light of this, so that the 'clergy home' was managed in a way that discouraged rather than heightened this sense of high religious and moral expectations. His elder siblings had had to 'forge their own way', while he had enjoyed a much more 'open-minded parenting experience than they did'. The perception of high expectations, it seems, can have a significant influence not just on clergy children but also on the clergyman and his wife as they negotiate the problems of parenting, yet another aspect of the negotiation of spiritual capital as a resource generated within the clerical household.

The Episcopal Factor

We mentioned earlier that most of the experiences invoked by our respondents as significant to their upbringing could be described with reference to the vicarage context. And yet they are distinctive in being the children of bishops, those elevated to a position of leadership in the Church of England. How this impacted upon their childhood and development is a complex question, and several different threads need unravelling. First, we need to distinguish between the impact of having a father as a bishop during one's formative years (a description which applies to 47 per cent of our sample) and the significance one's father's episcopal status might have in ongoing narratives of identity constructed during adulthood. Both may be important in making sense of current attitudes to professional or religious identity, but while the first has to do with the social context of upbringing the second appeals to the father as an enduring conversation partner as both parent and representative of the hierarchy of the church. Engagement with the latter is likely to be more sober and distant, although no less relevant, as we shall seek to demonstrate in the following chapters.

Second, we need to distinguish between the significance of being raised by an upwardly mobile clergyman and being raised within the context of the material and social peculiarities of an episcopal residence. The first is entwined in the various experiences charted earlier on, and is a difficult aspect to pin down. But it is significant that the qualities ultimately recognized as worthy of episcopal status within these men were present in their lives and work well before their consecration. The impact of living in an episcopal residence is easier to chart, and responses appear to be polarized between those clergy children who enjoyed and celebrated the material and social benefits associated with their father's status and those who were embarrassed by what they came to see as unwarranted wealth and opulence. One bishop's daughter claimed she 'wouldn't bring people back to our huge house as I felt it was morally wrong that a bishop should live in such privilege'.

The feeling that the outward trappings of their father's status were a backward step was not restricted to comments about luxurious residences. One respondent contrasted her experience of being a 'bishop's daughter' with the life her family had enjoyed when in a close-knit working-class parish: 'When you become a bishop it all changes, because people start kowtowing and being sycophantic.' For her the deference conferred on her father after his consecration revealed what she saw as the hypocrisy of the Church of England, and actually detracted from her own spiritual experience of worshipping in the Anglican Church. Another respondent felt his father's status adversely affected how others reacted to his own Christian faith, as it was interpreted as inevitable rather than something based on his own personal commitment. His status as a Christian was ascribed rather than achieved, and he felt that his 'own profession of faith was diminished when people found out my dad was a bishop'.

But elevation to the episcopacy confers social advantages as well, such as the dislocation of the clergyman from the geographical centre of his ministry. This is especially the case with suffragan bishops as their residences carry no necessary significance for their episcopal responsibilities, and even those who have an area remit are unlikely to be as explicitly associated with this area by local residents as the parochial clergyman. The wife of one suffragan bishop, reflecting on her children's upbringing, commented that 'it was easier for them than for vicarage children as their father rarely appeared on home ground to embarrass them'. In such situations the problems associated with the clergy home as a 'public space' are unlikely to apply to anywhere near the same degree as with a parochial clergyman. The bishop's work is not bounded by the area close by his residence, he is not directly responsible for a population of parishioners and his house is not linked to a local church, being thereby potentially identifiable by passers-by as a clergyman's residence. Because of the wider geographical remit of the bishop's ministry he is also less likely to have connections with his children's school. Hence, the cases that stand out as not impinging negatively upon the lives of the children are the families of suffragan bishops, whose ambiguous status is here a potential advantage because of the geographical and possibly vocational detachment of home from ministerial responsibility.

The foregoing is offered as a kind of axial discussion, as it raises numerous themes that will be taken up again in the following chapters. Specifically, while here we have aimed to highlight the kinds of capital that are generated within a clerical upbringing – both positive and negative – we will now turn our attention to how such resources are reflected upon as significant by clergy children as they make sense of their identities in adulthood. We begin with their religious lives.

Chapter 7

Clergy Children and Religious Identity

The image of the rebellious clergyman's son or daughter has become a common cultural stereotype. Much like that of the vicar or bishop's wife, these stereotypes are often far from the truth, saying more about cultural perceptions of religion than those they claim to describe. As far as clergy children are concerned it is often supposed that the institutionalized constraints of the church upon them will either trigger a thirst for freedom, marked by a rejection of Christianity and the embracing of a more individually focussed – inevitably 'modern' – lifestyle, or else will foster an emulation of the father's traditionalism and piety. The predictable outcome of a polarized twofold scheme of saint and sinner seldom matches the complex reality of actual individuals, as demonstrated in this chapter with its focus on the religious identities of the bishops' children who took part in our study. Drawing from questionnaire and interview data we set out to explore changing orientations and paths of personal development. As in the previous chapter our approach concentrates on the ways in which clergy children draw from the resources bequeathed them by their childhood in making sense of their religious identities as adults. Mapping patterns of religious affiliation and practice and then showing how clergy children construct narratives about their religious identities in dialogue with their youthful experience yields a complex picture that, inevitably perhaps, frustrates those simple stereotypes of the 'clergy child'.

Religious Identity: Statistical Patterns

While acknowledging that religious identity is more accurately and subtly addressed through a longitudinally qualitative approach, there is also much to be gained from our use of questionnaire surveys coupled with appropriate interviews. Accordingly, our survey data provide an impression of descriptions that individuals feel best capture their current lifestyle and value orientation. Our information is drawn from questionnaire returns completed by the 122 bishops' children received during the course of 2002–2003 and designed to generate an overall picture both of religious affiliation and of comparative levels of religious commitment.

We began by asking, 'Do you regard yourself as belonging to any particular religion?', offering four optional responses: 'No, I consider myself an atheist'; 'No, I consider myself an agnostic'; 'No, I do not see myself as *belonging* to any particular religion but nevertheless see myself as religious' and 'Yes, I do belong to a particular religion.' The aggregated responses are shown in Table 7.1.

Table 7.1   Current orientation of bishops' children to religion

Response	Number	% (adjusted)
No – atheist	7	5.7
No – agnostic	12	9.8
No affiliation but still religious	12	9.8
Yes, I belong to a religious tradition	91	74.6
Total	122	100

This shows a clear majority (75 per cent) seeing themselves as belonging to a particular religion. The 'No affiliation but still religious' option was included in recognition of recent research indicating that more and more people identify with a non-institutional religiosity. The 2001 census results, for example, revealed that 72 per cent of the English population consider themselves to be Christian, while less than 10 per cent regularly attend a Christian place of worship (Brierley, 2000). It was clearly worthwhile including the 'No affiliation but still religious' response, as nearly 10 per cent of our population felt that this best described their religious identity. We will explore later the kinds of religious convictions and patterns of participation that this broad response appears to have implied. Atheists and agnostics make up a significant minority, and both figures show notable similarities with national trends. If we take the evidence from the Soul of Britain survey of 2000, for example, 8 per cent of the population said they were 'convinced atheists' – 5.7 per cent for our group – while the figure of 10 per cent for agnostics is exactly the same as the proportion of agnostics among our clergy children (Bruce, 2002: 193; also see Greeley, 2003). Again, it is important not to make overly clear-cut assumptions here, for our interviews revealed that even when individuals opted for these identity markers their convictions were often far more complex and multi-faceted than we might at first assume.

We also sought a more detailed picture of religious identities by asking those who had claimed they belonged to some kind of religious tradition to tell us which tradition this is. Respondents were asked to choose one option from among 'Christianity (no denomination)', 'Roman Catholicism', 'Church of England/ Anglicanism', 'Baptist Church', 'Methodist Church', 'United Reformed Church' and 'Other Christian church', with room for them to specify a named group. An additional option allowed respondents to align themselves with a 'non-Christian group', again with an opportunity to provide details. The aggregated responses are detailed in Table 7.2.

Some 57 per cent aligned themselves with the Church of England, a figure that contrasts dramatically with that for the British nation as a whole, measured by the British Social Attitudes Survey as 27 per cent in 1999. That figure had itself suffered a 13 point decline throughout the 1980s and 1990s (Jowell et al., 2000: 123). That Anglican majority increases to 75 per cent when all other Christian denominations are taken into account (counting Quakers as 'Christian'). This is clearly not a group that exhibits immense religious diversity, at least not at first sight. Only single

Table 7.2   Bishops' children by affiliation to religious tradition

Tradition	*Number*	*% of all Respondents*
Church of England	69	56.6
Christian (no denomination)	21	17.2
Buddhist	1	0.8
Quaker	1	0.8
Roman Catholic	1	0.8
Total	93	76.2

individuals align themselves with Roman Catholicism and the Society of Friends; there appears to be no gravitation into the Nonconformist churches, and only one person has opted for an entirely different world religion, in this case Buddhism. It was clearly a good decision to include the 'Christian (no denomination)' category, as it attracted 17 per cent of all respondents. These 21 individuals will have had their own reasons for opting for a non-denominational Christian identity marker, perhaps reflecting the claim that in our post-Christian society denominational markers are less important to some than a shared pan-Christian identity (Richter, 2004: 169). Indeed, our interviews suggest that some associate a new-found evangelical commitment with a Christian authenticity that is beyond denominational identities, viewed as at best irrelevant to Christian faith and at worst as a set of redundant institutional distractions, associated with petty personal politics or pointless bureaucracy. As we discuss below, for many it is only by moving beyond the institutional forms of the Church of England that they achieve a sense of personal autonomy, a new-found freedom that allows the emergence of a more authentic religious life.

But how do these individuals express and embody their religious identities? In a later survey with a smaller sample of 51 of our bishops' children,[1] we asked about frequency of church attendance. The results are given in Table 7.3.

Table 7.3   Bishops' children and frequency of religious worship

Church Attendance	*% (Adjusted)*
More than once a week	31
Once a week	17
Once a month	6
At major festivals/special occasions	25
Rarely	13
Never	8

As can be seen, levels of church attendance among this group of clergy children are much higher than we would expect to find among a randomly selected sample of the national population. Brierley's English Church Census measured weekly church

---

1   This survey was conducted via email to elicit further information after the main postal survey and focussed on issues of religious practice.

attendance in 1998 at 7.5 per cent of the population. When broken down into weekly and twice-weekly attendees, the resultant figures are 5.95 per cent and 1.55 per cent respectively (Brierley, 2000: 27) and compare with 17 and 31 per cent in our sample. On less frequent attendees, Brierley found that 10.2 per cent of the nation attend monthly – slightly more than the 6 per cent in our sample – and 23.9 per cent attend either quarterly or twice per year, a figure which, when conflated for the convenience of comparison, is very close to our 25 per cent who attend church for 'major festivals/special occasions'. In addition, 13 per cent of our sample say they attend church 'rarely' (as Brierley's figures are based on clergy observations, they do not include a measure of 'rare' attendance). Only 8 per cent of our clergy children claim never to attend church, a figure that is 50.1 per cent for the general population (Brierley, 2000: 77).

While the low sample size demands that we treat these figures with some caution, it is obvious that there are unusually high numbers of clergy children demonstrating levels of church participation above weekly attendance, and unusually low numbers willing entirely to distance themselves from the church.[2] Perhaps this is unsurprising given the occupation of their fathers and the consequences of this for the socialization process – we might expect those raised in a home environment so closely integrating ecclesiastical and family concerns, and regularly exposing children to Christian teaching, to attach a great deal of importance to the church in adulthood. Even those who do not commit themselves wholeheartedly to an active life in their local parish church appear unwilling to disaffiliate themselves from the Church of England. Certainly, this is supported by the atypically high level of identification with Anglicanism. Indeed, the common understanding that clergy children are likely to respond to an intensive childhood experience of Christianity by rebelling and rejecting the church is not reflected in our evidence. Levels of personal alignment with irreligious categories – atheism and agnosticism – are entirely consistent with those for the national population as a whole. However, what these figures also tell us is that the socialization process peculiar to the clergy household is not entirely successful in steering its subjects into a life of active Christian commitment. Moreover, while it is clear that the vast majority of the group see themselves as having some affiliation to Christianity, subsequent interviews and a re-analysis of the questionnaire returns suggest that these 75 per cent represent a huge diversity of orientations. To understand this range of positions, we complement our statistical material with more discursive data. Furthermore, we introduce the notion that religious/spiritual identity is most authentically presented by deploying dynamic categories to capture processes of development and change throughout life.

---

2   Essentially, the variance in distribution within our own sample on the one hand, and the national population on the other, is down to those at either end of the church attendance spectrum. That is, 31 per cent of our sample attend church more than once a week (1.55 per cent for the nation); 8 per cent of our sample claim never to attend church (50.1 per cent of the nation) (cf. Brierley, 2000).

Accessing the Spiritual Journey

In seeking to make sense of religious identities in contemporary western society we do well to use language that allows for the dynamic, changeable and more fluid realities. Never before have labels traditionally associated with religious identity been treated with such suspicion, as mainstream religious traditions are challenged by individuals who are less willing to embrace them uncritically and who often wish to move beyond their conventional boundaries of belief and practice. This shift in the religious landscape calls for an analysis of emerging non-traditional, syncretistic and non-Christian, religious forms and demands that we broaden our conception of what Christian identity might mean. Most obviously, there is a need to take account of Christian religion that operates *outside* of the churches (Jamieson, 2002). One way of doing this is to focus on the different orientations people have towards centers of religious authority and meaning. For example, Jackson Carroll and Wade Clark Roof, in their study of generational change within US congregations, draw from Robert Wuthnow's distinction between 'dwellers' and 'seekers':

> Dwellers live in a stable place and feel secure within its territory; for them the sacred is fixed, and spirituality is cultivated through habitual practice within the familiar world of a particular tradition. Not that they are untouched by social change, but they are relatively well anchored amid the flux. By contrast, seekers explore new vistas and negotiate among alternative, and at times confusing, systems of belief and practice; for them, the sacred is fluid and portable, and spirituality is likened unto a process or state of becoming. The language of the journey fits their experience. (Carroll and Roof, 2002: 39)

In recent studies of contemporary religion and spirituality much has been made of a persistent blurring of boundaries between traditions and within them. The shift is from the affirmation of and commitment to inherited and relatively immutable religious traditions to the eclectic appropriation of religious resources, chosen and adapted to meet the individual's subjective needs. This more consumerist orientation inevitably invites a new use of metaphors of the spiritual pilgrimage, journey or path, the emphasis placed on development, change and an openness to future possibilities. But the emergence of this orientation is not restricted to what might be called 'alternative' religions, nor is it the preserve of those on the margins of the religious mainstream. Indeed, the adoption of such dynamic conceptual categories illuminates the extent to which the identities of those within mainstream religious traditions are also actually subject to change, evolution and creative development.[3] Christian churches as well as New Age outlets may be interpreted as evolving contexts through which the spiritual journeys of individuals take shape and assume new meaning. In this sense we need to stress the dynamic nature of identity in the ongoing spiritual careers of individuals.

---

3   The conception of religious identity in such processual terms has been more recently incorporated into the Anglican liturgy. For example, in the rite of public baptism, more 'static' family models such as 'the congregation of Christ's flock' in the *Book of Common Prayer* are complemented by *Common Worship*'s more mobile model of those who 'walk' as a pilgrim people 'journeying into the fullness of God's love' (*Common Worship*, 2000: 345).

Our approach in this study has been to use extended interviews to explore themes that emerged in our larger questionnaire survey, and to build up a picture of the narratives that bishops' children were constructing in making sense of their current identities. Here the relationship between history and personal development is complex, because our interviews formed the present-day context for the recollection of past events and their recruitment into a process of identity construction. Our study is therefore not longitudinal in the strict sense, but focusses on an individual's retrospective narrative as a lens through which patterns in the generation, evolution and deployment of spiritual capital may be discerned. Particularly in this chapter we are interested in how resources bequeathed by virtue of a 'clerical' upbringing, as described in the previous chapter, shape how these clergy children understand their religious identities as both present convictions and evolving journeys. We will develop these ideas later but, for the moment, we trace one individual's spiritual journey in a case study that illustrates the advantages of adopting a dynamic approach to identity, and highlights some recurring patterns that we found across a range of other cases.

Case Study: Stephen's Spiritual Journey

Stephen, born in 1947, is a social worker, the son of a former suffragan bishop who was a parochial clergyman in a rural region of England during his son's childhood. He recalls most keenly the sense of being separate, different from the local villagers, with an impression of class difference accentuated by the family's large, isolated rectory. He describes his father as a liberal Anglican, whose faith – as with his mother's – was entirely 'implicit'. There was no discussion about the nature or content of Christian faith or belief, merely a habit of following established parochial conventions, including church on Sunday and greeting parishioners there.

Stephen traces his first experience of what he calls 'spiritual awareness' to boarding school, involving worship at the local cathedral, where he eventually became a server. His spiritual development was within the Anglo-Catholic tradition – 'smells and bells and confessions' – through the period of his Confirmation, his experiences at public school, and a retreat to Walsingham arranged by the school chaplain, which he noted in particular. A key change in Stephen's life came when, in the mid-1960s, he went to university in London. Its lively, cosmopolitan life was dramatically at odds with the almost monastic existence of his schooling, whose Anglo-Catholicism had left little room for emotional expression. It had also been all-male, a factor that he now sees as holding him back in his personal development, and which added to the shock of moving to a metropolitan environment. In London Stephen encountered the university's Christian Union and underwent what he describes as an evangelical conversion experience and, like many converts, he was zealous in his new faith: 'I think [I] viewed my parents' religion as not clear, not explicit, not personal, impersonal, about religious observance rather than personal commitment and faith.' He accounts for his dramatic conversion partly with reference to his realization that God loved him, and that this was a personal, expressive love that had been largely absent from his experience of life thus far. Upon a visit home, he announced to his parents that he had become a Christian. His father was not pleased, and Stephen believes he took this as a criticism of the model of faith he had sought to instill in him. Being an introverted person, and given that Stephen was intimidated by his father, they did not discuss this experience further, and he says that it is only now, with his father in his eighties, that they have managed to resume a relationship in which they are able to communicate genuinely with each other.

Over the years Stephen's evangelicalism has softened: he has actually been asking himself whether he is still a Christian. He has looked into what he calls the 'cross-fertilization between Christianity and other religions' and is particularly interested in the Buddhist notion of detachment from worldly concerns. He is convinced now that there is a common set of ideas that lie behind all religions and behind humanity's search for the sacred. He is unsure about whether his investigations will steer him back into a life of religious observance because he feels that religion in the past has helped but also misled him. His attitude to religion in later adulthood is one of questioning and open exploration. He recalls happy times as a recent participant in a church attended while being trained as a therapist. He comments:

> I was lucky enough to go to a city centre church where there was a great deal of tolerance and interest in discussing things ... we had a theology discussion group not a Bible study group. I had some really good conversations that gave you permission to think outside the box of Christian orthodoxy.

He still feels he is in a different place from his father, who would prefer to believe his son was still firmly within the Christian fold. But they have found some common ground, particularly in their commitment to exploring new spiritual ideas in an open-minded way, an orientation common to both liberal Anglicanism and Stephen's post-Christian spiritual seekership. Stephen even feels that his father is proud of him for reaching this place, and it is clearly a source of healing and the basis for a resumed family relationship.

Making Sense of the Spiritual Journey

Stephen's story captures several recurring themes that feature in the spiritual journeys of many of our respondents. Unsurprisingly, he is fairly typical in having experienced a childhood in which parochial church life was central, although the importance he attaches to the religion he experienced at boarding school is also something mentioned by others as highly important to their development. Fifty (41 per cent) of our respondents attended a boarding school, many of them attending traditionalist institutions with long-standing connections to local church and cathedral life.[4] Given the comprehensive and integral role that boarding school often plays in the socialization of children, it is unsurprising that early religious identity

---

4   While some recounted how the financial sacrifices of parents – often with mother going out to work – helped fund such opportunities, other respondents attended such schools with assistance from bursaries reserved for the children of clergy. This is a long-standing tradition, and exemplifies how the cultural capital enjoyed by many clergy children is actively

should also have its locus in this environment. Indeed, this appears to have been so for many of their fathers too.[5]

As with many of his peers, Stephen's childhood was characterized by an unquestioning acceptance of patterns of religious participation presented to him as normal, with religious convictions only questioned when a radically new environment triggers a personal crisis. His transition from closeted boarding school to metropolitan city life provokes a dramatic awakening. While for some this kind of change leads to a period of skepticism and doubt, Stephen discovers and embraces evangelical Christianity, a move perhaps more shocking to his father than had he become an atheist, in his claiming a more 'authentic' Christian faith than that associated with his childhood. This is Stephen's 'conversion' experience and, as a dramatic milestone in his personal history, it is used to reject rather than reaffirm his earlier convictions. This is not always the case, as we shall see below; with some individuals 'conversion' is best interpreted as an 'intensification' or 'augmentation' of existing convictions rather than a defection from an earlier position.

Stephen's 'conversion' has another profound consequence. It appears to exacerbate an existing sense of alienation from his parents, something he associates with an ongoing emotional detachment on their behalf and with difficulty in communicating openly about personal matters. We may invoke generational differences here, between a more reserved, aloof disposition associated with the upper middle classes raised before the Second World War and the emotional literacy and open expressiveness of the 1960s, the culture into which Stephen was thrown as a young adult and from which he has drawn many of his attitudes and expectations. His frustration at his parents' austere and withdrawn approach to family life is also no doubt fed by his movement into social work, a profession premised on the importance of open communication and emotional attachment within the family. In this respect his career has become a channel for his reservations and, in many ways, emphasizes the persistent distance between his parents and himself, and between the generations that separate them.

In reflecting on their spiritual journey through the life course many of our respondents recalled a period of doubt and questioning, of challenging the traditions in which they had been raised and which had become normative for them. Stephen is no exception, although his period of questioning comes later than most; indeed, during our interview he expressed a sense that he is still, in middle age, working his way through this transitional period. He is no longer comfortable with the exclusivist claims of Christianity and wants to be open to the good that he discerns in all religious traditions. It is difficult to deny the profound impact that living within a pluralist culture has had on Stephen; the diversity of religion and of experience appears to have disturbed his earlier convictions about truth, so that he seems most comfortable now in a mode of questioning and spiritual exploration. In this he is also

---

preserved by the public school system, again effectively distinguishing clergy families from other families in a similar income bracket.

5   Some 62 per cent of our bishops attended public schools, many of them prestigious ones, and 50 per cent were boarders. Several emphasized the importance of boarding school as an influence on their formation as Christians and, for some, a shaping influence in their emerging ministerial vocation.

not alone among our population of clergy children. Disillusionment with the notion that Christianity has sole access to truth and can provide answers to all ultimate questions is widespread, although in different degrees and triggered by different experiences. Moreover, while Stephen has responded to this realization by adopting an open, critical spirituality which is at its heart grounded in subjective experience, others have reacted differently, some finding themselves exploring new possibilities but within the boundaries of the Anglican Church. Still others are moved by their disillusionment to a position of non-belief.

While Stephen's case illustrates several key themes recurring throughout our population of clergy children, it also highlights major points of divergence which distinguish cases from one another. We found, for example, a significant variety of moments of crisis triggering enduring personal change. While Stephen emphasized his move to London and encounter with evangelicalism as life changing, others focussed on the sage advice of a spiritual advisor, meeting their life partner, the birth of their first child or experiencing a crisis of faith following personal tragedy. So too with moments of religious doubt, which arose at different times for different individuals, for some in adolescence, for others after bereavement, overseas travel or following a process of serious personal reflection. These are moments within a complex lifecourse, recalled as significant by those attempting to make sense of their lives in narrative accounts. What interests us here is whether we can identify any patterns in the ways in which these events and experiences are interpreted, in how they are accorded meaning within the context of an ongoing spiritual journey?

Here we find Pollner and Stein's (1996) notion of 'narrative maps' helpful. 'Narrative maps' are the structures one uses to navigate and recount experience and psychological development. These are the narrative frameworks and signposts one has at one's disposal when talking or writing about one's self and life. Given the common patterns of experience shared by our bishops' children, described in some detail in the previous chapter, we may enquire whether they appeal to a common set of 'narrative maps' in making sense of their current religious identities and spiritual journeys? And we find that they do, and do so in a way that reveals an interesting capacity for self-interpretation (Taylor, 1989). In other words, while much in their accounts reflects the spiritual capital they have inherited, this capital is neither static nor its holder passive; rather, it is a set of resources active in the process of self-reflection and the forging of new identities. Bishops' children are revealed as individuals who are engaged in a conversation with the past, and with their early experiences of the clerical home and the church, as they try and invest meaning in their current lives. Moreover, the emerging 'narrative maps' of identity take us further in our understanding of the nature of capital as it circulates within the structures of the Church of England. First we turn to one background resource influential upon our respondents as they reflect upon religious orientation.

Liberal Christianity – An Ambiguous Resource

In a study of how adolescents from fundamentalist homes become alienated from religion, Roger Dudley refers to the argument that the more 'religious' the home, the more committed to religious certainties, the more likely is its rigid and autocratic nature (Dudley, 1978: 390). That assumption is one foundation for claims that clergy homes breed rebellion and a rejection of faith on the part of those raised within them. Our research among the children of Anglican bishops revealed a far more complex picture, not least because of a general absence of any such fundamentalist ethos. Rather, as earlier chapters revealed, we found a prevailing episcopal commitment to a more liberal theological tradition, marked by openness to intellectual reflection, resistance to fixed or ideological commitments and a cautious moderation in matters of inter-personal politics.[6] Indeed, one could argue that such are the qualities sought in Anglican bishops, with Edward Norman recently arguing that the 'avoidance of controversy', for example, was practically a 'golden rule' of contemporary church leadership (Norman, 2004: 38). Some would even say that those of a distinctively non-liberal persuasion, or at least those who unremittingly and rigidly align themselves to a 'party' position, are excluded from office.[7] This is not to rehearse the accusation, directed in the 1980s at Archbishop Runcie, that there is a 'liberal conspiracy' in the Church of England that prevents the episcopal appointment of evangelicals and Anglo-Catholics, or to concur with Edward Norman's further claim that the church is 'riddled with liberalism, and unable to speak authoritatively on any issue' (2004: 152). It is, rather, to speak of a dominant culture of leadership, that has, for complex reasons, come to reflect such 'liberal' qualities so that those who occupy the position of bishop, from whichever church party or tradition, have come to embody them. We are reminded of our earlier account of how an evangelical clergyman had changed his orientation to the church and its traditions following his episcopal appointment, while also seeking to retain his evangelical credentials. Liberalism did not replace his evangelical convictions, rather, a new set of priorities was absorbed into a broader perspective because of his translation into a different part of the institution.

Our interest here is in how the 'liberal' outlook associated with these churchmen is manifest in family life, and how its tendency towards tolerance and inclusivity was enhanced by the efforts of bishops and their wives to minimize the extent to which things ecclesiastical intruded into the home. Effectively, this seems to have shaped an upbringing in which Christianity, while always present, was not always articulated. Indeed, Stephen's example suggests that an emotional reserve more characteristic of the pre-1960s generation may also be a salient factor. Such reserve, expressed in an unquestioning observance of the largely liturgical practice of Christianity without necessarily offering open comment on its meaning, clearly has important consequences for the resources bequeathed to the next generation. One bishop's daughter, who subsequently embraced a more evangelical commitment, drew attention to the fact that 'though I had been brought up in clergy home, [I] knew very little of the Christian Gospel and wondered why I had never been taught to read the Bible'. What is at stake here is the space given for open verbal

---

6   A theological account of the virtues of liberalism, written by a bishop in episcopal office during our period, is offered in John Habgood's *Confessions of a Conservative Liberal* (1988).

7   Indeed, only 13 per cent of our bishops said they had aligned themselves with a 'church faction' for much of their time in office.

expression of Christian beliefs within the family, although this in turn raises related understandings of the status of the church within British culture. The place given to the articulation of religious ideas in the home – especially those ideas clearly shaping its day-to-day life – is important not just in furnishing clergy children with a vocabulary of resources with which to construct their identities (Wright-Mills, 1940) but also in communicating something about the place of religion in the broader scheme of things.

For example, one case illuminated how the lack of conversation and explicit religious teaching in the childhood home led to a later sense of not having ever believed anything, because nothing was ever consciously articulated or affirmed. It was just done. When we asked this respondent whether she had, as a child, shared the same Christian faith as her parents, her response was striking:

> I was never aware of having any … I went to church, yes, but I don't remember a time when I believed in God at all … never had any belief, no not at all … Religion was just not spoken about, and I can see why now I never had any belief, and I think my father probably would think differently about the way that we were brought up because I think his idea was not to force it on us, but it meant in fact that it was never there … I don't know any Bible stories, for example, it was just never something that was mentioned.

This kind of restraint may later become rationalized as empty conformity and rejected on these grounds, as has indeed become the case with this particular woman, who stopped attending church during her teenage years, bemused by '… all these people sitting around doing this same thing every week and not seeming very interested by it, seeming to do it out of obligation'. She remains cynical, though less so than during her youth, and states her orientation to religion as 'agnostic'. In addition to highlighting the significance of an early perception of religion as empty conformity, this case also illustrates something of the changing status of religion represented by these two generations. In his influential study *The Death of Christian Britain* Callum Brown argues that: '… the generation that grew up in the sixties was more dissimilar to the generation of its parents than in any previous century' (Brown, 2001: 190). He also emphasizes how this difference was in part expressed in a change in what Christianity and Christian piety was understood to entail. Around 1800, religion became 'overwhelmingly discursive' (2001: 195), emphasizing evangelical themes of purity and virtue, made sense of in moral oppositions – light and darkness, godliness and worldliness – and affirmed in popular literature and common understandings of respectability. He places particular emphasis on the role of women, who largely sustained this discourse through their appointed place as guardian of the family and its salvation. With the change in women's roles from the 1960s onwards, these structures were compromised, and the subsequent generations ceased to be articulate in this evangelical discourse. They began to see religion more in terms of churchgoing rather than as a series of regimes and customs which were adhered to strictly, and which embodied a deep piety. To extend this argument further, Christianity comes to be about regular practice and conscious and deliberate commitment, rather than something more intimately and seamlessly tied to the cultural conventions of being British. Brown traces these changes through oral history data, culminating in the 1960s, by which time the interviewee had become 'inarticulate about religion' (Brown, 2001: 183).

As such, it is perhaps unsurprising to find that some clergy children recall some dissonance between the conduct of their parents and their own sense of religious authenticity. The woman cited above abandoned the church in her teenage years during the early to mid-1970s, the period following immediately upon Brown's axis of cultural change, and so attracting a ready explanation for the dissonance she felt. However, it is important not to oversimplify matters, for the details of this specific case suggest that its muted, unquestioned domestic piety was influenced, amongst other things, by the father's liberal catholic churchmanship. This represents an interesting case within Brown's schema, for while he identifies women as the central guardians of a Christian discourse in the home, here it is men who occupy a dominant position, because of their embodiment of what Bourdieu calls 'knowledgeable mastery'. However, when filtered through liberal sensibilities, this embodied theological and ecclesiastical knowledge appears muted, or at least resistant to codification or closure. Indeed, at that time, the heyday of the charismatic movement, this tradition maintained something of an identity by *not* conforming to an outwardly evangelical discourse. But what is most interesting in applying Brown's discussion to this case is the issues it raises about how discourse generates shared identities, specifically within contexts relevant to socialization. Are the religious sensibilities of one generation only successfully passed on to the next when explicitly and systematically taught to them through some kind of rhetorical instruction? In light of this possibility we might ask whether the liberal Anglicanism affirmed by many of our bishops is self-defeating because its boundaries of meaning are insufficiently clear and produce, as Steve Bruce (1989) argued, a secularizing tendency among the next generation. But simplicity once more eludes us, for yet others have been brought up in this tradition, sometimes having its non-directive flavor enhanced by a deliberate effort on the part of clergy to keep prescriptive theological discourse within family life to a minimum, but have maintained an active commitment to Christianity and to the church. A key factor here might be whether there were contexts during childhood and adolescence, as in Sunday school, school itself, or perhaps dinner table conversations, in which religious and moral issues could be discussed openly and comfortably.[8] In cases which attest to the presence of such contexts, often involving supportive peer groups and mentors, any thoroughgoing rejection of the church appears to have been prevented, perhaps because there is less obviously something concrete to rebel against, or because the Christianity engaged with is something negotiated, thought through independently, accommodated and adapted to a person's changing circumstances. Indeed, the woman cited above recalled when she had first encountered more positive feelings towards things religious, it was when spending time in a French Roman Catholic family, for whom 'eating and talking [was] a way of being'.

---

8   Robin Gill's analysis of national survey data at least suggests a positive correlation between churchgoing and Christian belief, and between churchgoing and one's sense of moral order (Gill, 1999).

The changes charted by Callum Brown include a sense that the once almost seamless link between Christianity and British culture was radically undermined in the 1960s, and this is reflected in the narrative accounts which assume a different understanding of religion. While this was evident in some of our interviews, in others something like this religio-cultural synergy appears to have been rediscovered and embraced as a resource in adulthood. Some bishops' children have found themselves adopting a perspective on religion that, upon reflection, they view as in general agreement with the values of the Church of England. Their impression of what the church stands for is obviously a construction based on a variety of sources, including their current experience in a parish and observation of church leaders in the media, although most draw a great deal from the personal impression imprinted on them by their father. The Church of England effectively becomes an institutional expression of their father's personality, theological convictions and moral values.[9] Consequently, those who appeal to this outlook tend to recall and maintain a warm and positive relationship with their father, and hold a high opinion of his work as a churchman and member of the episcopate.

Some found they aligned themselves with the values associated with the Church of England when faced with the challenge of bringing up their own children. The Anglican Church, while acknowledged as imperfect, is nevertheless perceived as representing the values of decency, sincerity, restraint, altruism, equity, fair play, responsibility towards one's fellow humans and a healthy respect for tradition which is taken as a welcome curb against the *laissez-faire* excesses of late modern life. It is these values that are held together as a desirable framework within which to raise children, and are often sought after within the institutional contexts of the church school and parish congregation. Here it is important to note that, while a statistical analysis of our questionnaire data suggests that those who professed a clear religious identity were most likely to judge the religious teaching of their own children to be important, the category of 'clear religious commitment' is actually far from clear, encompassing a wide variety of perspectives. It includes, for example, those who view the Church of England in utilitarian terms, as valuable in so far as it is a sound moral resource for their children's socialization, whether or not they are personally committed to its tenets as an institution. As one respondent commented: 'I don't know whether [these values] are religious beliefs, or whether they're just very middle class English beliefs ... I'm not particularly bothered, actually, where they come from. I just like them, and I seek to find the same for my children.'

The perception of the Church of England – its institutions, leaders and traditions – as a source of sound moral values is by no means exclusive to the children of clergy. Indeed, in a culture with so few institutions willing to maintain moral principle over pragmatic or economic expediency, we might expect more and more frustrated parents to depend upon religious organizations as sources of moral teaching.[10] That they do not – at least not through congregational involvement – is an indication of

---

9   When the reverse is invoked as a narrative device – that the father embodies the values of the church, rather than the church evoking the values of the father – this tends to be used as part of a critique focussed on family neglect.

10   Hence the popularity of church schools amongst parents in the general population.

the diminishing social presence once enjoyed by the church, but also of the fact that the values listed above are so diffused into our general culture that they are not always linked with the Church of England. Indeed, if an embracing of these values is indicative of a stance of conformity, this is not merely conformity to a particular image of the church but to a particular vision of British identity. A theology of Anglicanism may propose that this blurring of boundaries between Anglicanism and British culture is far from accidental and captures the inclusive, communitarian ethic at the heart of the Church of England. A more cynical perspective may find in this the old image of the Tory party at prayer, driven by traditionalism and a pragmatism that avoids change and ideological commitments (Burgess, 2005).

What is interesting here is what such trends tell us about how strands of thought and value become detached and associated with various institutions and traditions over time. In this case values may be viewed as essentially the same as one's parents', though different generations take them to have different origins.

> ... this is where I differ from my parents actually, is that I think I have the same values as my parents, but they believe that they are centred on God, on Jesus, on the Trinity, whatever, and I would say, well, we've got all these values and they're fantastic. I'm not actually sure whether that's because people need to be nice to each other, or whether it all comes from God. You end up with the same values because you end up with forgiveness and you end up with, you know, it's not sensible to steal ... but ... I'm not sure how religious my values are.

Embracing such a liberal, almost 'golden rule' version of Christianity also allows the individual to retain their faith alongside a questioning stance towards the institution associated with it. However, this appears to have been tempered by issues to do with the quality of the parent–child relationship. When relationships with parents are associated with warmth, openness of expression and emotional connectedness, liberal Christianity is appropriated positively, as representing a healthy openness to debate and an admirable tolerance towards positions other than one's own. When relationships with parents are recalled in terms of emotional distance and a lack of authentic inter-generational communication, then liberal Christianity appears as one 'narrative map' with which to make sense of this. In these cases, as in Stephen's above, it is not the intellectual openness of this tradition that is emphasized, but a dedication to high liturgy and tradition of a kind that tends to foster a personal experience that is disconnected, cold, unemotional and open to interpretation as inauthentic. Liberal Christianity, itself a complex tradition, is here appropriated in the service of making sense of inter-generational value transmission. It reflects the values of the younger generation of clergy children in affirming tolerance, broad-mindedness and an openness to change, but can appear at odds with the emerging generation when coupled with a high Anglicanism that is perceived to be overly ceremonial, cold and distant, rather than tactile, emotionally fluent and open to the language of feelings.

Family, Order and Identity

In Chapter 6 we explored how being raised in a clerical household generates a peculiar constellation of experiences shared by many bishops' children, and argued that this has an impact on developing religious identities. Erving Goffman's (1959) notion of the 'interaction order' offers one fruitful means of understanding this process. This claims that the self is active in producing identity as it works *with* others at its 'dramatic realization' (Holstein and Gubrium, 2000: 36). The self performs this activity within an interaction order, a living framework that shapes the process of identity construction. Within the context of our study the primary interaction order must be that of 'growing up clerical' within an Anglican ethos, as outlined in the previous chapter. According to Goffman the self's engagement with the interaction order is moral in that it is committed to it and its performance is evaluated in terms of the order. This casts new light on how clergy children have high expectations projected on to them by those both within and outside of their families, as the interaction order encompasses norms and values partly emerging from an ecclesiastical, rather than domestic, source. Expectations of behavioral conduct and religious piety are heightened because the self is asked to perform a distinctive role, shaped by a Christian and ecclesiastical order which the father represents. This kind of analysis also highlights the dissonant status of the clergy family *vis-à-vis* its surrounding culture; it functions according to a different set of rules to those outside of it, and this appears to produce some feelings of disorientation and uncertainty about identity on the part of clergy children. This may be expressed with reference to Clifford Geertz's distinction between 'experience near' concepts – those which people might effortlessly use to describe what they see, think and do – and 'experience distant' concepts – those technical terms used by specialists (Geertz, 1983: 57) – although here it is instructive to consider specific *experiences* using the same framework. To expand, one distinctive feature of the clergy upbringing is that what is strange and distant to most people – for example, ceremony and priesthood – is made familiar, and what is conventionally 'near' – the family and its home – is infused with the movements of 'distant' outsiders. This peculiar arrangement is often made plain to clergy children after becoming exposed to the cultural norm, perhaps through school or friends.

What is interesting is how these individuals continue to engage with this inversion of social realms as they make sense of their orientations to religion and values in adult life. For example, one bishop's daughter interpreted decisions she had made about her own family life in light of her determination not to emulate her mother's practice of compromising her own ambitions in deference to her husband's. Her mother had 'certainly influenced [her] choice of career', through a common passion for literature, but she had also had, through her negative example, an influence on her choice of lifestyle:

> I mean my husband … he's worked abroad a good deal. And I've at times taken leave from my job and gone abroad with him. But I've never given it up, I've never lived abroad with him. And that's had its problems because as a family we've lived a very divided life, but that was a quite conscious decision. Not to be like Mum, giving up everything for the husband's career … I thought that giving up my career to be a wife and mother like Mum

did isn't me. But on the other hand, of course, you learn how to be a parent from your parents.

Here, the family structure recalled from childhood and focussed around the clergyman's ministry is consciously inverted. Identity is sought through a route that symbolically emphasizes difference from the clergy home, in part out of protest against a childhood in which the church loomed larger than family intimacy. Our respondent now claims to be an agnostic, although she retains what she sees as sentimental links to the Church of England, appreciating its liturgy and the symbolism of its calendar as reminiscent of the ecclesiastical rhythms that shaped her early life. However, she maintains a thoroughly cynical perspective on the church's structures of authority and culture of leadership, recalling how the expectations it imposed on her father prevented him from entirely fulfilling his responsibilities as a parent. Given the cynicism recounted in Chapter 6, grounded in a childhood experience of the church as an unwelcome and unhealthy invasion into domestic space, we might be unsurprised to find some of our respondents distancing themselves from the institution that, in some cases, was held directly accountable for childhood problems. As this respondent comments, reflecting on her father's frequent absences: 'I do and I don't blame him for this ... you could as well blame the institution that he was part of, which sort of took it for granted that a professional man's first duty was with his work.'

Others expressed a distance from their childhood by focussing on formalities associated with the Anglican Church, which, as in the case of Stephen, cited earlier, became associated with emotional distance and a lack of authentic feeling. One bishop's daughter, while not wishing to formally separate from the Church of England, found that this was what happened after a teenaged spiritual awakening inspired by the evangelical movement. Symbolically, she makes sense of this separation in terms of a difference between liturgy and personal faith: 'I wanted Christianity and I didn't particularly want the formality of the services.' Here there is a sense of realizing the meaningfulness of Christianity only after detaching it from the formality of the religion on which she was raised. Interestingly, this same individual went on to affirm her evangelical commitment, and a significant symbolic break from her father's churchmanship, in undergoing adult baptism. Her sense of difference from her ecclesiastical background was thus affirmed and emphasized in thoroughly ritual, not to say public, terms.

In some cases this rejection of the Church of England as an institution is affirmed by a shift to a non-denominational Christian identity, which was affirmed by 17 per cent of our bishops' children. Here, Christian values are disconnected from the institution of the Church of England – and by extension, possibly, from all structures representing denominational difference – and offer a way of affirming faith without the trappings that these structures might represent. One respondent had, as an adult, embraced a more evangelical style of Christianity, inspired by the emphasis that this tradition places on personal vocation and faith expressed in practical effort. His description of his religious values focussed on social justice and followed his experience of the Greenbelt festival and being inspired by his wife's activist perspective. While his father, a former suffragan bishop, clearly represents a very different tradition, affirmed as 'catholic', he maintains that both his parents and himself are actually 'very similar' in terms of their 'faith and … theology'. His departure, which he summarizes as an attempt to engage more openly and actively with 'the world', he interprets as a reflection of his personality. He therefore attempts to minimize the differences between himself and his parents, and goes on to comment that the 'evangelical' and 'liberal' labels he has been using do not truly reflect what is most important. Such differences, he suggests, are often simply 'a reflection of what type of people [they] are, or the traditions in which they are brought up'. His own convictions, while passionately held, do not extend to the need to make such distinctions and he prefers to see himself simply as a 'Christian', rather than as affiliated to any particular denomination or church party. However, he does hint at what distinguishes his faith now from his childhood experience, and it appears to amount to being a visible and world-transforming presence within a local context.

> … there were, very much, people who took their faith seriously in our middle of the road Anglican church that I went to when I grew up, but I guess, you know, a church like [ours], which has, you know, a very … full sort of vision of its ministry and it's excellent for the children's work, and full of people who are really willing to give time, you know, and money and resources to … furthering the kingdom of God. You know … we wanna be a part of it.

This illustrates a trend among some clergy children who have moved into a faith orientation liberated from denominational commitments. Such cases invariably involve individuals whose father embodied a liberal version of Anglicanism: associated with tolerance, inclusivity and an English restraint worthy of that generation. However, unlike the cases cited in the previous section, this sentiment is invoked here as the basis for personal change in someone's life.

For some, this intensification has meant a transition into a form of Christianity that is counter-cultural. Rather than emphasize the continuities between the church and the British context, they stress the proper role of the church as a medium of moral critique and stalwart of values that have become unpopular in a consumerist culture. One respondent had moved away from the more liberal Christianity associated with her father after having experienced an evangelical style conversion. Her faith became focussed upon radical commitment put into practice in one's daily life. While subsequent life experience has made her appreciation of the boundaries of Christianity more flexible and less judgmental, she still retains a sense of occupying ground which is very much counter to the dominant secular culture, and to the values expressed by her generation. Indeed, she struggles with this dissonance most keenly in reflecting on the exposure of her own children to wider cultural pressures:

> I find that almost everything we are being told goes against what I believe in. And I find it extremely difficult with the pressures that are on our children, and the pressures on us, actually. The materialism, the violence, the aggression, all the TV … the computer games, this sort of bombardment of consumerism … especially now with teenaged children, I find it really hard, really hard to know how to help them live their lives the right way, you know, the pressure on girls to be skinny and beautiful, the obsession with sex [in]

every video, the music videos I think have a lot to answer for, because most of them, the message is, money and sex, and I don't like it ...

While it is difficult to provide an accurate social profile of our bishops' children, questionnaire data add weight to the contention that they profess a set of values that are not radically different from their parents. Particularly in terms of the family, there is a sense that many – often after facing the challenges of raising their own children – seek to order their lives according to a set of values that is not supported by wider cultural trends. For example, we asked bishops, wives and children whether they felt that, generally speaking, young people today do not have enough respect for traditional British values. The responses are given below.

Table 7.4   'Youth disrespect traditional British values' – responses from bishops, wives and children

Response	*Bishops (%)*	*Wives (%)*	*Children (%)*
Strongly agree	3.3	7	10.7
Agree	31.7	37.2	27
Don't know	26.7	20.9	20.5
Disagree	35	27.9	25.4
Disagree strongly	3.3	–	9

In spite of the fact that this question is deliberately worded so as to evoke reactionary notions on morality and moral standards, often presumed to be the preserve of older, perhaps more right-wing, members of society, it has not divided the generations along simple lines. Roughly the same proportion of bishops disagreed or disagreed strongly with the statement as did their sons and daughters, although their wives were more sympathetic to this viewpoint. Aside from inter-generational parity, Table 7.4 also shows that a reasonably large proportion (38 per cent) of bishops' children were in some agreement with the notion that young people ought to show more respect for traditional British values, a level of support for 'traditionalism' which exceeded their fathers, who might be seen as symbolically participating in this very notion of 'British values'. Moreover, 11 per cent 'strongly agreed' with the statement given, representing a larger proportion of firmly committed 'traditionalists' than appeared among either bishops or their wives. Clearly, a concern with the moral state of contemporary culture was shared by a large number, although responses to this drew from different resources, some happy to affirm the Church of England, others radically distancing themselves from it.

Feelings of long-term resentment towards the church as an institution can run deep, and had informed the framework within which many of our respondents constructed their current religious identities. One recounted her disillusionment with the church after meeting so many clergy who were, in her eyes, totally ill equipped to be spiritual advisors. Her emphatic rejection of the institution was doubly affirmed in her choosing to affirm, immediately following these comments, her subsequent conversion to Roman Catholicism: 'I converted and I've been a Catholic for fifteen years. And I'm at home now. And as soon as I decided I knew I'd come home. For me it's the real thing.' The choice of words here is striking, suggesting that proximity to the everyday functioning of a religious institution may do more than simply expose its banalities; it may undermine a sense of spiritual authenticity.

If collective structures are a common focus of protest, it is not only religious institutions that are invoked by clergy children for this purpose. Indeed, recalling our comments on the clerical household as an 'intellectual household', it is interesting to consider how other ideologies enter into this process. For example, due to her childhood experience, one respondent could not totally separate Christianity from her father's socialism, so that when she rejected socialism she also rejected Christianity: her recent contact with evangelicalism had helped her to detach a basic Gospel message from her father's worldview. She makes particular note of her contact with wealthy evangelical churches in London, from whom she has learned that it is acceptable to be both middle-class and Christian, a notion with which she had long-standing issues because of the anti-materialist connotations of her father's Christian socialism.

Of course, rebellion can take on many forms, and while some have responded to their childhood experience by distancing themselves from the Church of England as an institution, others focus on their father's churchmanship. This was the case with one bishop's son who had become a clergyman himself but who had adopted an entirely different outlook to his liberal Anglican father. As his sister comments:

> My eldest brother was extremely rebellious, like me, but then became a clergyman … he's chosen a totally different line of faith to my father. So in a way he's still rebelling, you know, 'cause he's saying I'm not gonna do it like you. And I think he lives in the shadow of dad … I think my eldest brother admires my father the least, thinks he's a bit of an old fool, doesn't agree with his attitudes, but then my brother's pretty extreme, you know, he's … dead against this whole gay bishop thing, and actively against it, and that's just one example of his attitude. He's a very exclusive Christian, I think. So it's quite upsetting for my father to experience that, you know.

Here, Christianity becomes the site for the struggle over spiritual capital, a stock of ideas the definition of which is in dispute, and the difference between definitions representing both generational difference and the need for inter-generational distance, to which we now turn.

The Quest for Autonomy

The apparent quest by many of these bishops' children to deconstruct and disentangle the values inherited from their upbringing reflects a need to re-interpret spiritual capital within their own adult context. By engaging in this process of self-interpretation they are able to free the associations and ideas bequeathed to them by their background from the institutions and ideologies that make them initially unpalatable. One striking way in which this is done is by separating learnt values from any connection with Christianity or the institutions that represent it. One bishop's daughter, when asked whether she had taken on the values of her parents, said that morally she had, but these were not Christian beliefs. She respected her mother and father as good people, but 'I don't believe they're good people because they're Christian people ...', therefore separating moral and religious integrity from their ecclesiastical roots. Indeed, the need to separate values from institutional and traditional contexts in order to render them more 'authentic' was a pattern that extended beyond the 10 per cent of clergy children who explicitly affirmed a 'non-affiliated' religiosity.

Such reflections on values were especially striking when we asked bishops' sons and daughters to comment on the religious teaching of their own children, when such matters might be expected to take on yet new significance. One hoped that their children would 'appreciate that much of Christian teaching has intrinsic values, whether or not you are a Christian'. Another claimed her son was a pagan, 'although his values are totally Christian'. In both cases there is an implicit desire to separate sound values, whatever these might be, from outward or institutional expressions of them. By preserving values from institutional forms, there is a sense that they may remain pure and have integrity. One respondent expressed this in terms of a need to expose his children to 'spirituality', 'not religious teaching', although he goes on to share his concern that by failing to give them a dogmatic framework of any sort, which he adds he had, he is 'depriving them of an important touchstone for their own development'. Clearly, as generations pass and new ones emerge, the paradoxes associated with integrity and the fallibility of institutions are re-visited.

But if the relative independence of values is important to these individuals, so is their own autonomy as individuals distinct from their own father's and from his church connections. We are reminded here of the comment referred to in the last chapter, of the man who resented the fact that his own faith was diminished when people found out his father was a bishop. The deliberate and conscious act of commitment, central to his evangelical ethos, was undermined by the patronising expectation of inevitability. Echoing this, the self is constructed in these emerging narratives in a way that emphasizes the importance of autonomy, of sitting loose to religious institutions – especially the Church of England – and perhaps of ontological distance from the theological traditions and ecclesiastical connections associated with the father. In this sense, clergy children may be seen as disempowered, as they are inevitably defined in relation to their father's position. However, they may also be viewed as empowered by the spiritual capital that encourages them to challenge and reconfigure the values and ideas of their upbringing. Interview transcripts revealed a repertoire of motives, symbols and references, important to the process of reflecting on, critiquing and rethinking the clerical home within the context of present-day needs and circumstances. In part, this process depends on cultural capital, on education and intellectual prowess, which certainly shaped the capacity of clergy children for theological discussion and critical self-interpretation. In this sense the resources of identity-construction have much to do with the benefits of social class status. A further dimension relates to confidence, and the benefits of having a lofty institution such as the Church of England laid bare with all its faults and imperfections during their formative years. It is easier to draw selectively and discriminately from the church when it has already been exposed as a human institution.

Some bishops' children have responded by rejecting the narratives of their youth for an alternative story, perhaps embracing the Roman Catholic Church, Baptist tradition,[11] Evangelicalism or a more informal notion of family, to make sense of their situation. Others remain more focussed on the importance of transforming the self, including those who embrace a conversionist model of faith. Indeed, this understanding offers a narrative device for challenging any institutional inheritance, by sweeping clean the memories of what has gone before in the name of new experience. One respondent thus linked his own evangelical faith with his existential need for independence from his father:

> … my own faith was formed in an evangelical stable in a way my dad's wasn't, and really that became the way I think I expressed my own independence through my teenaged years. Dad and I were at our least close during my teens, and I became quite involved in the charismatic movement and became quite militant in my evangelicalism, and really thought my dad's liberal Catholicism was worthless. But my own sense of my values and my self as a Christian person were very much clearer for me …

A clarification of self was achieved through other routes as well, the most notable being wider cultural experience, which was reflected upon by some as a route into a more personal, experiential kind of spirituality. Our bishops' children are not caught up in networks of alternative or 'New Age' religion,[12] but they do participate in a broader cultural trend focussed on individual fulfillment and a freedom to shape one's own personal, professional and family life (Rose, 1992: 157), in this case in dialog with past experience and inherited resources. For one bishop's son, a broadening of his experience had empowered him to reject all that he had previously learned from others and, instead, acquire new knowledge by his own thinking and experience. He has incorporated these themes into his own creative writing:

> [I] thought a lot about the departure from the standard religion of your youth, which is essentially being told things basically about religion, and the sort of spiritual quest or journey of being older, almost having to knock that down and start again and work it out for yourself because … I found it totally unhelpful. So quite a lot of [my] writing is about sort of getting rid of that and yeah, trying to work out things for yourself, away from a sort of construct which was instilled in you when you hadn't been really been able to think for yourself.

What is interesting about this case is how this individual's reflections on theological discussions with his father had helped him in thinking through the problems of pluralism and cultural difference. In theoretical terms, a personal spiritual quest was triggered as a counter-response to his clerical upbringing, but advanced by virtue of the spiritual capital acquired through that very context. As with the clergy wives we

---

11 While none of our questionnaire respondents formally chose 'Baptist' as an identity marker, we became aware through interviews that one of those opting for the 'Christian (no denomination)' category had moved into an evangelical faith through her involvement with a Baptist church.

12 Only 10 per cent claimed to be currently involved in any kind of 'alternative therapy' group, mostly yoga, and none expanded on a non-affiliated religiosity in obviously 'New Age' terms. Our one Buddhist respondent affirmed a commitment to this tradition as a way of life, rather than as one 'spiritual resource' among many.

addressed in Chapter 5, the bishops' family appears to generate an ambiguous stock of experiences and resources, which both lock individuals into a continuing personal dialog with the church, while offering opportunities for empowerment of a certain kind. For bishops' wives this took form through harnessing social capital – networks and interactive experience – for their children, more significant is the emergence of a religious discourse, resourced by forms of cultural capital learnt in the clerical environment, although certain factors may conspire to block the development of such capital, as we have discussed above with reference to the management of family life and the liberal tradition. Here, our focus has been on religious identity as a personal, discursive phenomenon, to do with how one makes sense of one's place in the world. In the next chapter, we advance this discussion by focussing on practice, specifically, on professional life.

Chapter 8

Clergy Children, Work and Professional Identity

A distinguishing characteristic of the clergy home is the fact that it is not merely a domestic space but one also focussed on professional ministry. So much was argued in Chapter 6, where we saw how, from the perspective of the clergy wife and children, the vicarage and palace may serve their domestic needs as a secondary concern to the primary business of running and serving the parish or diocese. This perspective features prominently in the memories of childhood confided in us by the majority of our respondents, and even the 22 per cent minority who had not spent formative years within a vicarage cite experiences that are still characteristic of this environment. With bishops increasingly assuming the primarily role of 'pastor-manager' this arrangement is increasingly replicated in the bishop's palace. From the point of view of clergy children, their home is both domestic dwelling and professional space, a peculiar arrangement that naturally affects their emerging perspectives on their own working life, and such is the topic of this chapter.

To explore what these bishops' children have taken from their parents in forging a professional life for themselves, we examine the careers they chose and the attitudes they adopt towards their work. We ask whether there are parallels with the ways in which their parents viewed such things, or patterns of influence that can be traced back to their experience of being raised in a clerical home. In keeping with the approach to inter-generational influence developed throughout this book, we focus on the resources, or spiritual capital, they have inherited, asking if these are mobilized as professional skills or motivations, or whether, perhaps, they become a focus for the rejection of parental influence or of the learned model of working life associated with the clergy home. We also have in mind the issue of the inalienable quality of some values, embodied in the life of father and mother, and bequeathed to these children, and the ways such values may be transformed in and through patterns of work.

The Working Lives of Clergy Children: Statistical Patterns

The questionnaire sent to bishops' children included a section devoted to 'career life', containing closed and open-ended questions about past and current occupational activity. A question on 'current occupation' was left open-ended so that we could gather as much information as possible from the career description offered: the responses we were able to codify into the 12 categories shown in Table 8.1.

Table 8.1 Clergy children by current occupation

Occupational Group	% (Adjusted)
Business/management	20
School teaching	20
Caring professions	8
Media	7
Other	7
Civil servant and related	6
Clergy	6
Expressive arts	6
Social work and related	6
University teaching	5
Law	3
Housewife/mother	6
Total	100

The wording of the question – What is your *current occupation*? – was deliberately left ambiguous, with no suggestion that this necessarily meant paid work. This was so that those who consider voluntary work or responsibilities as a housewife or househusband, for example, to be their chief 'occupation', could feel able to say so. As is clear, 6 per cent identified themselves as housewives or mothers, although follow-up interviews and cross-analysis of questionnaires suggested that the question had been interpreted differently by different respondents, with some current housewives citing as their occupation their previous career for which they were trained and to which they intended to return. Other women working part-time did not cite any paid work, preferring to see themselves first and foremost as housewives or mothers. This is not a phenomenon specific to clergy children but reflects broader cultural trends that demand a new approach to the politics of identity.

The remaining categories cover occupations broadly associated with the upper middle classes, which is unsurprising given that respondents were from families of upwardly mobile clergymen who were themselves largely from upper-middle-class backgrounds. Social class identity is rarely challenged between generations (Barrett and McIntosh, 1982: 44–5) and while there are a few cases of clergy children taking up blue-collar occupations, they are in a small minority. This continuity of class identity is also reflected in educational opportunities, with 59 per cent attending a public or independent school and 75 per cent holding a bachelor's degree or more advanced academic qualification. It is, then, unsurprising that when their career choices are translated into social class categories, 86 per cent of our clergy sons and daughters fall within social classes 1 and 2, reserved for those occupying professional and managerial posts.[1]

---

1   Classification of social class adopted from Goldthorpe (1980) (also see Davies et al., 1991: 53–4). The 'other' category encapsulated a broad range of responses, including 'student', 'administrator', 'computing engineer', 'translator', 'lorry driver', 'caterer', 'pharmaceutical research' and 'architect'.

Beyond issues of wealth and status, these career choices also indicate something about the kind of work that these individuals do during their everyday lives and the values embodied in their choice of occupation. To explore this more fully we divide their range of careers into categories according to three types of working practice: caring and nurture (including education), leadership and governance, and expression and creativity. The results are presented in Table 8.2.

Table 8.2   Current professions of clergy children re-coded into types of working practice

Caring & Nurture (%)	Leadership & Governance (%)	Expression & Creativity (%)
School teaching (20)	Business/management (20)	Media (7)
University teaching (5)	Law (3)	Expressive arts (6)
Caring professions (8)	Civil servant and related (6)	
Social work and related (6)		
Housewife/mother (6)		
Clergy (6)		
Total: 51	Total: 29	Total: 13

One reason why this re-classification is possible is that many of those categorized within 'business/management' are in fairly senior managerial posts, or at least in posts that require the use of leadership skills, and are therefore easily placed within the leadership and governance column. This categorization also highlights sectors of the working world not generally represented within our population: all of the typically blue-collar professions, including manufacturing and skilled trades, and, beyond the expected class boundaries, those in small business, the retail sector, clerical and junior white-collar work, not to mention the world of finance. Apart from two policemen, there are no members of the uniformed occupations, including the fire service and the military. This is especially interesting as a potential marker of cultural change, given Medhurst and Moyser's (1988) finding that many of the bishops from earlier in the twentieth century had fathers who were military men. It is difficult to show exactly how our population of clergy children differs in its career choices from patterns across the general working population of Great Britain, although a rough comparison with national trends suggests that the clergy children of our sample show an unusually high probability of pursuing a career in a field focused on public service, rather than a career in private business,[2] and are at least three times more likely to pursue a professional occupation.[3]

---

2   Proportionately speaking, there are twice as many of our clergy children working in the public sector than are doing so in the wider population, and roughly half as many working in the private sector (Park et al., 2003: 298).

3   Comparisons made on the basis of Office of National Statistics Data, which indicate that in Spring 2001 (the closest data set to our own), 11.7 per cent of the total population

What they do show is a marked tendency to gravitate towards certain kinds of work. The first is characterized by caring and nurture, includes school teachers, nurses, medical doctors and social workers: public sector workers whose professional lives embody a sense of public service. The second is typified by leadership and governance, and embraces senior business managers and directors and those involved in local or central government, including civil servants and one MP. We also include lawyers and solicitors in this group, because although not necessarily concerned with the direct management of others, their work involves the application of English law and represents an alignment with the state. In this sense they represent the central power structures of society, something they share with their fathers to a certain degree. The third category governs expression and creativity, it gathers together all those whose work is focussed on their own creative endeavors, including artists, writers and those involved in the production side of the media. If the first category represents a commitment to the care and nurture of others (the personal and the pastoral) and the second represents an embrace of leadership (institutional governance), then the third represents a desire for autonomy, an independence of thought and deed and a concern for the non-material. We have classed 'clergy', who make up 6 per cent of our group, within the caring and nurture category because of obvious overlaps in the area of pastoral care. However, there are aspects of the clergyman's work that may be placed in each of the three categories, as we saw in earlier chapters.

The three categories are presented in descending order of appeal, with over half, some 51 per cent, currently engaged in work focussed on caring and nurture, 29 per cent in leadership and governance, and 13 per cent in expressive or creative work. However, if we take into account the entire career history of these individuals rather than merely their current occupation, a slightly different picture emerges. The questionnaire survey asked about all forms of paid work undertaken at some point in their lives. This excluded voluntary work and home life, and enables us to gain some impression of patterns of career development beyond recent choices and current circumstances. This is particularly advantageous for an understanding of roughly 75 per cent of our female respondents who had taken career breaks to raise a family.[4] Retaining the same three broad categories of work practice, the results are shown in Table 8.3.[5]

Again, the most popular category is the first, with a clear majority of 72 per cent having experienced work caring and nurturing others. In other words, at some point in their lives most had held positions as an educator, social worker or within the medical field. In second place this time, however, comes the 'expression and creativity' category, with a significant minority of 45 per cent having taken up paid

---

worked in professional occupations (<http://www.statistics.gov.uk/statbase/Expodata/Spreadsheets/D7917.xls>, accessed 25 April 2006).

4   Despite changing cultural attitudes to the management of parental responsibilities, this only applied to 16 per cent of the males in our survey.

5   The categories are slightly different here from those employed in Table 8.2, as these data are generated from a multiple-choice question. As such, Table 8.3 should be read as a picture of the extent to which these specific categories of career were pursued by our respondents, rather than a total picture of their aggregated career lives.

Table 8.3 Paid work experienced by clergy children at some time during their lives

Caring & Nurture (%)	Leadership & Governance (%)	Expression & Creativity (%)
School teaching (30)	Business/management (38)	Media or writing (32)
University teaching (17)		Expressive arts (13)
Caring professions (17)		
Social work and related (8)		
Total: 72	Total: 38	Total: 45

work at some point focussed on the expressive arts, broadcasting, journalism or some other kind of writing. Close behind come those with experience in business management or commerce, comprising 38 per cent of the total. Perhaps the most significant finding here is that while only 13 per cent are currently engaged in occupations within the expressive/creative category, 45 per cent have actually worked in this field at some point. This clearly represents a popular career choice, if one not always sustained in the long term.

The Appeal of Occupations

Why are these individuals attracted to occupations emphasizing caring and nurture, leadership or expressive creativity? Here their life experience may provide some potential answers. If, for example, they never had any childhood experience of the world and ethos of business they would, perhaps, be less likely to pursue careers in this area. Indeed, the morality associated with their upbringing, with its sense of altruistic service and community focus rather than self-advancement, may rule out such a career path for some people. Questionnaire responses do seem to support this, with 42 per cent, for example, associating the appeal of their work with the importance of building relationships with people, while 18 per cent saw their occupation as enabling them to work towards a public good or service. Tellingly, perhaps, only 7 per cent said that their work appealed to them because it allowed them time for their personal or family lives, and only four individuals mentioned any kind of remuneration as a motivating factor. What emerges is a population of individuals committed to their jobs, articulate about their professional values, and who largely frame their commitment with reference to values associated with the broader public good. They are, in short, attracted to work allowing them to make a valuable contribution to human communities, be they schools, the socially deprived, business colleagues or society as a whole.

One bishop's daughter, for example, employed as an educator of excluded children, saw her job satisfaction as consisting in 'making a difference for the kids who I work with'. She emphasized the value of working with young people disenfranchised from society and the education system, helping them build self-esteem and realize their ambitions. This sense of satisfaction at providing a service to the community was widespread, with many affirming a feeling that their jobs ought to 'make a difference' to the well-being of others. This echoes some of the bishops' comments on civic duty, colored by the post-war climate and justified with reference to theological teaching or their sense of calling to the priesthood. They made sense of their vocation by seeing their Christian identity and experience as members of a particular generation. Their children express a different perspective for, while affirming a similar commitment to altruism through work, they do so within a more individualistic culture shaping a more secularized outlook. These are more likely to justify morality within their working lives as a necessary corrective to what they see as the culturally dominant perspective which places profit before people, material gain before interpersonal well-being. Here the inalienable sense of the value of persons is strongly evident.

While many of our respondents value their careers in terms of such relational, altruistic and inter-personal dimensions, these sentiments are affirmed differently within different career types. Within the options different professional cultures offer for the expression of moral convictions we found a widespread tendency for respondents to discern a strong moral element within their career path, and to justify their work in terms of its moral integrity. Careers are treated as a channel for the expression of deeply held moral convictions and, as such, are viewed as an essential aspect of personal identity. Accordingly, a significant minority of 27 per cent regarded their career as 'essential' to their identity or purpose in life. The majority are, however, more cautious, with 56 per cent preferring to talk about their career as 'fairly important', a hesitancy that may reflect a tendency to interpret the question in a particular way – as referring to careers as income-driven, to the exclusion of a wider project of moral or civic responsibility. This may of course reflect a need to affirm a space for family time, or for voluntary work or religious commitment, more readily associated with the civic ideals shared across our population. However, many do appear to place their professional work at the center of their lives, and even those hesitant about affirming work as an essential priority do not thereby detach work from their sense of moral and civic commitment. Indeed, professional life appears as a key context in which such values may be expressed, furthered and fostered in others. This phenomenon is one we now examine in more detail, focussing on the significance these clergy children attach to their commitment to professional life. This is especially interesting when compared with their fathers' comments on their ministry and sense of responsibility to the public. With this in mind, we are able to trace the principal ways in which inter-generational resources appear to have been mobilized, showing how patterns in occupational engagement represented by the clergy father and by the context of his profession have been taken up within the professional lives of their children.

Recalled Exemplars: Altruism

There are as many ways of interpreting inter-generational influences as there are complications in identifying influences through empirical evidence. This we saw in Chapter 6. We are often presented with parallels between generations, common beliefs, habits, dispositions or practices, but whether there is a causal relationship between them is an issue altogether more contentious. From one perspective, much depends upon how this pattern is consciously conceived by those supposedly acting in response to it. Do those supposedly influenced by the previous generation conceive of themselves as being so moved? Again, perceptions of influence may change over time as childhood memories are re-interpreted in the light of ongoing life experience. For example, negative memories of an aloof and distant father once associated with emotional neglect may assume a sympathetic perspective as the adult grows older and appreciates the pressure their father was under at that time. It is just such changing perspectives that make straightforward patterns of inter-generational influence difficult to chart.

One approach to this problem is through 'exemplars', models of life constructed from past experiences or childhood memories and expressed in narrative accounts. Rather than assume that inter-generational influence may be charted in linear form on a blurred but ultimately unchanging map, we argue that if we are interested in influence as an aspect of identity construction, then we would do best to illuminate patterns of influence within the context of the narrative construction of identity. This approach was developed in the previous chapter in terms of religious identity, and we again turn to our extensive semi-structured interviews for emerging models of professional practice. These 'exemplars' usually, but not always, take the form of individuals whose memory persists into adulthood and serve as models of and for behavior, or as reference points invoked to make sense of life situations. Our questionnaire survey revealed such figures within the personal development of many clergy children. While we received a wide variety of answers, including God, friends, teachers and 'self,' some 63 per cent placed their parents in this category. Apart from exemplars in the form of significant individuals noted for their character, intimacy or charisma, we may also speak of exemplars in the form of social skills or practices associated with particular life experiences or events that have taken on significance over time. A discussion of some cases will allow us to develop this idea for the home as an exemplary context.

Our respondents commonly characterized the clergy household as a home that was also a public place concerned with the pastoral care of others. Whether these 'others' are viewed as outsiders or members of the community largely depends on whether this domestic peculiarity is recalled as a positive or negative experience. In Chapter 6 we cited those who viewed this tendency as an intrusion into their family life; the public nature of the vicarage compromised the privacy they hoped to maintain in their own homes, and in some cases, generated a feeling of coming second to the needs of the parish or diocese. Others, however, recalled the constant coming and going of parishioners through the vicarage from a different perspective, focussing on its inherent altruism through which they were able to construct a model for social responsibility in adult life. This focussed on the importance of providing for others in need and of handling them responsibly and with sensitivity whether within a family, church, general social life or the workplace. For example, one suffragan bishop's son, whom we call Peter, talked about his approach to dealing with the workers for whom he is responsible as an operations manager at a major transport facility. While seeing himself as an atheist, who now maintains a degree of cynical distance from the church, he nevertheless consciously traces the moral values influencing his work to his experiences of being raised in a vicarage. In his view, it was through confronting the strange but frequent presence of needy parishioners that he learnt valuable lessons about hospitality and coping with the needs of others. He reflects on the priority he gives to making time for those within his care, and relates this to the 'open door' of his childhood vicarage home, in which all would be welcome, including 'the tramps and the poor and the needy'. Moreover, he consciously and deliberately conducts his working life in this way because it is his conviction that this is the right thing to do. His job as a manager clearly involves a duty of pastoral care to the people who work for him.

This is by no means our only example of a clergy child approaching their occupation with a strong sense of moral responsibility towards others. In this case altruism is focussed upon more junior staff, with the relationship of manager to managed taking on a pastoral dimension. Another case took the form of a research scientist identifying parallels between his own duty of mobilizing his research team and his father's duty as bishop to mobilize and empower the clergy. For others their sense of altruism is directed towards those whose welfare is the object of their work, such as the surgeon who claimed his job allowed him to 'get close to people's humanity and human suffering', or the woman mentioned earlier, who works with children who are disenfranchised from the education system or, again, the school teacher driven by her mission to inspire and encourage her pupils to bring 'out the best in them'.

In other cases, rather than the experience of the clergy home, it is the father himself who is invoked as exemplar. One bishop's son reflected on his father's patience and kindness in dealing with people as an inspiration for his own professional medical practice. Most notably, he holds him as a figure of authentic moral conviction, without pretension, hypocrisy or cynicism: his father is 'enormously kind and patient', and 'genuinely values people in whatever level or position he finds them'. Though framed in a different way, one woman who had experienced a difficult personal relationship with her father because of what she saw as his authoritarian personality still viewed him as a valuable role model whose example had been essential to her working practice as a teacher. She mentions, in particular, 'listening to people', commenting on her father's ability 'to make everybody feel important and special', regardless of their social background. She goes on to recall his 'values of hard work, honesty, integrity, reliability, trustworthiness'.

Stephen, the social worker introduced in the previous chapter, perceives direct parallels between his own pastoral responsibilities in caring for children from difficult backgrounds, and his father's responsibilities as a parson. In fact, he even described his role as like a 'secular priest', focussed on the building of communities and helping people take control of their lives. He draws a correlation between his father's skills, inspired by clinical theology and focussed on counseling, and his own, focussing on a common passion for the therapeutic, for working alongside people facing their problems in a relationship of care and support. He sees 'close parallels' in their interests, which have emerged 'in different ways', through different professional routes. In developing his own interpretation of this connection, he suggested that those who entered the emerging field of social work in the late 1960s came from either 'a working-class background with socialist ideals or we were from an educated background with Christian ideals'. Hence his motivation for entering this career is traced directly to the values instilled in him as a clergy child. However, he also views the emotional distance that characterized his upbringing as a problem to be 'worked out' through his career, particularly by ensuring other children do not suffer from the same experiences. Some of these problems he attributes to boarding school, others to the emotional aloofness of his parents.

Here, the memory of boyhood's home is a focus for both positive and negative reactions in adulthood; theoretically speaking, it shows how the negotiation of spiritual capital can involve processes of both conformity and rebellion, as well as a complex selection of resources deployed to varying purposes in adult life. Altruism appears as part of a positive response to exemplars learnt through one's upbringing, but is also inspired by a counter-reaction to emotional distance. In this sense it highlights the positive moral resources, and the personal anxieties, associated with being raised in a clerical home. One deeply engrained conviction among the clergy children was less ambiguous, though also acted upon in a variety of different ways: the importance of public service, which deserves its own attention.

Public Service

If altruism refers to a personal orientation to those close by, public service, also embracing a constellation of ideas, values and activities, encompasses a more abstracted sense of duty to a wider community. As a key value motivating orientation to professional work it was expressed almost as a visceral, compulsive tendency: one emphasized how this value had remained a key 'driver' well into middle age:

> That powerful sense of duty within the family, within institutions and boarding school is still an important driver for me now. If you catch me around meal-time, you'll find me washing up. Not because I feel like doing it but because of my duty and before I can stop myself, my hands are in the water. I think for goodness sake leave the thing, watch telly instead, let it pile up. At the age of 56 being driven by [a] childhood sense of duty, but it's really potent.

While this illustrates an embodied orientation to general behavior, other respondents focussed on how their commitment to public service had led them to particular careers, as with the teacher who spoke of how her work made her feel she was 'doing something useful, putting something back into society'. Another who, after years as a translator, had made a decision to channel her talents and sense of the importance of public service into a new career in teaching likened herself to her mother in having 'very rigid ideas about what I think are valuable jobs', saying she could not do a job that was not serving in some way. In this respect, she feels 'teaching is an obvious vocational job'.

We shall return to the issue of vocation later, here we simply note how these comments reflect a common perception that careers pursued primarily for the sake of material wealth are somehow lacking in integrity. This tendency to gravitate towards careers concerned with the non-material may in part explain why so many of our respondents (45 per cent) had worked at some point in a creative, expressive field such as art, music or writing. This focus on 'giving something to society' is, of course, open to interpretation, and public service is perhaps less associated with art and the expressive than with education, and what has been called 'civic service', work that actively and materially enhances the well-being of a community (Bellah and Sullivan, 1987). The 72 per cent who had worked at some point within 'caring and nurture' may fall into this category, including careers in education, medicine and social work embodying the commitment to public service so frequently invoked as a moral priority. If professional life is an obvious outlet for this commitment, another is voluntary work. Indeed, if there is a discernible tendency towards affirming a sense of civic responsibility within the workplace it is, if anything, more apparent outside of that context. For example, one bishop's daughter refused to be led by a question that spoke of careers as 'vocational', preferring instead to speak of her voluntary work in her local church: 'it's not work, really, it's service, you know. I have a very strong sense [of] duty.' Indeed, it is the behavior of our bishops' children within the voluntary sphere that lends most weight to the argument that clergy children express a distinctive moral commitment. When we compare responses within our questionnaire survey to data available from the British Social Attitudes Survey, some interesting findings emerge. For example, while only 6 per cent of our population of clergy children claimed they were at the present time members of a political party – five Labour Party members, one member of the Socialist Workers' Party, and one member of the Conservative Party – this is still twice the percentage for the British population, of which only 3 per cent were members of any political party in 2000 (Park et al., 2001: 177). Our sample of bishops' children are also around 75 per cent more likely to belong to a trade union or staff association than the average British citizen,[6] and are four times more likely to take an active interest in environmental concerns, as expressed in membership of organizations such as the National Trust and Friends of the Earth.[7]

These figures indicate civic commitment through organizations whose work represents a public service of some kind. An important complement lies in the extent to which individuals commit their time and effort to these causes. Questionnaire respondents were asked whether they had engaged in any voluntary work during the past twelve months: political work, charitable work, religious/church-related work, or voluntary work of another kind. The results, compared with national figures, are represented in Table 8.4.

This shows the bishops' children as far more likely to engage in voluntary work than the average British citizen, especially where religious/church-related work is concerned. In other words, their commitment to moral causes, expressed in

---

6   Thirty-four per cent of our group are currently members of a trade union or staff association. BSAS have national figures for membership of trade unions and staff associations, but we would have to count the two values separately in order for our data to be directly comparable (figures for the two are combined here). However, this refinement will only serve to raise our figure, and so a large difference between the two groups is indisputable.

7   According to the BSAS 18th Report (Parkes et al., 2001), in 2000, taking all environmental organizations together, 13 per cent of the population were members, and that is not allowing for multiple memberships; 39 per cent of our population are members of at least one of these organizations, four times the national figures.

Table 8.4 Voluntary work by bishops' children compared with national trends

Type of Voluntary Work	Bishops' Children (%)	British Population (%)
Political work	7.4	3.6
Charitable work	32	20.5
Religious/church-related work	39.4	13.7
Other voluntary work	18.7	18.6
No voluntary work at all	37.7	77.25

institutional membership, is matched by a practical contribution to furthering these causes, a trend that may be explained with reference to a number of factors. First, one might relate the results to religious identity and ask if churchgoers at large are more likely to engage in voluntary activity. What little research exists in Britain suggests a tentative affirmative, with churchgoing positively associated with giving and volunteering in the wider community.[8] Social class, too, must be a salient factor, as is the related issue of expendable time and social networks.[9] It is also possible that the ideals associated with civic responsibility are somehow instilled more deeply in those raised within a clergy household, especially given the ideals of service and altruism clearly worked out and exemplified in the family life of many clergymen.

It is not surprising that the sons and daughters of senior Christian leaders have a keen sense of moral responsibility to the wider community, reflecting a stock of spiritual capital that figures prominently in their father's role as an advocate of the Christian faith and practitioner of its teachings, an exemplar that is especially powerful when filtered through its practical expression in a parochial context. It is one thing to be taught the importance of providing for the less fortunate, it is quite another to live within a home in which such provision regularly takes place. What is more interesting, however, is that there are cases when this spiritual capital is experienced as a negative resource, as something that constrains rather than empowers. In Chapter 6 we outlined aspects of upbringing that are often later perceived as having an ambiguous influence, such as the experience of living in a home that was very much a public space, or being subject to the inflated expectations of others. These are social factors, experiences shaped by the behavior of others that are beyond the clergy child's control. What we encounter here is something different: moral dispositions that have been internalized, and then later rejected, or at least modified, in light of subsequent life experience.

For example, for some respondents, their sense of moral duty was so deeply embedded that it later threatened to compromise other responsibilities. One woman,

---

8   Helen Cameron's examination of statistics gathered from the English 2001 Church Life Profile Survey suggests that 21 per cent of churchgoers are involved in social action through their congregation, 24 per cent outside of their congregation, with donations to non-religious causes practiced by 61 per cent (Cameron with Escott, 2002).

9   The 2001 British Social Attitudes Survey found that levels of organizational membership – including churches, sports clubs, trade unions and political parties – were lowest among the poor and less educated (Park et al., 2002: 205).

whom we call Helen, described her situation with some passion, emphasizing both her commitment to voluntary work and to the community, but also stressed her eventual realization that this amounted to a compulsive constraint upon her adult life. Her voluntary work had started to have a detrimental effect on her own career and, in some respects, upon her own family. She sees this compulsion to serve as directly inherited from her parents, saying: 'I've come to realize that this good works thing, sense of duty, service to others, is really deep in me, and that comes from my parents.' She adds, tellingly: 'there isn't a shred of business-mindedness in either of them'.

It is interesting that Helen articulates her parents' attitude not in terms of moral strength, but as a lack of 'business-mindedness'. There is a sense in which she views their pietistic evangelicalism as naïve and unworldly. She also speaks of her need to distance herself from them to achieve a sense of personal and spiritual autonomy that she sees as a precondition for realizing a sense of identity. It might be reasonable to view her effort to 'unlearn' the uncritical altruism associated with her childhood as part of the same process. In other words, personal tendencies traced to childhood upbringing are seen as constraints in the adult world, as barriers to achieving fulfillment and personal ambition. Strikingly, her attempts to 'unlearn' what she was taught as a child are self-conscious and deliberate, presented as a mature decision to liberate herself from an engrained *habitus*: 'it's almost like an addiction you know, to stop doing things for other people'.

Here, then, we encounter a complex process incorporating both an embrace of some childhood resources and a rejection of others. Public service, like altruism, can be associated with a wide-ranging constellation of ideas and experiences, some positive, some negative; some perceived as empowering adult life, others as a constraining influence. It may take the form of an engrained compulsion to adopt a mode of behavior that reflects ideas of service to others, whether expressed in a general moral disposition or in specific activities or a career. Such occupations often fall within the caring and nurture category, but may also be an interpretation of art and expression as a worthwhile engagement and celebration of the non-material. A third mode of response is also in evidence, among those clergy children who develop their commitment to public service through grander moral or political ambitions, set on a larger canvas, and often combined with a professional identity within the leadership/governance category.

Here, public service becomes moral leadership, sometimes enhanced by a sense of vision and a desire to change society for the better. For example, one suffragan bishop's daughter had pursued a lucrative career in marketing, and though she cites it as fulfilling it did not enable her to realize her long-standing ambitions of a moral and political kind. She reflects on her plans for life subsequent to her career break taken in order to raise her two children. Having earned her money, she says: '… now's the time to kind of put that back together with what I always did want to do which was, do something to move the world on a bit really'. She relates this to her long-standing ambition for political involvement which she traces to her upbringing both in terms of her father's ambitions for her, and his own example as a political animal within the church. She reflected on the fact that her father had always felt at a disadvantage in the church for not having an Oxbridge degree, and that this strengthened his determination that his children not suffer from the same prejudice. He nurtured high ambitions for them, as his daughter comments, with some humor: 'I know that my dad always wanted me to be prime minister, and I don't think I'll ever be prime minister, but I think I will go back some way towards what he wanted me to in the end.'

Counter-cultural Ethics

Values derived from a clerical household may also be applied in a professional context through what might be called 'business ethics' – the conscious and deliberate affirmation and application of an ethical framework within one's professional career. This is an interesting area in which clergy children are distinguished for their *continuity with* their parents, and the intention of some to distance themselves from the values of their own generation (Stewart, 1994: 231). In this respect they see themselves as affirming values which are counter-cultural, hence the comments of the respondent cited in the previous chapter on her 'battle with consumerism' and 'materialistic culture'. Another cited his mother's belief, itself inherited from her own parents, that material things are at best neutral and at worst bad, and related the inculcation of this value amongst her three children to the fact that none of his siblings had gone into 'big business', even though they possessed the skills to do so. While our culture may be characterized by a materialist consumerism, the clergy children of our study have deeply engrained in them a moral resistance to the values affirmed and celebrated by this culture.

Some felt a dissonance between their own values and those of 'the world' most acutely within a professional context, especially when they had pursued careers which have a reputation for being either 'amoral', that is, professional fields that do not generally or regularly appeal to a moral framework, or which are often viewed by outsiders as explicitly immoral, usually because of their tendency to prioritize profit above all other factors. Such accusations are most readily associated with business in the private sector, especially in large corporations that may have a dubious reputation with respect to ethical trading, management of employees and consumer accountability. One striking case study emerged in the figure of a successful London businesswoman, whom we shall call Vicky, whose father had been a suffragan bishop. She had worked in marketing, market research and in advertising, and considered her line of work to be one in which moral integrity was a relatively alien notion. Conscious of this, she deliberately toned down her moral convictions so as not to alienate her colleagues or appear too far wide of the professional norm. In this respect she reflects a capitulation to the privatization of morality within late modern Britain, and the idea that business practice might be held to account on moral grounds sits most uncomfortably with the enterprise culture of the 1980s, when this individual was entering the corporate world. Perhaps this partly explains her reticence to introduce any moral reasoning into her business practice in a way that was too obviously connected to her religious background. As she says: 'I would never invoke Jesus Christ in a meeting, but I think people would always have been pretty clear that I had a different moral view.' She offers examples of taking a salary cut when she was a director in order that some of her employees could keep their jobs, and asking her fellow board members to do the same, and of protesting about an advertising campaign featuring scantily clad women which she felt was inappropriate when it would be seen by children. She describes both stances as unpopular and unusual within her profession, but all the same they were issues upon which she felt compelled to make a stand, in part because of her father's example and teaching. She refers to her father's 'quasi political New Testament values', saying that these 'have been very much a part of how I've done my job'.

Another example is presented by a diocesan bishop's son who, after considering a vocation to the Roman Catholic priesthood, actually went into the media, producing television advertisements and short films. When asked whether he saw any of his father's values in his own job, he affirmed his determination to be 'scrupulously honest ... in a business where people are not', adding that he had decided he would 'rather go bankrupt than do things dishonestly'. He refers to the practice of using bribes to secure business deals, a convention he has come across repeatedly in his line of work, adding: 'I've always been completely straight about it [business]. There are serious boundaries that I will not cross.'

In this sense the corporate world provides an ideal arena for the affirmation of counter-cultural values, especially those deeply engrained moral convictions that are concerned with inter-personal conduct. In offering a context that is at best morally lukewarm and at worst morally bankrupt, it provides a setting in which strong moral convictions, especially those grounded in religious commitment, can gain legitimacy, vitality and novelty, simply by being counter to the norm. Both of the examples given above refer to individuals who are committed members of the Church of England, and while they affirm a strong moral stance within their professional identity, it is interesting that both seek to separate the expression of their moral values from their Christian roots, admitting that they would resist making an explicit connection between business ethics and their Christian commitment in the work context. As such, while their faith is not privatized, it is to a degree domesticated to the more secular conditions of the business world in which they work. It would appear that the spiritual capital inherited by clergy children allows for a creative and diverse appropriation when it comes to its application within a professional context.

Work as a Spiritual Pursuit

One of many distinctive aspects of being a clergy child is that Christianity and the church are issues on which one almost inevitably has a stance. It is unlikely that such a central dimension to one's upbringing – especially when one's father is a bishop – could generate an apathetic or utterly dispassionate response in adulthood. One instructive illustration might refer to the question of ordination; given their father's status, this possibility would for many of our respondents have been bound up in the high – sometimes unreasonable – expectations others projected on to them as they were growing up. Some clearly felt significant pressure to follow in their father's footsteps, and not just as a clergyman but as a senior and high-achieving one. While those bishops' daughters who are now middle-aged would probably not have considered this during their early years, the ordination of women in the Anglican Church post-1992 may have caused them to think again. Treating this as perhaps the most obvious means of integrating a professional and spiritual life, we asked our respondents whether they had ever considered becoming ordained. Some 12 per cent said they had, 82 per cent said they had not, while 6 per cent had actually considered the possibility and subsequently taken holy orders. This might be viewed as a very high rejection figure, and when asked why they had not considered ordination, the most common responses focussed on three distinct ideas. First, many felt what might be described as a dissonance of identity, that they were simply not appropriate candidates for the ministry. Some appealed to the language of vocation, explaining that they did not feel a sense of 'calling'. This theological concept was even applied by some to their chosen (non-clerical) profession: 'I was obviously "called" to do something else.' For some, their reservation at the notion of being ordained had less to do with a God-driven calling or its absence than with feelings of inadequacy: either their faith they judged to be insufficiently strong, or they unfavorably compared themselves and their ministerial potential to their father. As one put it:

> I always knew that I didn't want to be a priest because I never thought I'd be able to do it as well as my father did. I was always very impressed with how well ... he performed the role, he obviously had a tremendous faith ... I thought I'd never be able to match his abilities and I'd always be measuring myself and falling short.

Here, a distinctive role model had impressed a sense of radical difference and, while still seeing himself in continuity with his father's Anglican tradition, this individual has become resigned to a difference in personal gifts and skills. Another respondent felt his own faith was not 'sophisticated enough to communicate to others', suggesting the absorption of a role model perhaps centered around theological articulacy, rhetorical eloquence and depth of spiritual reflection. These qualities are often associated with an 'ideal type' of the Anglican bishop, and it is interesting to reflect on how these forms of spiritual capital are passed to bishops' children as Christian aspirations. In other words, does having a bishop as a father generate a particular image of 'the good Christian', perhaps focussed on theological sophistication, which informs processes of self-evaluation?

Second, some respondents explained their resistance to ordained ministry with reference to their reservations towards institutional religion. This applied to sons and daughters who had expressed an agnostic or non-affiliated religious identity and to some who situated themselves within the Christian, and in some cases, Anglican community. This reflects the increasingly cited tendency among the British population to remain 'religious' while harboring significant cynicism, and perhaps suspicion, towards its institutional forms, not least the established Church of England. Some clues as to why these individuals should hold such a view may be found in the third idea cited: that the experience of living in a clerical household had a negative impact upon their view of the church. One respondent said they had never considered becoming ordained, 'because one's life is never one's own in a parish and I did not want my family to grow up in a goldfish bowl!' Another mentioned the hours their father had worked, describing them as 'appalling', while one respondent commented that they had 'seen it from the inside – it's not nice!!' Here, it is the domestic reality of living in a vicarage that is focussed upon, and we explored in the previous chapter how such reservations may lead individuals to distance themselves from the church generally.

But such a negative response was not offered by all of our respondents: 12 per cent had positively considered the possibility of ordination, and 6 per cent (7 individuals) had actually entered into ordained ministry of the Church of England, including four in parochial ministry, one cathedral functionary and a college chaplain. In reflecting on this small minority, two cases reveal some interesting themes that are pertinent to a wider analysis. The first is the daughter of a diocesan bishop whom we shall call Elizabeth, the youngest of four who considers herself to be the most positive among her siblings when it comes to her view of her father's profession and the Church of England. While she affirms her ambitions to be a teacher as vocational, she prefers to connect her own vocation to her voluntary work within the local parish church. Her contribution to parish life, incorporating PCC membership, worship groups and helping to lead services, is something she considers to be an important service proceeding from her Christian faith. She has a belief that she should use the gifts given to her and associates this with a 'very, very strong calling, need, desire'. Her interpretation of this in terms of a vocation has led her to reflect on whether she may have a calling of a different kind, although she says her thoughts on the matter are unclear.

Elizabeth's comments are reminiscent of the almost visceral sense of duty that was invoked by one of our other respondents earlier in this chapter, reflecting a deep-seated obligation to serve, but in this case it is an obligation that is not resisted but is positively affirmed, and interpreted in vocational terms. In this case Christian commitment is conceived in practical terms, and we may speculate about whether a presentation of Christian vocation in the clergy home encourages an orientation to Christian identity that is work-focussed, measured by effort, service, labor and practical demonstration. For those with a strong parish connection, the local church may provide an ideal context in which this orientation may be put into practice.

By contrast, David (not his real name) is the son of a suffragan bishop, a clergyman of liberal catholic churchmanship. During his teenage years David had a radical conversion experience, and became a rather zealous evangelical, simultaneously arriving at a conviction that he wanted to become a clergyman. Interestingly, the difference in churchmanship between himself and his father has always informed their relationship, and has shaped the way in which David affirms a narrative of his calling. He is both aware of the fact that his father's position naturally invites the suggestion that he has followed in his footsteps, but also of his own need to affirm an autonomous experience of God's calling – conceived in evangelical terms – which has its own integrity. He resolves this problem by separating his father as role model from the dramatic experience of being called, which generated feelings of compulsion that have never wavered.

> At the very least you'd have to say that my experience of growing up in a vicarage opened up the possibility that that's something I could do … I had a role model in my head, and

it fell within my experience, my expectations of what a person might do ... but my sense of calling came, it felt to me, out of the blue ... I don't ever remember trying on the possibility for size – this is something I might do – until in the same instant that I found my own faith, I found a conviction that this is what I was supposed be, and that conviction has never wavered, and I find it very difficult to explain it or analyse it at all, but it's always felt to me as if doing anything else in my life would be running away from what I was made to do, and I don't think there was anything automatic about that; there were four of us children, we're not all ordained. I'm sure it stands in relationship to my dad's work but it is my vocation.

There is here a sense that David feels a strong need to distinguish his own vocation from the influence of his father, in order that his own commitment might maintain its own integrity. It is based on experience and personal volition, rather than on family inheritance that has an unpalatable inevitability about it. Here, vocation is conceived as something based on a divine force that intrudes into one's life and undercuts forces associated with family structure, childhood upbringing and inter-generational value-transmission. Unlike Elizabeth, who is content to affirm that the positive role model of her father has instilled the sense of service so central to her Christian commitment, David seeks ontological distance from his father's ministry, in order that a sense of genuinely personal commitment can be expressed. For Elizabeth, vocation is what unites the generations in a continuity of Christian service; for David, vocation divides them on grounds of churchmanship. While both describe very positive relationships with their fathers now, their orientations to work illustrate how those relationships can generate very different understandings of vocation.

The relationship between spirituality and work extends beyond the question of ordination. While the vast majority of our population had not considered going into ordained ministry, a much higher proportion nevertheless perceived a spiritual dimension in their professional lives. When asked in the questionnaire survey about the relationship between work and spirituality, 4 per cent felt their work hindered their spiritual development, 32 per cent felt their work was a channel for the expression of their spiritual values, while 59 per cent felt neither of these responses was appropriate. Within the 32 per cent who positively related work and spiritual life, there was a variety of occupations, although the vast majority (30 out of 39 individuals) slotted into the 'care and nurture' category described earlier, and no company managers or directors viewed their working lives in this way. In terms of how the two worlds were related, various patterns were in evidence, although most could be mapped onto a spectrum with 'implicitly informed by spiritual values' at one end, and 'explicitly deployed in the service of the expression of spiritual values' at the other. At one extreme we have those who, while affirming a clearly defined spiritual or religious identity, express a desire to keep this identity quite separate from their professional lives. For example, the media producer we mentioned earlier acknowledged that his Christian beliefs informed his business ethics but treated them as separate spheres of his life as much as possible. He also links his own reservations about explicitly affirming his own beliefs to his father's reservations about 'proselytizing', adding: 'I don't feel that part of my religious faith is to instruct or encourage other people to get involved ... I'd rather lead by example, frankly, and ... I think that that was probably what my dad was like.'

Most respondents were not so determined to privatize their faith, and yet for some the nature of their professional work allowed a more subtle engagement with spiritual matters. There were six individuals committed to an artistic or creative occupation, and four of them viewed their work as a channel for their spiritual values. While this is a low number, it should be read in light of the relatively high proportion (45 per cent) who had engaged in the creative sphere in a professional capacity at some point during their lives. It is a moot point whether certain careers lend themselves to spiritual engagement more than others, and whether those former artists would perceive a spiritual engagement if they were still pursuing this kind of career. However, it is undeniable that the creative arts allow for a personal expression that is less reducible to rational process and to an instrumental means to profit than many others field of work. Indeed, for those artists we spoke to, their work was presented as a site for the exploration and celebration of things spiritual, whether this is attached to a commitment to the Christian church, or part of a more open quest for identity. One diocesan bishop's daughter had rediscovered her talent for artistic expression after raising her children, and interpreted this as a god-given gift that is now central to her fulfillment in life: 'I've realized that I do have a gift, and I'm not using it, and God wants us to use our gifts, so my faith is really central to the fact that I've now come back to my art ...'. By contrast, we spoke to the youngest son of a diocesan bishop who was developing a professional interest in creative writing. On reflection, he was finding that his passion for writing allowed a kind of spiritual expression which reflects his rejection of religion as an external, institutional phenomenon and his embrace of a more open, spiritual journey, grounded in cultural experience.

A more explicit attempt to link spiritual values with conduct at work was affirmed by the many respondents who work in education. One school teacher saw her work as 'a way of being of service to other people' and associated it with 'living life as [a] faith process'. One head teacher said she tried 'to be a role model for my pupils and the staff I lead. I hope that my spiritual values are evident.' One respondent linked her orientation to working with excluded pupils to her commitment to Buddhism, which 'emphasizes taking action in your own community to improve people's lives'. Another had deliberately chosen to work in a school situated in a demanding area because she felt there was more need there for a Christian example. There are obvious links between the teaching profession and that of the clergyman, not least those related to pastoral duties, and we explored some of those links earlier on in this chapter. Whether one views one's moral commitment to public service as colored by spiritual values may depend on one's view of the relationship between Christianity and ethical responsibility, which raises the question of whether one can be committed to one without the other. Cases examined earlier suggest that they clearly can, and we may recall the example of Peter, whose atheist stance had not prevented him from viewing his upbringing in a clerical home as a positive moral resource, from which he had drawn exemplars which now inform his orientation to his professional responsibilities. In this sense, the difference between those who affirm a positive engagement with spiritual values at work and those who affirm these values as merely ethical may be small indeed, and the difference in practical consequences may be minimal.

A more distinctive orientation is found among those at the far end of the scale, who find themselves consciously and deliberately making room for the expression of spiritual values within the workplace. Hence one respondent, who works as a primary school office manager, said: 'I see my job as a form of Christian witness … [seeking to provide] Christian witness within commercial, political and educational environments.' Here, spiritual values make their way into working life in a more explicit fashion, and in a practical expression that may move well beyond the conventional expectations of the job. This was certainly the case with one school teacher, for whom school was a legitimate site for the expression of her Christian convictions. Occasionally she had found herself adopting an impromptu pastoral role. When relatives of staff and pupils had been ill or were experiencing a period of struggle, she had organized prayers in a way that non-Christians in her school clearly appreciated. When asked whether she sees much of a separation between values at home or at work, her answer, in polar opposition to the media producer cited earlier, was: 'a separation? No, no I wouldn't really.' For her, a practical, devotional style of Christian commitment had generated a particularly pro-active approach to maintaining a spiritual dimension to school life.

Chapter 9

Conclusion

Description is its own form of interpretation that explicit theories seek to enhance. Previous chapters furnish an interplay of people's interpretative accounts of their own lives and of our attempts at further analysis of the bishop and bishop's family as a multiple resource for the Church of England and for British society at large. Throughout this volume we have explored the nature and consequences of this resource in the priestly formation and episcopal ministry of late twentieth century bishops, in the dynamics of their family life and its influence upon the beliefs and values of their children. Such a focus on the family has a special relevance within wider debates about the fate of religion in the contemporary context. We are reminded of Danielle Hervièu-Léger's conviction that 'the collapse of the traditional family, wholly dedicated to biological reproduction and the transmission of a biological, material and symbolic inheritance from generation to generation, probably counts as the central factor in the disintegration of the imagined continuity that lies at the heart of the modern crisis of religion' (Hervièu-Léger, 2000: 133). There are, of course, major contextual differences between France and England, between clerical families and families at large and, more obviously still, between celibate Catholic and largely married Anglican priests and bishops. There are, too, major issues surrounding how the continuity of tradition is 'imagined'. Even so, our own study reflects Hervièu-Léger's concern, and in exploring the dynamics of family life within a specific ecclesiastical context, contributes to this broader debate about the dynamics surrounding the transmission of religious identity and religious values.

In doing so, this book offers a distinctive kind of sociological study of the Church of England in which large-scale generalizations have served as the background for a more detailed analysis of individual lives. We have employed a variety of perspectives in the hope of capturing something of the complexity inherent in the way these individuals and families have lived. Such complexity demands we move beyond conventional survey techniques, and our concern to take account of processes of meaning-making in proper context has highlighted shared narratives as sites for the construction of identity. We wanted to hear the accounts people gave of their own lives and of those of their relatives and, as we did so, we also came to see the importance of place as a context-shaping narrative. A picture began to emerge in which boys learned from parents, from their school, church, military service: their formation continued through university and theological college and from influential mentors in many of these contexts. They married, and their wives entered into their life and ministry to varying degrees as they also started families of their own as well as sometimes engaging in other work. From intense and successful parish life each gained advancement as dignitaries in the church with consequences for where and how they lived and also for their wife and children's style of life. Their children grew, were educated, and in some very particular ways and were, themselves, religiously influenced by their family background. They, in turn, took decisions on their own family life and mode of employment, many then having children of their own as the process of generational flow continued.

Interviews and questionnaire returns gave us access to a great deal of material on these individuals and families and the places that helped structure them. The tone of conversation was as vital as any statistics produced, the memories of vicarage and palace as significant as national committees chaired. To benefit from the qualitative knowledge acquired and the quantitative information gathered, we sought to combine approaches from both social anthropology and sociology, especially theories of symbolic exchange and spiritual capital, which helped furnish an illuminating analysis of the resources passed between generations, one sensitive to both the social construction of power and the quality of inter-personal relationships. While our aims here have been primarily sociological, we have sought to highlight broader implications for adopting this perspective, particularly at the interdisciplinary boundaries between the social sciences, history and theology. Not least, our analysis highlights how an examination of the lives of religious leaders within the context of family and domestic circumstances may provide the basis for a multi-dimensional approach to ecclesiastical power, important both for theologies of episcopacy, as illustrated in Chapter 3, and for discussions of the evolving values driving the Anglican communion in the later twentieth century.

Many diverse values and social trends have been complicit in the formation of the bishops, wives and children in this study. There is, in particular, the growth of pluralism. During the late twentieth century Britain became both more multi-cultural and multi-religious and the growth of mass communication through globalized media has brought people in touch with a broad range of cross-cultural information. In terms of religion, this has accompanied an expansion in the number of traditions, new religious movements, new spiritualities and quasi-religious New Age movements, all adding their wares to a diverse spiritual marketplace, and each competing for the interest of the late modern spiritual consumer. Partly as a consequence of pluralism, the spiritual consumer is also more empowered than ever before and yet the very plurality of religious products can, for some people, undermine the truth claims of any one of them, making it increasingly difficult for any to claim validity to the exclusion of all others. At the more liberal, open end of the spectrum, this has engendered a re-conception of the idea of participation with an emphasis not on exclusive and enduring membership but on involvement as often and however best meets the needs of the individual. In sum, religion is widely appropriated as a resource for meeting the subjective needs of the self: the self is the judge of the authenticity of each religious or spiritual phenomenon. This runs counter to the traditional world of receiving, maintaining and transmitting religious verities through self-sacrificial service, into which most of our bishops were born, trained and served. What is more, the generations covered in this study have been those most marked by this overlap of tradition and pluralism, serving as an ideal case study for the emergence of spiritual capital as a 'liquid resource' (Verter, 2003).

Accompanying this has been the increasing marginalization of the church after the 1960s. The church as an institution, and especially perhaps the established Church of England, has undergone a change of status. Officially it may still be regarded as central to the identity of the nation, allied to its political structures and committed to its moral and cultural needs, but in practical terms its power and significance has been seriously curtailed. This is reflected in the changing self-understanding of bishops, as detailed in Chapters 2 and 3. These leaders tended no longer to perceive their role in terms of the moral and religious leadership of the nation, but rather in terms of the pastoral needs of clergy and parish congregations within their own diocese. It is a process of change from nation to locality, from proclamation to nurture, and from worldly engagement to ecclesiastical insularity. Chapters 3 and 4 described how the bishops we spoke to considered themselves to have been functioning in a time of transition; the church they knew as children, students and curates was radically transformed by the time they were its episcopal leaders. Most importantly, there is a perception of cultural dissonance, of perceiving a church capitulating to a culture that has become increasingly cynical towards its traditions and moral standing.

And yet this is where our study becomes significant, as it focusses upon an axis of change, for the children of these bishops may be viewed as caught between the traditions of the church and the conventions of late twentieth century British culture. They were raised in close proximity to the church, exposed to its functions and day-to-day traditions, but have entered a culture that is largely detached from, perhaps even incredulous towards, these same things. While most adults will recognize a degree of difference between the values instilled during their childhood and the values which prevail in their current lives, this dissonance is more radical for clergy children because values associated with childhood were not simply reflective of parental convictions; they are associated with and partly expressed by an institutional presence that was all-consuming. Moreover, this institution, the Church of England, is a religious one, and as such imbued the values associated with childhood with a sense of profound and ultimate importance. When one's cultural surroundings imply the increasing irrelevance of these values, and of the institution that they represent, we might expect a dramatic response, perhaps of disillusionment and rejection, perhaps of traditionalist retrenchment. In this confrontation of value systems, we can see how this study provides some insights into the heart of the secularization process.

Family and Church

In the clerical and episcopal family, we encounter a distinctive arena for the interplay of religious and other values and for their transmission across generations. In some of these families, largely but not always those where a liberal theology drives the father's outlook, the children gain experience in discussion and are taught values of the importance of thinking for themselves. That intellectual capital comes into its own in the complex process of rejecting some and retaining and transforming other beliefs and practices. In that process the 'capital' is complemented, or perhaps it is better to see it as 'interpreted', through the appropriation of inalienable values derived from the example of their parents' lives. In relation to Hervièu-Léger's concerns, these adult clergy children afford concrete examples of how, in processes of religious change, 'continuity is capable of incorporating even the innovations and reinterpretations demanded by the present' while also partly challenging the idea that 'a characteristic of modern societies is that they are no longer societies of memory, and as such ordered with a view to reproducing what is inherited' (Hervièu-Léger, 2000: 87, 123). Indeed, part of the value of employing symbolic exchange theory is that it provides one means of assessing the impact of person-derived values upon other individuals. Of course we acknowledge recent changes in society and religion in Britain, but we are wary of overly rigid notions of what it is that is changing. At the level of individual lives, even those of a narrowly focussed group such as bishops and their children, the nature of change involves what might be called 'transformed retention'. And it is precisely the nature of transformed retentions that underlies our study of the individuals in the preceding chapters. We use this oddly paradoxical term to describe the critically creative process of adaptive change by which beliefs and values pass from parents to children, or from mentors to those they influence. In some respects this notion reflects our discussion in Chapter 1 of Beckford's idea that religious symbols and meanings may 'float free' from their traditional origins and 'be appropriated by non-religious agencies', not to mention Verter's (2003) conception of spiritual capital, which informs our understanding of religious influence in terms of a liquid and mutable species of capital. Our concern is, however, to draw attention to the fact that it is individuals who appropriate potentially floating values. Within this study these are not just any individuals but people close to the centre of one major religious tradition in Britain, a point to which we return in a moment. The relative freedom of attitude towards belief and practice often encountered in both these episcopal parents and children should not be taken too much for granted but should, at least, be seen as both part of cultural change and a feature of the church's life in the later twentieth century.[1]

We argue that the central axis of these processes is the family, and while this reflects recent work in social scientific circles, it is not an uncontroversial issue when considered within an ecclesiastical context. As such, it is worth highlighting Edward Norman's critique of the Church of England, its doctrine, ritual and leadership, precisely because of his identification of 'family values' as a preoccupation of the contemporary church. He argues that Anglican clarity over sexual morality only emerges in an 'explicit and articulate' way when it addresses 'family values', and even then it does so not on the basis of a biblical base, not 'inspired by the example of the Holy Family of Nazareth', but by a general social convention of families as a stable arena for rearing children and, ultimately, by a cultural grounding in 'patriarchy' (Norman, 2004: 54–5). For him 'family values' constitute the 'centrepiece of such social doctrine as the Church possesses at the present time', but they are, essentially, the values of 'the bourgeois concept of the family' whose 'key concept is stability' (2004: 40–41). It may, perhaps, be unfair to criticize Norman too much for his nostalgically sad and haunting image of the Church of England

---

1 It is worth noting that one of the most interesting, widely published, yet least read essays on religion and social change is that entitled 'Of Ceremonies: why some be abolished and some retained', and is present in the *Book of Common Prayer*, a text as fully alert to a 'reverence … for antiquity' as to 'new-fangledness and innovation'.

as a liberally half-captained, anchorless ship, lost on a groundswell of cultural and historical relativism, since it is obviously intended as a generalization that contrasts with his usually detailed historical scholarship. Still, his *Anglican Difficulties* book does give pause for thought and, in the light of our studies, it is difficult to agree with his claim that 'family values' are not 'derived from within the family unit at all', but comprise 'whatever social or moral values achieve ascendancy in the surrounding culture' (Norman, 2004: 55). While it is obviously the case that any family, or any other group for that matter, participates in its wider society, the individual members of a family have a great deal of influence on one another in how they appropriate and implement, accept or reject wider social values. The family appears as both a resource for, and a site for the negotiation of, emerging beliefs, values and commitments. In the human sciences life is just as complex as is doctrine in theology. Norman's suggested inspirational case of the Holy Family of Nazareth, for example, would offer very little indeed by way of a practical model for contemporary Christian ethics of marriage and family life. He invokes the current divorce rate and matches it with the suggestion that continuing relationships are, probably, equally as 'deeply unsatisfactory as working partnerships': all to the effect that 'the family can scarcely be considered all that stable as a nurturing environment for children'. Such generalizations have their place in certain types of social commentary and are valuable as potential benchmarks against which to compare and contrast our detailed, empirical observations. But they must also be open for criticism from the detailed case. In particular, we have been able to identify several values absent from Norman's descriptions yet vital for the families of church leaders we studied, and not without strong theological roots. These include service, altruism, hospitality, civic-mindedness, moral restraint, a critical perspective on culture – all notions arguably contingent on inherited and acquired spiritual capital, but fully understood only in light of symbolic exchange theory, which illuminates their positive and communitarian direction by emphasizing the inter-dependent nature of social life.

Members of bishops' families have often spoken of the family as a source of serving and helping others, most especially at the parish level. This has, quite often, involved the wife in a complementary or even 'shared' ministry with that of their husbands, sometimes to the apparent detriment of any career of their own. While it would be easy to interpret this in Norman's terms of patriarchy, it is often more complex than that and involves the wife in her own orientation to Christian service. Children too have spoken of the family as a context within which they were involved in some kind of concern for other people who came and went, even though, for some, this meant a relative lack of privacy and quite contradicted Norman's notion of 'tight, small units of modern bourgeois practice' (Norman, 2004: 41). Of course, we have noted how such clerical families are different from many others in society, others into which clergy children sometimes wished to escape. It may be that this very fact of difference, with the family serving a distinctive occupational purpose for priests and bishops, furnishes one reason why 'family values' may have been of high significance for Church of England leaders' concerns, even though that is not the explicit rationale advanced for the importance of 'the family' in their theological thinking. This would be expected if, as previous chapters have demonstrated, the clerical family is itself a complex resource of and base from which the priest and the bishop operate within society. Its social and theological importance is enhanced by its practical usefulness within ministry.

We have presented sufficient evidence to indicate that the family itself serves as a kind of validating arena from which the bishop moves out into his ecclesiastical and social ministry. The family, conceived in a certain form, lends legitimacy as well as practical utility to the processes surrounding the Anglican bishop. Here we recall Talcott Parsons' (1956) argument that the family serves the two functions of socializing the young and stabilizing the personalities of the parents, although within this context, a notion of 'stability' acquires the function of partially validating the father's work. 'Stability', often constructed in some cultural and ecclesiastical circles in terms of traditional gender roles and a wife and children compliant with the norms of respectability associated with the Church of England and its hierarchy, becomes a byword for legitimacy. Here, the innovations of Rosalind Runcie as an 'unorthodox episcopal wife', recalled as liberating by some bishops' wives, take on new meaning, indicating as they do the ways in which the conduct of the partner (and children) is brought to bear on perceptions of whether a clergyman is suitable for episcopal office (Carpenter, 1996: 49). As such, when the family's 'stability' serves the function of providing a basis for validation, it can become a force for conservatism in the church, a point not insignificant in broader western contexts where 'family values' frame an intolerant attitude towards cultural innovations such as homosexuality and female empowerment that challenge the social order of the traditional nuclear family.[2]

The limited amount of material we possess on unmarried bishops also reinforces this point in that they have reflected upon the potential limits placed upon their work by the fact of not being married, an area ripe for fruitful research in comparing, say, Anglican and Catholic episcopates. As one bishop commented, '... it might have helped being married. [Being single,] people seem less sure of coming to you with problems, especially marital ones ... The church [now] wants a good family man.' This, in some ways, marks a significant development in how the episcopal role and its symbolic associations have evolved in recent years, working steadily away from the bachelor archbishops of Lang and Garbett, and the childless married archbishops, Temple and Ramsey. Indeed, Geoffrey Fisher (Archbishop of Canterbury, 1945–61) might be seen as something of an innovation in this respect, being the only Archbishop of Canterbury in the later twentieth century whose public status was also expressed through the extended embodiment of a large nuclear family.[3]

And yet the vicar's and bishop's family differs significantly from the tight, bourgeois unit, the divorced middle-class family, the single-parent family and the

---

2   In this sense, Edward Norman (1976) is right to highlight the 'bourgeois family' as a model that informs how families are evaluated in the Church of England. Our departure from his analysis has to do with his insistence that associated emerging values are derived exclusively from the broader culture, rather than partially nurtured and negotiated within the structures of the family itself.

3   Archbishop Geoffrey Fisher, himself the son of a parson, was the youngest of ten children (although two died early); he married in his thirtieth year – four years after being ordained as a priest – and he and his wife, Rosamond, had six sons.

co-habiting partnerships that grew in number significantly during the later decades of our period of study. The clerical family may even display features more characteristic of a kind of 'extended' family, not in the accepted kinship sense but in terms of the fictive kinship inherent within a particular conception of Christian social life. Unlike the celibate Catholic 'father' of a parish, the ordinary Church of England vicar and, in the ways we have described, also the bishop works out of the context of an actual family 'into' the church-family. Here, symbolic exchange theory aptly accounts for the inalienable values that pass within families and becomes their own form of both cultural and spiritual capital available for deployment within church and society.

One prime theological rationale for the supra-familial 'family' also relates to the anthropological concern with symbolic exchange as expressed, for example, in the phrase 'making the stranger less unknown'. This 'sacramental phrase', as perhaps we might view it, was employed by Jacques Godbout to describe the purpose of symbolic exchange or the gift-system as opposed to the goals of the market and of the welfare state that tend to depersonalize individuals (Godbout with Caillé, 1998: 62). Indeed, recognition of this is, for example, inherent within the British Government's more recent desire to relate to local charities and what are regularly described as 'faith communities' as potential agencies mediating between impersonal governmental policies and local populations. At the church's theological and ethical heart, one that beats strongly in the narratives of our bishops, lies the personal service one person 'renders' to another, and not a service 'dispensed' to a 'client', the latter situation seen by Godbout as being increasingly the case in agencies of the Welfare State. This is the problematic challenge of and for the bishop as both pastor and manager within the church. But it is also deeply significant when we ask how a bishop can be a 'father' of Christians – whether as Christ's flock or pilgrims journeying into God's love – and also be a father of his biological family. For flocks, pilgrims and families all take time and energy, as previous chapters have shown.

Family and Capital

Though the clerical father may not have always vested as much time in his children as did his wife, the clerical home that was created through his occupation nevertheless bequeathed certain benefits. Its busy interaction with many sorts of people, despite the frustration that caused to some family members, still generated considerable spiritual capital from which the children benefited in later life, just as it added to the working spiritual capital of their father. Accordingly, while processes of identity construction among our population of clergy children are many and varied, they tend to share a common set of concerns that they need to negotiate through their narratives as adults and which runs counter to the cultural norm. To expand on this, modernization has brought with it a separation of work and family, so that ties between family members were weakened and the familial intimacy which was a consequence of working together in an integrated environment was replaced by a greater tendency towards individualization (Bengtson, Biblarz and Roberts, 2002: 45–6). Hargrove, drawing from Christopher Lasch's influential study, takes this analysis further, arguing that:

> while both family and church were in earlier times institutions that linked individuals with the larger society, they are now sought out as refuges from that society. Lasch's *Haven in a Heartless World* (1977), makes this case for the modern experience of the family. It can also be applied to the church: In modern society, both are havens in which people expect to be protected from the ravages of the impersonal public arena, and in which they seek help in the pursuit of a meaningful self-identity. (Hargrove, 1983: 29)

Evoking Edward Norman's description, the modern family is presented as privatized, focussed primarily on the intimacies and subjective concerns of its members. It is no longer concerned with matters of work, education or health, and perhaps of religion, all of which have been deferred to specialist agencies, allowing the family to be treated as a refuge from the uncertainties of the outside world, a 'refuge' also open, of course, to enclosed abuse. Still, if we can argue that this trend had become entrenched by the second half of the twentieth century, we may view the clergy family as a peculiar exception to the cultural norm. Work is maintained as a family concern to a much greater extent than might be expected in most other careers: the clergy wife, as we saw in Chapter 5, is often expected to be the other partner in a 'shared ministry' with her husband, the children are often expected to attend and take active roles in their father's church, and the clergy family is very much viewed by outsiders as representing the work of the clergyman, so that family life and pastoral work become overlapping spheres. The clergy home may be presented as a haven from secularity, and yet it is an imperfect haven in so far as it does not offer a clearly delineated territory that is set apart from other social spheres. Rather, the nature of the clerical role, in both its parochial and episcopal forms, means that other spheres are allowed to intrude into family life, as both embodied in the figure of the father, and to a degree the mother, and through external agents who impose expectations and introduce processes which are alien to conventional family life.

This does not inevitably amount to feelings of alienation on the part of clergy children. As many who took part in our study were keen to point out, many of their experiences were welcome and positive and are now looked back on with considerable favor. Furthermore, this arrangement of family life was 'normal' to them and in many cases has never been perceived as problematic, not least because of the lack of any comparable alternative. And yet expressions of discomfort of a particular kind – emphasizing intrusion, exposure and a confusion of roles and expectations – are so prominent in our data that it is impossible to dismiss Lasch's arguments as irrelevant. In other words, there is some evidence for the claim that clergy families, while bequeathing significant stocks of capital, also generate an environment that sits uneasily with broader changes in western culture, and perhaps at times works against processes of positive adaptation.

To be more specific, clergy families appear to live within a peculiar kind of domestic structure, one that blurs the boundaries between spheres of experience that, otherwise, are kept relatively discrete. The three main spheres of social life that are confused are those of family, work and religion, and that confusion is felt all the more keenly when clergy children become old enough to encounter the cultural norm, offering its more clear-cut delineation. Hence the searching out of a surrogate family by one daughter, a family in which life could be discussed outside of an evangelical discourse. Hence the growing awareness of clerical peculiarity through experiences at school, where the distinctiveness of the clergy child's situation is sometimes uncomfortably unveiled. Hence the comments of one bishop's son, who was especially aware of the peculiarities of his upbringing because he had become a clergyman himself and faced the complications that his father had. He even went so far as to say that he and his siblings had been 'subsumed into the pastoral process, not necessarily with our consent'.

The problem of boundary confusion is well cited in the limited literature that exists on the peculiar experiences of clergy children. Hardy expresses this in terms of an 'ethic of self-sacrifice', possessed by the clergy family, that 'tolerates repeated instances of ambiguity or intrusion.' (2001: 549) The blurring of emotional boundaries in the clergy home is viewed as a negative experience, demanding a more clear delineation of boundaries in order to facilitate 'authentic self-expression and self-identity exploration.' (Hardy, 2001: 548). The need for clear boundary distinctions between professional ministry and family life is acknowledged within pastoral theology, as a necessary prerequisite for the effective deliverance of pastoral care (Strange and Sheppard, 2001). It is also implicit in Moy and Malony's recommendation, based on a psychological study, that ministers need to insulate their families from the multiple pressures of their vocation if healthy family life is to be sustained (1987: 63). In her study of pastors' children among Seventh Day Adventists, Anderson (1998) found that those most likely to report thoroughly positive views of their upbringing 'described a loving home with involved parents who gave them the freedom to be themselves. They described their parents as genuine, sincere, loving God, and *having the ability to separate church from home*' (Anderson, 1998: 401; our emphasis). Indeed, Anderson goes on to argue, on the basis of her data, that clear boundary maintenance is a crucial factor in determining whether a clerical upbringing leads to a religious commitment in adulthood (1998: 404). Based on a British study of clergy stress, Burton calls for clearer boundaries to be drawn between the job and home life, and argues that stress is in part down to a blurring of boundaries between work and home life, and to a lack of support from the church hierarchy (Burton, 1999). And in a book aimed at assisting clergy children through their 'identity crisis', Cameron Lee highlights importance of clear boundaries within the clergy family, and of dangers of boundary violations (Lee, 1992: 33). He even lists the six most common boundary violations within clergy families, including the demands of the pastor's professional role and image being allowed to contaminate the parent–child relationship, and the congregation expecting too much of the clergy family's time and energy (1992: 53).

It is our contention that the negotiation of spiritual capital by the clergy children of our study can be understood in many ways as a response to this blurring of the boundaries of work, religion and family life which was so central to their childhood experience. Moreover, their attempts to forge an orientation to religion and professional life can be interpreted in many cases as an attempt to separate out these spheres in their own lives in a sustainable way. Indeed, this may explain some respondents' perception of a direct link between their own values and those of their father's vocation, alongside a determination to make sense of their worth as purely moral, social or applied professional skills. Work and religion converge around the same values, but are structurally separated, producing an alternative moral order. We are also reminded of how some clergy children have affirmed a religious identity only after separating themselves in some way from the institution of the Church of England, which is associated with both a lack of spiritual authenticity and the confused boundaries of childhood family life. This is not to argue for a negative presentation of a clerical upbringing, from which individuals liberate themselves as adults. Rather, it reflects a desire to map the complex ways in which clergy children negotiate the spiritual capital bequeathed to them on the basis of their father's position and their experience of a clerical household, and which they deploy in their narrative constructions of professional and religious identity. Here, we might mention Jon Davies' argument, that in the modern context the family is centered around and defined by a voluntary contract between husband and wife (Davies, 1993: 88–9). Children, as 'involuntary members', are then forced to compensate for their relative marginalization by maximizing their freedom from the family. In other words, there is a wider cultural impetus to realize identity by seeking *independence from* one's biological family, so that in seeking to disentangle themselves from the blurred boundaries of the clerical home, clergy children are re-aligning themselves with the cultural norm. What we highlight here is that, while this is a fair analysis, it is easy to overemphasize the element of detachment. Our case studies suggest that the primary context of identity development is indeed not the family as a bounded entity, it is the wider society, but with the family remaining significant as a site beyond which and in relation to which one's identity is ultimately realized.[4]

In light of this dominant trend, it is worth noting that a minority of clergy children have embraced the integrated model of religion, family and work associated with their parents. They have adopted this arrangement as a source of meaning and stability in a changing and morally dubious culture. The most obvious examples of this are of those women who have themselves married clergymen and adopted a family and professional lifestyle that is the mirror image of their parents' pattern. Here, the family may be interpreted as perpetuating experiences associated with the original clerical home, in which spiritual and domestic concerns were fused, possibly heightened further by the symbolic status elevation to the Episcopate and the social consequences that this entails. Some have taken this model further, and adopted a more radical version of this inherited family model in order to express a more counter-cultural form of Christianity. Archetypal here are those evangelicals – some of them clergy – who have rebelled against the more liberal Anglicanism of their fathers; these display a certain acceptance while nevertheless re-applying their spiritual capital in a fresh direction. Indeed, one might argue that within an inter-generational framework, capital is expressed with more symbolic effect when it stands in opposition to other sources of power, and within such a context the father and his status is an obvious focus of self-assertion.

---

4   As also supported in the work of Bengtson, Biblarz and Roberts (2002) and Furlong and Cartmel (1997), discussed in Chapter 1.

The Bishop as a Site of Cultural Intensification

This status is perhaps worthy of further comment, in terms of the significance of defining oneself in relation to an imposing parental role model. While psychological studies might focus on the implications of being the son or daughter of a religious leader in terms of the need for boundaries and a sense of independent identity, our study also highlights the issue of the bishop as, himself, a symbolic figure. More than representing just patriarchy and authority, he participates in a constellation of values and associations by virtue of a public status conferred both by society and the church. To conclude our analysis of this phenomenon we recall and develop the notion of cultural intensification, already alluded to in Chapter 7. This will provide one helpful way of thinking about the place of symbolic persons and places within everyday life. It starts from the assumption that major cultural values tend, ordinarily, to be implicit and assumed, they underlie custom and convention and are simply taken for granted. But this idea of taken-for-grantedness of life is one that, itself, requires some attention. As Alfred Schutz demonstrated in his phenomenological studies 'the expert, the man on the street, and the well-informed citizen', each possessed their own form of taken-for-granted ideas (Schutz, 1971: 123).

At specific times and places or through particular events and experiences such taken-for-granted values are brought to sharp focus or given some prominence. They may assume some symbolic form and be presented by ritual means. Experiences such as bereavement may also, for example, cause an unexpected disruption to the ordinariness of things, one might even expect moments within formal education to prompt similar experiences. More expectedly, formal ritual has the effect of causing a kind of pause within the ordinariness of life and invites popular engagement with the values its symbols enshrine and express. This is widely the case with rites of passage including marriage and, for example, the ordination of priests or the consecration of bishops. But we have even seen how the letter raising the issue of episcopal appointment caused just such a disruption within the ordinariness of things for many of our bishops. But a ritual pausing to focus on prime beliefs occurs on a much more frequent basis in connection with rites of intensification such as the Eucharist or daily prayer. This idea of rites of intensification has been practically ignored in liturgical studies whose interest has, for example, been more preoccupied with rites of passage. But rites of intensification, as with the Eucharist or other regularly repeated services, have the important function of drawing the participant's attention to prime beliefs and dominant values. This highlighting and pinpointing of beliefs is not, however, simply a rational or intellectual process but one in which the emotions are activated and energized and, perhaps, faith evoked in a renewed commitment.

From that specific use we have taken this notion of rites of intensification, originally developed by Chapple and Coon,[5] and developed it into the idea of 'cultural intensification' so as to broaden its application from specific rites to wider religious or cultural phenomena including bishops, their families, and even their

---

5   Chapple and Coon (1942: 410) believed that rites of intensification were far more significant than rites of passage within the development of 'complex religious institutions'. See also Davies (2002): 139–40.

palaces. We see cultural intensification as a notion helping us differentiate between the way people pursue ordinary levels of engagement with prime cultural values on the one hand and further levels elicited by particular circumstances on the other. For most church members bishops are relatively distant figures encountered at special ritual events; for many clergy, too, their bishop is likely to be a not particularly well-known figure. Part of the symbolic significance of bishops lies in their centrality to the key ritual of ordination, to their authority in making new priests and consecrating new bishops. Such 'authority is intrinsic to liturgy',[6] and became increasingly important in the Church of England as that institution became dramatically more Eucharist-focussed as the twentieth century progressed. To meet with such a man, then, as with any leader within society or of an institution, is to engage in a special event. In terms, for example, of Mary Douglas's anthropological way of thinking, it is to draw near to a source of power in society (Douglas, 1966), a power vested in a system that, as far as the Church of England is concerned, is grounded in a sense of tradition, albeit particularly conceived and invented, and one with bonds with the state that confer an additional dimension of influence. The church is not, however, simply a kind of technical memory 'storage system' (Douglas, 1987: 70) but one that is embodied in designated persons, most especially its bishops. It is in this sense that we may speak of a bishop as a person in whom there is a cultural intensification of Christianity. He is taken to embody the values of the faith, which are thereby, in a sense, enshrined in him.

Often, things associated with a focus of cultural intensification, with what the anthropologist Roy Rappaport called 'ultimate sacred postulates', share, to some extent, in that 'intensification', that 'ultimacy', that sense of deep import and significance (Rappaport, 1999: 287). This is what happens in the case of a bishop's family and palace. So, 'going to the palace', or 'meeting with the bishop', or perhaps even 'being at school with' a bishop's child, may be regarded by some in wider society as significant and in our terms expresses an aspect of 'cultural intensification', although one that is perhaps waning in our post-Christian context. But what of the views of a bishop's wife or children, those who are intimately and domestically familiar with him? We have shown how some of these dynamics of relationships work, and how they are complexly intertwined with personality factors. Some episcopal offspring spoke of their experience as one that demystified any 'intensification' that people at large might have. Others remained in awe of their father's qualities and abilities, sometimes feeling some distance from their father and his religion. Yet others needed to move into new forms of religious expression before personal authenticity seemed possible.

Vagueness and the Perpetuation of Tradition

Alongside this theme of cultural intensification, and its import for bishop, family and home, we come to a final reflection on a topic that emerged from the way some

---

6   Rappaport's study of ritual and the sacred is amongst the most extensive and incisive of any twentieth-century anthropological study, with many implications for Christian liturgy (1999: 284).

bishops evaluated their own theological position – that of vagueness. Though it might seem paradoxical to align the rather positive notion of intensification with what would seem the negative notion of vagueness, we wish to raise it here in a concluding speculation that offers scope for further research.

In Chapter 2 we saw how 'vagueness' was an appropriate description for two broad contexts: one concerned bishops who found it hard to pinpoint a close party alliance within the churchmanship scheme of the church from the outset of their ministry, another accounted for their self-awareness of having changed theological stance during the course of their ministry. This sense of vagueness embraced an inclusive attitude to religion, to different kinds of people and to God. We did not interpret this in any negative sense nor align it with any form of intellectual clumsiness or moral lassitude but, rather, spoke of its potential adaptive significance for men having to operate with and amidst a variety of committed personnel both within the church as an institution and across wider society. In this respect the bishop emerges as a multivocal symbol, and those men who occupy this status often self-consciously and deliberately embody this multivocality, resisting codification and any straightforward alignment with any single tradition. This tendency invites various explanations, not least relating to the diplomacy demanded of high office, the fact that long-term experience, not to mention intellectual capital, fosters an awareness of complexity which leads to a resistance to being 'pinned down', and the dominance of a liberal/pragmatic culture of leadership in the Church of England that is centered around these very qualities. In one sense such 'vagueness' could also be interpreted in terms of the broad English attitude of reticence over the expression of personal belief and an accepting attitude towards the varied views of others. This is, in part, a cultural response to previous centuries' religious antagonisms[7] as well as to religious developments in the twentieth century. Certainly this is a complex issue demanding its own detailed account for any era.[8] We might also view 'vagueness' in terms of the taken-for-granted nature of religion embedded in society, perhaps a cultural survival from the Christian Britain that Callum Brown argues was dramatically challenged by the 1960s. On this understanding, people simply hope that religion will be adopted by others, including their children, as a matter of course, especially when there exist regular forms of religious attendance and ritual participation, as was the case for

---

7   See Leslie (1933: 91) for the late nineteenth-century 'victory of tolerance' following the Oxford Movement and subsequent legal cases over ritual expansion in Anglicanism.

8   In the earlier nineteenth century, for example, there was considerable doctrinal debate, and not a little animosity, surrounding Newman's Oxford Movement. Its Tract 80, one of the many theological essays that prompted 'Tractarian' as one name for this group, was entitled *On Reserve in Communicating Religious Knowledge*, and advocated its own form of caution over inappropriate parading of religious doctrine. It prompted vigorous opposition from more Protestant Anglican clergy who decried any sense of hidden feature or *Arcani Disciplina* to the faith, and advocated preaching 'without reserve … explicitly and prominently' key doctrines such as that of the Atonement (Townsend, 1838: 40–41). Whether such 'reserve' influenced subsequent pastoral practice would demand further research; certainly, Anglo-Catholicism influenced significant sectors of the Church of England and, for example, heightened the status of priesthood and fostered the centrality of bishops interpreted in terms of the Apostolic Succession.

most of the bishops and families in our study. But, finally, there may be another aspect to 'vagueness', one that relates it to 'cultural intensification', and it is with this speculation that we conclude our reflections. It may be that 'vagueness' in this church's leaders affords a means of framing cultural intensification. This complex situation allows a bishop to operate over a wide liturgical scheme of churchmanship, to entertain a spectrum of doctrinal schemes, to extend his ecclesiastical identity into a wide range of social worlds and to convey a sense of divine engagement with history and humanity.

Appendix

The Clergy and British Society, 1940–2000: The Study

From the outset, our study had three main, interrelated, aims: (a) to chart the ministerial development of senior Anglican clergymen; (b) to assess how the responsibilities of leadership shape the home life of clergy families, and (c) to trace how each of these factors contributes to the developing identities of the sons and daughters of these clergy. All require the collection and analysis of empirical data, and as our intention was to furnish a sociological study of living individuals, this data was to be gathered via survey and interview methods. It is only in communicating with the individuals in question, and thus generating primary data, that we may piece together a thorough and authentic study of the social influence of the Church of England.

Pilot Studies

In order to gauge initial ideas and test our working hypotheses, we first interviewed six retired Anglican bishops as pilot studies. These were selected on the advice of a professional colleague who knew these individuals personally, although an effort was also made to arrive at a broad range of churchmanship and experience. These interviews were transcribed and analyzed as a means of developing initial ideas and as a basis for the development of our research methods. Questionnaires and interview frameworks were subsequently constructed in light of important lessons learnt from these pilot studies, although the studies were also valuable in their own right and were later incorporated into our general analysis.

The Survey

Our next step was to plan a postal questionnaire survey, which would encompass all living retired clergy who had served as bishops in the Church of England, their wives and their adult offspring. We first wrote to all of these bishops, gathering their contact details from *Crockford's Clerical Directory*, to inform them of our intentions. This was a useful exercise, as several responded saying they would rather not be involved, and we received letters from families informing us that some of the bishops on our list had recently passed away. This reduced our population to 95 individual bishops, 66 of whom had living spouses, and 87 of whom had living children. We constructed a questionnaire for each group. Questionnaire A was addressed to married bishops, and included questions on their early life, ministry as a clergyman and bishop, reflections on the nature of the episcopal role, and on how their ministry has affected the life of their own family. Questionnaire B was addressed to unmarried bishops, included in this study as a comparison group, and included the same sections but without the questions on family. Questionnaire C was addressed to bishops' wives, and included questions on their early life, their professional life, and their own families, specifically focussing on how their husband's career affected home life. Questionnaire D was addressed to clergy children, and included questions on childhood in the clergy home, career and professional life, and on their own families, particularly how the values learnt during their own childhood are present in their current home life. In all four questionnaires we also included a section on general social and religious values, in order that patterns of agreement and difference could be measured across the generations and between families. For the sake of maintaining a straightforward and speedy correspondence, we sent all questionnaires in sealed envelopes in batches, addressed to each of the bishops on our list, with a request that they pass on the relevant questionnaires to their wife and children. These were sent out in the summer of 2002, and we received a steady stream of completed questionnaires over the following twelve months or so. The eventual response rates were 63 per cent for the bishops, 65 per cent for their wives, and 52 per cent for their children.[1] These returns were then analyzed using the SPSS program.

The Interviews

Given restrictions on finance and time, it was decided that we would attempt to conduct around fifty extended interviews, with half covering bishops (and, where possible, their wives) and half bishops' children. In as many cases as possible we would also seek to match up bishops with children, so that inter-generational comparisons could be drawn and correlations established on the basis of interview data. We would also restrict ourselves to one child per family, in order to maximize the spread of the sample. With this in mind, the selection of bishops was made first, and the selection of children partly based upon those bishops selected.

In selecting which bishops to interview, we were faced with a collection of 42 (that is, 72 per cent of those bishops who returned completed questionnaires were also willing to be interviewed). It was decided that a stratified random sample would be taken from these, taking into account the general distribution of generation (age), churchmanship (based on theological college attended) and episcopal status

---

1   These figures need to be treated with some degree of caution because of the method used to administer the survey. While sending batches of questionnaires to bishops simplified correspondence and arguably strengthened our response rate, it also meant that bishops were the effective gatekeepers: they had it in their power to withhold the questionnaires from their entire families if they so chose, and some clearly did. This is, of course, beyond our control, but it does mean that it is necessary to calculate the response rates as two separate sets of figures: (i) The level of response from among all those within a category who – as far we can tell – had an authentic opportunity to respond, that is, they received a questionnaire in the post, and (ii) the level of response as an indicator of the coverage of a particular population. Response rates of the first kind are given above, rates of coverage are for bishops 63 per cent, for their wives 59 per cent, and for their children 46 per cent.

(diocesan or suffragan) among the entire population of retired Anglican bishops in the Church of England. The generally idea was to acquire a body of interview data that could be seen as representative of the population of retired Church of England bishops and their families.

However, there were a few bishops whom we decided to interview regardless of this process because of their status and influence. We judged that these individuals might furnish us with important information about the development of the episcopate in general, and about the culture of the hierarchy of the Church of England, having themselves occupied its highest echelons. Moreover, these figures and their families present case studies for the impact of senior episcopal status (with all the pressures of power that this brings) upon the clergy family, and hence serve as potentially extreme cases of the kind of family dynamic we are principally interested in. For these reasons we decided to approach these figures for interviews apart from the general sampling procedure.

In addition to these figures it was deemed appropriate that we interview at least two non-married bishops. This way, comparative comments may be made on the difference that family life makes to the evolution of the episcopal role and its effect on personal values. Just over 10 per cent of our population had never been married, and only five individuals had completed questionnaires *and* agreed in principle to be interviewed. Interestingly, all were trained in a theological college associated with a 'central' or 'catholic' churchmanship. One bishop was randomly selected from each group.

This initial selection procedure presented us with 5 bishops. The remaining 20 would have to be randomly selected from the rest of the available population, but within certain boundaries so as to achieve a representative sample. We decided it was most important to achieve a range of bishops based on the spread of generations, churchmanship and Episcopal status represented in the wider population. Of course, this was subject to certain practical constraints: for example, not all bishops had agreed to be interviewed, and some strands of churchmanship were better represented than others. It was impossible to impose strict stratified sampling according to age, because – understandably – many of the very elderly bishops (born before 1920) had either not returned a questionnaire or had expressed a preference not to be interviewed. With that in mind, the random selection was adjusted merely so that broad trends were reflected, that is, that those born in the 1920s comprised the largest group, followed by the 1930s group, and with a handful of older bishops where possible.

The principal guidelines for selection were based on the distribution of episcopal status and churchmanship within the wider population of retired Anglican bishops in the Church of England. In reflection of this population, it was decided that 60 per cent of the interviewees would be former suffragan bishops, and 40 per cent would be former diocesan bishops. Each of these groups would then comprise approx 33 per cent of a central churchmanship, 33 per cent of a catholic churchmanship and 33 per cent of an evangelical churchmanship. (Questionnaire data confirmed that churchmanship is a complex issue; however it still embodies an important set of distinctions, and given the clear importance of theological training on future development and clerical formation, we decided to divide the bishops according to the identity generally professed by the college in which they completed their theological training.)

Rounding up numbers for convenience, we arrived at a total group of 21: 12 suffragans (4 evangelical, 4 catholic, 4 central) and 9 diocesans (3 evangelical, 2 catholic, 4 central). The imbalance of catholics and centrals in the diocesan category was due to the fact that only 2 of the former diocesan bishops willing to be interviewed had been trained in a catholic college. Together, this amounted to a total group of 26 interviewees, although due to changes in availability this was eventually reduced to 25. This may be referred to as Group 1.

During a telephone conversation, one bishop suggested that the wife either makes or ruins an episcopacy, and his had made his, and so was 'absolutely essential' to the issues we were interested in. This reflected other comments that had been made by bishops about the ministry they had 'shared' with their wives. Consequently we made a concerted effort to include the bishop's wife in the interview process. In some cases this was welcome and straightforward because, as with the individual cited above, there was a sense that we could not possibly understand the nature of episcopal ministry and its impact on the family without taking into account the experience of the wife and mother. In other cases things were more awkward, with the bishop sometimes clearly not wishing his wife to be involved, or the wife herself expressing this desire. In these cases, for reasons of sensitivity, we did not press the matter and sought to respect the wishes of our respondents. This means that we do not have a very large or representative sample of bishops' wives. However, we did manage to conduct several extended and most illuminating interviews, and when we did not, we attempted to engage the wives in casual conversation about our interests and have attempted to incorporate emerging insights and observations into our discussion.

The subsequent selection of bishops' children was more straightforward. The pool of potential interviewees was 82 (73 per cent of those bishops' children who returned completed questionnaires were also willing to be interviewed.) We aimed to arrive at a second group of 25, and to match children with bishops already selected for Group 1 wherever possible. Where several children from one family were available, only one was selected randomly. Group 1 did not provide us with automatic choices for the entirety of Group 2, because it included at least two unmarried bishops, and of those bishops who had families, not all had returned questionnaires, and not all of those had also agreed to be interviewed. So the remainder were selected randomly from the general population of bishops' children, taking into account the policy of only selecting one individual per family while also ensuring that the gender divide was not significantly biased one way or the other.

Thus, Group 2 was selected, which eventually amounted to a total of 24 bishop's children. All were children of bishops who had returned questionnaires; 17 were children of bishops who were also interviewed; 1 was a son of a bishop who had already been interviewed as a pilot study; 6 were children of bishops for whom we have no interview data. This way, we have maximized the extent to which interview data may be correlated across the generations so that inferences may be drawn on the basis of data beyond questionnaire returns.

Bibliography

Anderson, Carole B. (1998), 'The experience of growing up in a minister's home and the religious commitment of the adult child of a minister', *Pastoral Psychology*, 46 (6), 393–411.

Archbishops' Council (2001), *Working with the Spirit: Choosing Diocesan Bishops: A Review of the Operation of The Crown Appointments Commission and Related Matters*, London: Church House Publishing.

Armstrong, David (2004), 'Emotions in organizations: disturbing or intelligence', in Huffington, C., Armstrong, D., Halton, W., Hoyle, L. and Pooley, J. (eds), *Working Below the Surface: The Emotional Life of Contemporary Organizations*, London: Karnac, pp. 11–27.

Avis, Paul (2000), *The Anglican Understanding of the Church*, London: SPCK.

Barnes, E.W. (1927), *Should Such a Faith Offend? Sermons and Addresses*, London: Hodder and Stoughton.

Barrett, Michele and McIntosh, Mary (1982), *The Anti-social Family*, London: Verso.

Bauman, Richard (1986), *Story, Performance, and Event: Contextual Studies of Oral Narrative*, Cambridge: Cambridge University Press.

Bauman, Zygmunt (2000), *Liquid Modernity*, Cambridge: Polity Press.

Bebbington, David W. (1989), *Evangelicalism in Modern Britain – A History from the 1730s to the 1980s*, London: Unwin Hyman.

Beck, Ulrick (1992), *Risk Society: Towards a New Modernity*, London: Sage.

Beckford, James (2001), 'Social Movements as Free-floating Religious Phenomena', in Fenn, Richard K. (ed.), *Blackwell Companion to Sociology of Religion*, Oxford: Blackwell, pp. 229–48.

Beckford, James A. (1989), *Religion and Advanced Industrial Society*, London: Unwin Hyman.

Beckford, James A. (2005), *Social Theory and Religion*, Cambridge: Cambridge University Press.

Beesley, Peter (2001), 'The Legal Role of Bishops', in *Resourcing Bishops: The First Report of the Archbishops' Review Group on Bishops' Needs and Resources*, London: Church House Publishing.

Beeson, Trevor (2002), *The Bishops*, London: SCM Press.

Believing in the Church: The Corporate Nature of Faith (1981), A Report of the Doctrine Commission of the Church of England, London: SPCK.

Bellah, Robert N. and Sullivan, William M. (1987), 'The professions and the common good: Vocation/profession/career', *Religion and Intellectual Life*, 4 (3), 7–20.

Bengtson, Vern L., Biblarz, Timothy J. and Roberts, Robert E. (2002), *How Families Still Matter: A Longitudinal Study of Youth in Two Generations*, Cambridge: Cambridge University Press.

Berger, Peter L. ([1974] 1977), *Pyramids of Sacrifice: Political Ethics and Social Change*, Harmondsworth: Pelican Books.

Berlin, Isaiah ([1960] 1997), 'The Concept of History', in *Isaiah Berlin: The Proper Study of Mankind*, London: Chatto and Windus, pp. 17–58.

Bernstein, Basil (1971), *Class, Codes and Control, Volume 1: Theoretical Studies towards a Sociology of Language*, London: Paladin.

Bernstein, Basil (1975), *Class, Codes and Control, Volume 3: Towards a Theory of Educational Transmissions*, London: Routledge and Kegan Paul.

Bloch, Maurice (1992), 'What Goes Without Saying: The Conceptualisation of Zafimaniry Society', in Kuper, Adam (ed.), *Conceptualizing Society*, London: Routledge, pp. 127–46.

Booty, John (1988), 'Standard Divines', in Sykes, Stephen and Booty, John (eds), *The Study of Anglicanism*, London: SPCK/Fortran Press, pp. 163–74.

Bourdieu, Pierre (1977), 'Cultural Reproduction and Social Reproduction', In Karabel, J. and Halsey, A.H. (eds), *Power and Ideology in Education*, Oxford: Oxford University Press, pp. 487–511.

Bourdieu, Pierre, ([1979] 1984), *Distinction: A Social Critique of the Judgement of Taste*, trans. Richard Nice, London: Routledge.

Bourdieu, Pierre (1987), 'Legitimation and Structured Interests in Weber's Sociology of Religion', in Lash, S. and Whimster, S. (eds), *Max Weber, Rationality and Modernity*, London: Allen and Unwin, pp. 119–36.

Bourdieu, Pierre (1991), 'Genesis and structure of the religious field', *Comparative Social Research*, 13, 1–44.

Bourdieu, Pierre and de Saint Martin, Monique (1982), 'La Sainte Famille, L'épiscopat Français dans le Champ du Pouvoir', *Actes de la Recherche en Sciences Sociales,* 44/45, 2–53.

Brierley, Peter (2000), *The Tide is Running Out: What the English Church Attendance Survey Reveals*, London: Christian Research.

Britton, Joseph (2003), 'The evangelicity of the episcopate', *Anglican Theological Review*, 85 (4), 609–21.

Broderson, Arvid (ed.) (1971), *Collected Papers of Alfred Schutz*, vol. 3, The Hague: Martinus Nijhoff.

Brown, Callum G. (2001), *The Death of Christian Britain: Understanding Secularisation 1800–2000*, London and New York: Routledge.

Bruce, Steve (1989), *A House Divided: Protestantism, Schism and Secularization*, London: Routledge.

Bruce, Steve (2002), *God is Dead: Secularization in the West*, Oxford: Blackwell.

Bryman, Alan (1985), 'Professionalism and the clergy: A research note', *Review of Religious Research*, 26 (3), 253–60.

Bryman, Alan (1992), *Charisma and Leadership in Organizations*, London: Sage.

Burgess, Neil (1998), *Into Deep Water: The Experience of Curates in the Church of England*, Bury St Edmonds: Kevin Mayhew.

Burgess, Neil (2005), 'Geoffrey Fisher's ghost – the 'liberal conspiracy' in the Church of England', *Modern Believing*, 46 (3), 63–70.

Burkitt, F.C. (1908), 'Theological Liberalism', *Anglican Liberalism*, by Twelve Churchmen, London: Williams & Norgate, pp. 18–34.

Burton, P. (1999), 'People before the Public: A Study of Stress in Clergy Families', unpublished Ph.D. thesis, University of Bristol.

Cameron, Helen with Escott, Philip (2002), 'The community involvement of church attenders: Findings from the English Church Life Profile', paper presented at the ISTR Fifth International Conference, Cape Town, 7–10 July 2002.

Campbell, Colin (1972), 'The Cult, the Cultic Milieu and Secularization', in Hill, Michael (ed.), *A Sociological Yearbook of Religion in Britain*, vol. 5, London: SCM Press, pp. 119–36.

Carey, George (1995), 'Michael Ramsey's Response to Honest to God', in Gill, Robin and Kendall, Lorna (eds), *Michael Ramsey as Theologian*, London: Darton, Longman and Todd.

Carpenter, Edward (1991), *Archbishop Fisher – His Life and Times*, Norwich: The Canterbury Press.

Carpenter, Humphrey (1996), *Robert Runcie: The Reluctant Archbishop*, London: Hodder and Stoughton.

Carpenter, S.C. (1949), *Winnington-Ingram*, London: Hodder and Stoughton.

Carroll, Jackson and Roof, Wade Clark (2002), *Bridging Divided Worlds: Generational Cultures in Congregations*, San Francisco, CA: Jossey-Bass.

Cavalli, Alessandro (2004), 'Generations and value orientations', *Social Compass*, 51 (2), 155–68.

Chadwick, Owen (1983), *Hensley Henson: A Study in the Friction between Church and State*, Oxford: Clarendon Press.

Chadwick, Owen (1990), *Michael Ramsey. A Life*, Oxford: Oxford University Press.

Chapple, Eliot and Coon, Carlton Stevens (1947), *Principles of Anthropology*, London: Cape.

Churches Information for Mission (2001), *Faith in Life: A Snapshot of Church Life at the Beginning of the 21st Century*, London: Churches Information for Mission.

Coleman, J. (1990), *Foundations of Social Theory*, Cambridge, MA and London: Belknap Press of Harvard University.

Coleman, J. (2000), 'Social Capital and the Creation of Human Capital', in Dasgupta, Partha, and Serageldin (eds), *Social Capital: A Multifaceted Perspective*, Washington, DC: World Bank, pp. 13–39.

Coleman, Peter (1991), 'Ageing and Life History: The Meaning of Reminiscence in Late Life', in Dex, S. (ed.), *Life and Work History Analyses: Qualitative and Quantitative Developments*, London: Routledge.

Common Worship: Services and Prayers for the Church of England (2000), London: Church House.

Cornwell, Jocelyn (1984), *Hard Earned Lives*, London: Tavistock.

Cox, Jeffrey (2003), 'Master Narratives of Long-term Religious Change', in McLeod, Hugh and Ustorf, Werner (eds), *The Decline of Christendom in Western Europe, 1750–2000*, Cambridge: Cambridge University Press, pp. 201–17.

Cunningham, W. (1908), *The Cure of Souls*, Cambridge: Cambridge University Press.

Cupitt, Don (1979), *The Debate about Christ*, London: SCM Press.

Currie, Robert, Gilbert, Alan and Horsley, Lee (1977), *Churches and Churchgoers: Patterns of Church Growth in the British Isles Since 1700*, Oxford: Clarendon Press.

D'Antonio, William V. and Aldous, Joan (eds) (1983), *Families and Religions: Conflict and Change in Modern Society*, London: Sage.

Davie, Grace (1994), *Religion in Britain Since 1945: Believing Without Belonging*, Oxford: Blackwell.

Davies, Douglas J. (1981), 'Theologies in Code', *Research Bulletin*, Institute for the Study of Worship and Religious Architecture, Birmingham University.

Davies, Douglas J. (1985), 'The Charismatic Ethic and the Spirit of Post-industrialism', in Martin, D. and Mullen, P. (eds), *Strange Gifts*, Oxford: Blackwell.

Davies, Douglas J. (1986), *Studies in Pastoral Theology and Social Anthropology*, Birmingham: University of Birmingham Institute for Study of Worship and Religious Architecture.

Davies, Douglas J. (2000), *The Mormon Culture of Salvation*, Aldershot: Ashgate.

Davies, Douglas J. (2001), 'Health, Morality and Sacrifice: The Sociology of Disasters', in Fenn, Richard K. (ed.), *Blackwell Companion to Sociology of Religion*, Oxford: Blackwell, pp. 404–17.

Davies, Douglas J. (2004a), 'Purity, Spirit and Reciprocity in the Acts of the Apostles', in Lawrence, Louise and Aguilar, Mario I. (eds), *Anthropology and Biblical Studies, Avenues of Approach*, Leiden: Deo Publishing, pp. 259–80.

Davies, Douglas J. (2004b), 'Moral Somatic Relationships', *Tidsskrift for Kirke Religion Samfunn*, 2 (17), 97–105.

Davies, Douglas J. (2005), 'Anglican Soteriology: Incarnation, Worship and the Property of Mercy', in Keller, Roger R. and Millet, Robert (eds), *Salvation in Christ*, Provo, UT: Religious Studies Centre, Brigham Young University.

Davies, Douglas J., Watkins, Charles and Winter, Michael (1991), *Church and Religion in Rural England*, Edinburgh: T. & T. Clark.

Davies, Jon (1993), 'From Household to Family to Individualism', in Davies, J. (ed.), *The Family: Is it Just Another Lifestyle Choice?* London: IEA Health and Welfare Unit, pp. 63–103.

Douglas, Mary (1966), *Purity and Danger: An Analysis of the Concepts of Pollution and Taboo*, London: Routledge.

Douglas, Mary (1987), *How Institutions Think*, London: Routledge and Kegan Paul.

Dudley, Roger Louis (1978), 'Alienation from religion in adolescents from fundamentalist religious homes', *Journal for the Scientific Study of Religion*, 17 (4), 389–98.

Dunlap, Pamela and Kendall, Keith (1983), 'Two career clergy/lay couples', *Quarterly Review*, 3, 59–70.

Durkheim, Emile (1915), *The Elementary Forms of the Religious Life*, London: Allen and Unwin.

Dyhouse, Carol (1995), *No Distinction of Sex? Women in British Universities 1870–1939,* London: UCL Press.

Edwards, David L. (1978), *Leaders of the Church of England, 1828-1978*, London: Hodder and Stoughton.

Edwards, David L. (1987), *The Futures of Christianity: An Analysis of Historical, Contemporary and Future Trends within the Worldwide Church*, London: Hodder and Stoughton.

Erickson, Victoria Lee (2001), 'Georg Simmel: American Sociology Chooses the Stone the Builders Refused', in Fenn, Richard K. (ed.), *Blackwell Companion to Sociology of Religion*, Oxford: Blackwell, pp. 105–19.

Etzioni, Amitai (1975), *A Comparative Analysis of Complex Organizations*, revised edn, New York: Free Press.

Faith in the City: Report of the Archbishop of Canterbury's Commission on Urban Priority Areas (1985), London: Church House Publishing.

Faith in the Countryside (1990), Worthing: Churchman Publishing.

Finch, Janet and Mason, Jennifer (1993), *Negotiating Family Responsibilities*, London and New York: Tavistock/Routledge.

Fiske, Susan T. (2004), *Social Beings: A Core Motives Approach to Social Psychology*, Hoboken, NJ: Wiley.

Forder, Charles (1949), *The Parish Priest at Work*, London: SPCK.

Fromm, Erich ([1942] 1960), *Fear of Freedom*, London: Routledge.

Furlong, Andy and Cartmel, Fred (1997), *Young People and Social Change: Individualization and Risk in Late Modernity*, Buckingham: Open University Press.

Gallagher, Sally K. (2003), *Evangelical Identity and Gendered Family Life*, New Brunswick, NJ and London: Rutgers University Press.

Geertz, Clifford (1983), *Local Knowledge*, New York: Basic Books.

Geertz, Clifford (1988), *Works and Lives: The Anthropologist as Author*, Cambridge: Polity Press.

Giddens, Anthony (1991), *Modernity and Self Identity: Self and Society in the Late Modern Age*, Oxford: Polity Press.

Gill, Robin (1999), *Churchgoing and Christian Ethics*, Cambridge: Cambridge University Press.

Gilliat-Ray, Sophie (2001), '*The Fate of the Anglican Clergy* and the class of '97: Some implications of the changing sociological profile of ordinands', *Journal of Contemporary Religion*, 16 (2), 209–25.

Gillis, John (1985), *For Better, For Worse: British Marriages 1600 to the Present*, Oxford: Oxford University Press.

Godbout, Jacques with Caillé, Alain ([1992] 1998), *The World of the Gift*, trans. Donald Winkler, Montreal and London: McGill-Queen's University Press.

Godelier, Maurice (1999), *The Enigma of the Gift*, Oxford: Blackwell.

Goffman, Erving (1959), *The Presentation of Self in Everyday Life*, New York: Doubleday.

Goffman, Erving (1971), *Relations in Public: Microstudies of the Public Order*, New York: Basic Books.

Goffman, Erving (1974), *Frame Analysis: An Essay on the Organization of Experience*, Norwich: Harper and Row.

Goldthorpe, J.H. (1980), *Social Mobility and Class Structure in Modern Britain*, Oxford: Clarendon Press.

Goody, Jack (1995), *The Expansive Movement, Anthropology in Britain and Africa 1918–1970*, Cambridge: Cambridge University Press.

Gorer, Geoffrey (1973), *Sex and Marriage in England Today*, St Albans: Panther Books.

Greeley, Andrew (1997), 'Coleman revisited: Religious structures as a source of social capital', *American Behavioral Scientist*, 40 (5), 587–94.

Greeley, Andrew (2003), *Religion in Europe at the End of the Second Millennium*, New Brunswick, NJ: Transaction Publishers.

Guest, Mathew (2007), 'In Search of Spiritual Capital: The Spiritual as Cultural Resource', in Flanagan, K. and Jupp, P. (eds), *The Sociology of Spirituality*, Aldershot: Ashgate.

Habgood, John (1988), *Confessions of a Conservative Liberal*, London: SPCK.

Hakim, Catherine (2003), *Models of the Family in Modern Societies: Ideals and Realities*, Aldershot: Ashgate.

Handley, H. (1908), in 'Religious Liberalism', *Anglican Liberalism*, by Twelve Churchmen, London: Williams & Norgate, pp. 1–17.

Hankey, W.J. (1988), 'Canon Law', in Sykes, Stephen and Booty, John (eds), *The Study of Anglicanism*, London: SPCK/Fortran Press, pp. 200–215.

Hardy, Bruce (2001), 'Pastoral care with clergy children', *Review and Expositor*, 98 (4), 545–56.

Hare Duke, Michael (1982), 'Dr Frank Lake: expert on 'clinical theology', *Church Times*, 14 May.

Hargrove, Barbara (1983), 'The Church, the Family and the Modernisation Process', in D'Antonio, William V. and Aldous, Joan (eds), *Families and Religions: Conflict and Change in Modern Society*, London: Sage, pp. 21–48.

Hastings, Adrian (1987), *A History of English Christianity, 1920–1985*, London: Fount Paperbacks.

Headlam, Maurice (1944), *Bishop and Friend, Nugent Hicks*, London: Macdonald.

Heelas, Paul (1996), *The New Age Movement: The Celebration of the Self and the Sacralization of Modernity*, Oxford and Cambridge, MA: Blackwell.

Heelas, Paul and Morris, Paul (eds) (1992), *The Values of the Enterprise Culture: The Moral Debate*, London: Routledge.

Henshall, 'Steve' Ann (1991), *Not Always Murder at the Vicarage: A View of Clergy Marriage Today*, London: Triangle, SPCK.

Henshall, 'Steve' Ann (1994), *Is This a Daddy Sunday? Healing the Scars of Divorce*, Crowborough: Monarch Press.

Henson, Herbert Hensley (1939), *The Church of England*, Cambridge: Cambridge University Press.

Hervièu-Léger, D. ([1993] 2000), *Religion as a Chain of Memory*, trans. Simon Lee, Oxford: Polity Press.

Hinton, Michael (1994), *The Anglican Parochial Clergy: A Celebration*, London: SCM Press.

Hochschild, Arlie R. (1997), *The Time Bind: When Work becomes Home and Home becomes Work*, New York: Metropolitan Books.

Hochschild, Arlie R. (2003), *The Commercialization of Intimate Life. Notes from Home and Work*, Berkeley, CA, Los Angeles, CA and London: University of California Press.

Holstein, James A. and Gubrium, Jaber F. (2000), *The Self We Live By: Narrative Identity in a Postmodern World*, New York and Oxford: Oxford University Press.

Hooker, Richard (1865), 'The Laws of Ecclesiastical Polity', in *The Works of Mr Richard Hooker*, Oxford: Clarendon Press.

Hout, Michael (1984), 'Status, autonomy, and training in occupational mobility', *The American Journal of Sociology*, 89 (6), 1,379–409.

Hunt, Stephen (2001), *Anyone for Alpha? Evangelism in a Post-Christian Society*, London: Darton, Longman and Todd.

Hutch, Richard A. (1997), *The Meaning of Lives: Biography, Autobiography and the Spiritual Quest*, London: Ashgate.

Inge, John (2003), *A Christian Theology of Place*, Aldershot: Ashgate.

Jamieson, Alan (2002), *A Churchless Faith: Faith Journeys Beyond the Churches*, London: SPCK.

Jenkins, Timothy (1999), *Religion in English Everyday Life*, New York and Oxford: Berghahn Books.

Jevons, F.B. (1913), *Personality*, London: Methuen.

Josselson, R. and Lieblich, A. (eds) (1993), *The Narrative Study of Lives, Volume 1: Psychology: Biographical Methods*, Newbury Park, CA: Sage.

Jowell, Roger et al. (eds) (2000), *British Social Attitudes, the 17th Report*, London: Thousand Oaks, New Delhi: Sage.

Käsler, Dirk ([1979] 1988), *Max Weber: An Introduction to his Life and Work*, Cambridge: Polity Press.

Kavanagh, Dennis (1987), *Thatcherism and British Politics*, Oxford: Oxford University Press.

Kent, John (1992), *William Temple*, Cambridge: Cambridge University Press.

Kierkegaard, Søren ([1843] 1959), *Either/Or*, vol. 1, trans. D.F. Swanson and L.M. Swanson, Princeton, NJ: Princeton University Press.

Lake, Frank (1966), *Clinical Theology*, London: Darton, Longman and Todd.

Lasch, Christopher (1977), *Haven in a Heartless World: The Family Besieged*, New York: Basic Books.

Law, William ([1728] 1906), *A Serious Call to a Devout and Holy Life*, London: J.M. Dent.

Lee, Cameron (1992), *PK: Helping Pastors' Kids through their Identity Crisis*, Grand Rapids, MI: Zondervan.

Lee, Simon and Stanford, Peter (1990), *Believing Bishops*, London: Faber and Faber.

Leslie, Shane (1933), *The Oxford Movement, 1833–1933*, London: Burns Oates & Washbourne.

Lesthaeghe, Ron (1983), 'A century of demographic and cultural change in western Europe: An exploration of underlying dimensions', *Population and Development Review*, 9 (3), 411–35.

Linde, Charlotte (1993), *Life Stories: The Creation of Coherence*, New York and Oxford: Oxford University Press.

Living Faith in the City (1990), London: Church of England.

Lockhart, J.G. (1949), *Cosmo Gordon Lang*, London: Hodder and Stoughton.

Lyon, D. (2000), *Jesus in Disneyland: Religion in Postmodern Times*, Cambridge: Polity Press.

Mannheim, Karl (1952), 'The Problem of Generations', in *Essays in the Sociology of Knowledge*, London: Routledge, pp. 286–320.

Martin, David (1967), *A Sociology of English Religion*, London: SCM Press.

Martineau, Robert (1972), *The Office and Work of a Priest*, London: Mowbray.

Mauss, Marcel ([1925] 1954), *The Gift, Forms and Function of Exchange in Archaic Societies*, trans. I. Cunnison, London: Cohen and West.

McCown, D.E. and Sharma, C. (1992), 'Children in the public eye: The functioning of pastors' children', *Journal of Religion and Health*, 31 (1), 31–40.

McGregor Burns, J. (1978), *Leadership*, New York: Harper & Row.

McKie, Linda and Cunningham-Burley, Sarah (eds) (2005), *Families in Society: Boundaries and Relationships*, Bristol: The Policy Press.

McLeod, Hugh (2003), 'Introduction', in McLeod, Hugh and Ustorf, Werner (eds), *The Decline of Christendom in Western Europe, 1750–2000*, Cambridge: Cambridge University Press, pp. 1–26.

Medhurst, Kenneth and Moyser, George (1985), 'Lambeth Palace, The Bishops and Politics', in Moyser, G. (ed.), *Church and Politics Today: The Role of the Church of England in Contemporary Politics*, Edinburgh: T. & T. Clark, pp. 75–106.

Medhurst, Kenneth and Moyser, George (1988), *Church and Politics in a Secular Age*, Oxford: Clarendon Press.

Megill, Allan (1995), 'Recounting the past: "Description", explanation and narrative in historiography', *The American Historical Review*, 94 (3), 627–53.

Mehl, Roger ([1965] 1970), *The Sociology of Protestantism*, London: SCM Press.

Mellows Report (2001): See *Resourcing Bishops*.

Morgan, Dewi (ed.) (1959), *They Became Anglicans*, London: Mowbray.

Moscovici, Serge (1993), *The Invention of Society*, Cambridge: Polity Press.

Moy, S. and Malony, H.N. (1987), 'An empirical study of ministers' children and families', *Journal of Psychology and Christianity*, 6, 52–64.

Nazir-Ali, Michael (2001), 'Towards a Theology of Choosing Bishops', in *Working with the Spirit: Choosing diocesan bishops*, London: Church House Publishing.

Needham, Rodney (1980), *Reconnaissances*, Toronto: University of Toronto Press.

Nelson, John (1994), 'Suffragan Bishops and Cathedrals: De Jure Relationships', unpublished paper, University of Birmingham.

Nesbitt, Paula D. (1997), *Feminization of the Clergy in America*, New York: Oxford University Press.

Newman, John Henry (1835), *The Recommendation of Suffragan Bishops Recommended*, London: J.G. Rivington and Oxford: J.H. Parker.

Newman, John Henry (1946), *Apologia Pro Vita Sua*, London: Sheed & Ward.

Norman, Edward (1976), *Church and Society in England 1770–1970*, Oxford: Clarendon Press.

Norman, Edward (2004), *Anglican Difficulties: A New Syllabus of Errors*, London: Moorhouse.

Norris, Richard A. (1988), 'Episcopacy', in Sykes, Stephen and Booty, John (eds), *The Study of Anglicanism*, London: SPCK/Fortran Press, pp. 296–312.

Oakley, Anne (1981), 'Interviewing Women: A Contradiction in Terms', in Roberts, H. (ed.), *Doing Feminist Research*, London: Routledge and Kegan Paul.

Owen, Eluned, E. (1961), *The Later Life of Bishop Owen: A Son of Wales*, Llandysul: Gomerian Press.

Palmer, Bernard (1992), *High and Mitred: A Study of Prime Ministers as Bishop-makers, 1837–1977*, London: SPCK.

Park, Alison et al. (eds) (2001), *British Social Attitudes, the 18th Report: Public Policy*, London, Thousand Oaks, New Delhi: Sage.

Park, Alison et al. (eds) (2002), *British Social Attitudes, the 19th Report*, London, Thousand Oaks, New Delhi: Sage.

Park, Alison et al. (eds) (2003), *British Social Attitudes, the 20th Report: Continuity and Change Over Two Decades*, London, Thousand Oaks, New Delhi: Sage.

Parsons, Gerald (1989), 'The Rise of Pluralism in the Church of England', in Badham, P. (ed.), *Religion, State and Society in Modern Britain*, Lampeter: Edwin Mellen Press.

Parsons, Talcott ([1922] 1966), 'Introduction', in Max Weber ([1922] 1966), *The Sociology of Religion*, London: Social Science Paperbacks with Methuen.

Parsons, Talcott et al. (1956), *Family, Socialization and Interaction Process*, London: Routledge and Kegan Paul.

Paul, Leslie (1964), *The Deployment and Payment of the Clergy*, Westminster: Church Information Office.

Peart-Binns, John S. (1990), *Alfred Edwin Morris, Archbishop of Wales*, Llandysul: Gomer Press.

Perry Report: See *Working with the Spirit*.

Podmore, Colin (2000), 'The Choosing of Bishops in the Early Church and in the Church of England: An Historical Survey', in The Archbishop's Council (2001), *Working with the Spirit: Choosing Diocesan Bishops. A Review of the Operation of The Crown Appointments Commission and Related Matters*, London: Church House Publishing, pp. 113–38.

Podmore, Colin (2006), 'The Church of England's Understanding of Episcopacy', *Theology*, 109 (849), 173–81.

Pollner, Melvin and Stein, Jill (1996), 'Narrative mapping of social worlds: The voice of experience in Alcoholics Anonymous', *Symbolic Interaction*, 19, 203–24.

Preston, Ronald (1988), 'Christian socialism becalmed', *Theology*, January, 24–32.

Putnam, Robert (2000), *Bowling Alone: The Collapse and Revival of American Community*, New York, London: Simon and Schuster.

Ranson, Stewart, Bryman, Alan and Hinings, Bob (1977), *Clergy, Ministers and Priests*, London, Henley, Boston: Routledge and Kegan Paul.

Rappaport, Roy A. (1999), *Ritual and Religion in the Making of Humanity*, Cambridge: Cambridge University Press.

Reay, Diane (2004), 'Gendering Bourdieu's Concepts of Capitals? Emotional Capital, Women and Social Class', in Adkins, L. and Skeggs, B. (eds), *Feminism After Bourdieu*, Oxford and Malden, MA: Blackwell, pp. 57–74.

Rees, Robin L.D. (1993), *Weary and Ill at Ease: A Survey of Clergy and Organists*, Leominster: Gracewing.

Rees, W.G. (1906), *The Parson's Outlook: Studies in Clerical Life and Character*, London: Longmans, Green.

Resourcing Bishops: The First Report of the Archbishops' Review Group (2001), London: Church House Publishing.

Richmond, Lee J., Rayburn, Carole and Rogers, Lynn (1985), 'Clergymen, clergywomen and their spouses: Stress in professional religious families', *Journal of Career Development*, 12 (1), 81–6.

Richter, Philip (2004), 'Denominational Cultures: The Cinderella of Congregational Studies?', in Guest, M., Tusting, K. and Woodhead, L. (eds), *Congregational Studies in the UK: Christianity in a Post-Christian Context*, Aldershot: Ashgate, pp. 169–84.

Roberts, Richard H. (2002), *Religion, Theology and the Human Sciences*, Cambridge: Cambridge University Press.

Robinson, John A.T. (1963), *Honest to God*, London: SCM Press.

Roof, Wade Clark (1993), *A Generation of Seekers: The Spiritual Journeys of the Baby Boom Generation*, New York: HarperCollins.

Roof, Wade Clark (1999), *Spiritual Marketplace. Baby Boomers and the Remaking of American Religion*, Princeton, NJ: Princeton University Press.

Rose, Nikolas (1992), 'Governing the Enterprising Self', in Heelas, Paul and Morris, Paul (eds), *The Values of the Enterprise Culture: The Moral Debate*, London and New York: Routledge, pp. 141–64.

Rowatt, G. Wade (2001), 'Stress and satisfaction in ministry families', *Review and Expositor*, 98, 523–43.

Rubinstein, W.D. (1987), 'Education and the Social Origins of British Elites, 1880–1970', in *Elites and the Wealthy in Modern British History: Essays in Social and Economic History*, Brighton: The Harvester Press, pp. 172–221.

Russell, Anthony (1980), *The Clerical Profession*, London: SPCK.

Sanford, T.L. (1998), *I Have to be Perfect (and other Parsonage Heresies)*, Colorado Springs, CO: Llama Press.

Saward, M. (1987), *The Anglican Church Today: Evangelicals on the Move*, Oxford: Mowbray.

Schutz, Alfred ([1964] 1971), *Collected Papers*, edited and with an introduction by Arvid Brodersen, The Hague: Martinus Nijhoff.

Segalen, Martine ([1981] 1986), *Historical Anthropology and the Family*, trans. J.C.Whitehouse and Sarah Matthews, Cambridge: Cambridge University Press.

Sennett, Richard ([2003] 2004), *Respect: The Formation of Character in an Age of Inequality*, London: Penguin Books.

Sheppard, David (1983), *Bias to the Poor*, London: Hodder and Stoughton.

Sheppard, David (2002), *Steps Along Hope Street: My Life in Cricket, the Church and the Inner City*, London: Hodder and Stoughton.

Sheppard, Grace (1989), *An Aspect of Fear*, London: Darton, Longman and Todd.

Sheppard, Grace (1995), *Pits and Pedestals. A Journey Towards Self-Respect*, London: Darton, Longman and Todd.

Sherkat, Darren E. (2003), 'Religious Socialization: Sources of Influence and Influences of Agency', in Dillon, Michele (ed.), *Handbook of the Sociology of Religion*, Cambridge: Cambridge University Press, pp. 151–63.

Simmel, Georg (1997), *Essays on Religion*, New Haven, CT and London: Yale University Press.

Smith, Wilfred Cantwell (1963), *The Meaning and End of Religion*, New York: Macmillan.

Steer, Roger (1998), *Church on Fire: The Story of Anglican Evangelicals*, London: Hodder and Stoughton.

Stewart, Abigail J. (1994), 'The Women's Movement and Women's Lives: Linking Individual Development and Social Events', in Lieblich, Amia and Josselson, Ruthellen (eds), *The Narrative Study of Lives, Volume 2: Exploring Identity and Gender*, London: Sage Publications, pp. 230–50.

Stoffels, Hijme (2004), '"Preachers' Kids are the Worst": Results of a Survey among Dutch Clergy Children', paper given at the ASR Conference, San Francisco, CA.

Strange, K.S. and Sheppard, L.A. (2001), 'Evaluations of clergy children versus non-clergy children: Does a negative stereotype exist?', *Pastoral Psychology*, 50 (1), 53–60.

Suggate, Alan (1994), 'The Christian Churches in England since 1945: Ecumenism and Social Concern', in Gilley, S. and Sheils, W.J. (eds), *A History of Religion in Britain*, Oxford: Blackwell, pp. 467–87.

Summerfield, Penny (1998), *Reconstructing Women's Wartime Lives*, Manchester and New York: Manchester University Press.

Sykes, Stephen (1978), *The Integrity of Anglicanism*, London: Mowbray.

Taylor, Charles (1989), *Sources of the Self*, Cambridge: Cambridge University Press.

Temple, F.S. (ed.) (1963), *Some Lambeth Letters 1942–44*, Oxford: Oxford University Press.

Thompson, Francis (1913), *Selected Poems of Francis Thompson*, London: Methuen and Burns & Oates.

Thompson, Kenneth (1992), 'Individual and Community in Religious Critiques of the Enterprise Culture', in Heelas, Paul and Morris, Paul (eds), *The Values of the Enterprise Culture: The Moral Debate*, London and New York: Rouledge, pp. 253–75.

Towler, R. and Coxon, A.P.M. (1979), *The Fate of the Anglican Clergy: A Sociological Study*, London: Macmillan.

Townsend, George (1838), *The Doctrine of the Atonement to be Taught Without Reserve*, London: L. and G. Seeley.

Turnbull Report: See *Working as One Body*.

Verter, Bradford T. (2003), 'Spiritual capital: Theorizing religion with Bourdieu against Bourdieu', *Sociological Theory*, 21 (2), 150–74.

Watson, David (1983), *You Are My God: An Autobiography*, Sevenoaks: Hodder and Stoughton.

Watson, John (1896), The Cure of Souls: Yale Lectures on Practical Theology, London: Hodder and Stoughton.

Weber, Max (1958), *The Protestant Ethic and the Spirit of Capitalism*, New York: Scribner's.

Weber, Max (1963), *The Sociology of Religion*, Boston, MA: Beacon Press.

Weber, Max ([1922] 1966), *The Sociology of Religion*, London: Social Science Paperbacks with Methuen.

Weber, Max (1967), *From Max Weber: Essays in Sociology*, ed. H.H. Gerth and C. Wright-Mills, London: Routledge and Kegan Paul.

Weber, Max (1978), *Economy and Society*, Berkeley, CA: University of California Press.

West, Frank H. (1980), *'FRB' – A Portrait of Bishop Russell Barry*, Nottingham: Grove Books.

Wickham, E.R. (1957), *Church and People in an Industrial City*, London: Lutterworth Press.

Williams, Rowan (2000), *On Christian Theology*, Oxford: Blackwell.

Wilson, B.R. (1966), *Religion in Secular Society: A Sociological Comment*, Harmondsworth: Penguin.

Winquist, Charles E. (1978), *Homecoming: Interpretation, Transformation and Individuation*, Missoula, MT: American Academy of Religion, Scholars Press.

Working as One Body: Report of the Archbishops' Commission on the Organisation of the Church of England (1995), London: Church House Publishing.

Working with the Spirit: Choosing Diocesan Bishops (2001), London: Church House Publishing.

Wraight, Heather (2001), *Eve's Glue: The Role Women Play in Holding the Church Together*, Carlisle: Paternoster Press.

Wright-Mills, C. (1940), 'Situated action and vocabularies of motive', *American Sociological Review*, 5, 904–13.

Yamane, David (2000), 'Narrative and religious experience', *Sociology of Religion*, 61 (2), 171–90.

Young, Michael and Willmott, Peter (1975), *The Symmetrical Family: A Study of Work and Leisure in the London Region*, Harmondsworth: Penguin.

Index